Physical
Database Design
Using Oracle

Physical Database Design Using Oracle

Donald K. Burleson

AUERBACH PUBLICATIONS

A CRC Press Company

Boca Raton London New York Washington, D.C.

Library of Congress Cataloging-in-Publication Data

Burleson, Donald K.
    Physical database design using Oracle / Donald K. Burleson.
        p. cm.
    Includes index.
    ISBN 0-8493-1817-3 (alk. paper)
        1. Oracle (Computer file) 2. Database design. 3. Relational databases. I. Title.

QA76.9.D26B875 2004
005.75′65--dc22

2004049442

Visit the Auerbach Web site at www.auerbach-publications.com

© 2005 by CRC Press LLC
Auerbach is an imprint of CRC Press LLC

No claim to original U.S. Government works
International Standard Book Number 0-8493-1817-3
Library of Congress Card Number 2004049442
Printed in the United States of America 1 2 3 4 5 6 7 8 9 0

DEDICATION

This book is dedicated to Jean Lavender, a real survivor and feisty lady, whose courage has been an inspiration.

CONTENTS

PREFACE

The evolution of the Oracle® database has led to a revolution of design practices. As of Oracle Database 10g, the database physical structures have become more complex than ever before and database designers face a plethora of physical ways to implement the logical models.

The purpose of this book is to correlate the logical data model with the physical implementation structures provided by Oracle Corporation. Oracle Database 10g offers object-oriented data structures, pure relational data structures as well as specialized data structures such as index-organized tables. Given so many choices, Oracle designers must understand the appropriate use of each physical technology and how it maps to their logical data models.

This book targets the practicing Oracle professional who already has exposure to basic Oracle database administration. It is my hope that this text provides you with the insights that you need to choose the appropriate physical model for your mission-critical application.

Regards,

Donald K. Burleson

ABOUT THE AUTHOR

Donald K. Burleson is one of the world's top Oracle database experts with more than 20 years of full-time database administration (DBA) experience. He specializes in creating database architectures for large online databases and he has worked with some of the world's most powerful and complex systems.

A former adjunct professor, Don Burleson has written 32 books, published more than 100 articles in national magazines, and served as editor-in-chief of *Oracle Internals* and senior consulting editor for DBAzine and series editor for Rampant TechPress. Don is a popular lecturer and teacher and is a frequent speaker at OracleWorld and other international database conferences.

As a leading corporate database consultant, Don has worked with numerous Fortune 500 corporations creating robust database architectures for mission-critical systems. Don is also a noted expert on E-commerce systems and has been instrumental in the development of numerous Web-based systems that support thousands of concurrent users.

Don's professional Web sites include www.dba-oracle.com and www.remote-dba.net.

In addition to his services as a consultant, Don also is active in charitable programs to aid visually impaired individuals. Don pioneered a technique for delivering tiny pigmy horses as guide animals for the blind and manages a nonprofit corporation called The Guide Horse Foundation dedicated to providing free guide horses to the blind. The Web site for The Guide Horse Foundation is www.guidehorse.org.

Don Burleson's books include:

Oracle Privacy Security Auditing — Includes Federal Law Compliance with HIPAA, Sarbanes-Oxley & The Gramm-Leach-Bliley Act GLB, Rampant TechPress, 2003

Oracle Index Management Secrets — Top Oracle Experts Discuss Index Management Techniques, Rampant TechPress, 2003

Oracle SQL Internals Handbook, Rampant TechPress, 2003

Oracle Space Management Handbook, Rampant TechPress, 2003

Advanced SQL Database Programmer Handbook, Rampant TechPress, 2003

The Data Warehouse eBusiness DBA Handbook, Rampant TechPress, 2003

Oracle9iAS Administration Handbook, Oracle Press, 2003

Creating a Self-Tuning Oracle Database — Automatic Oracle9i Dynamic SGA Performance, Rampant TechPress, 2003

Conducting the Oracle Job Interview — IT Manager Guide for Oracle Job Interviews with Oracle Interview Questions, Rampant TechPress, 2003

Oracle9i UNIX Administration Handbook, Oracle Press, 2002

Oracle9i High Performance Tuning with STATSPACK, Oracle Press, 2002

Oracle Internals — Tips, Tricks, and Techniques for DBAs, CRC Press, 2001

Oracle High Performance SQL Tuning, Oracle Press, 2001

Oracle High Performance Tuning with STATSPACK, Oracle Press, 2001

UNIX for Oracle DBAs Pocket Reference, O'Reilly & Associates, 2000

Oracle SAP Administration, O'Reilly & Associates, 1999

Inside the Database Object Model, CRC Press, 1998

High Performance Oracle Data Warehousing — All You Need to Master Professional Database Development Using Oracle, Coriolis Publishing, 1997

High Performance Oracle8 Tuning — Performance and Tuning Techniques for Getting the Most from Your Oracle8 Database, Coriolis Publishing, 1997

High Performance Oracle Database Applications — Performance and Tuning Techniques for Getting the Most from Your Oracle Database, Coriolis Publishing, 1996

Oracle Databases on the Web — Learn to Create Web Pages that Interface with Database Engines, Coriolis Publishing, 1996

Managing Distributed Databases — Building Bridges between Database Islands, John Wiley & Sons, 1995

Practical Application of Object-Oriented Techniques to Relational Databases, John Wiley & Sons, 1994

1

INTRODUCTION TO ORACLE PHYSICAL DESIGN

PREFACE

Over the past 30 years, we've seen the evolution of a wide variety of systems analysis and design methodologies. We've seen the methodologies of Grady Booch, Ed Yourdon, Chris Gane and Trish Sarson, as well as the emergence of standard systems development methodologies such as joint application development and Unified Modeling Language (UML).

Regardless of the methodology, at some point in the systems implementation, the database designer must be able to convert a logical data modeling for data into physical data structures. From a database point of view, it is incidental whether you're dealing with a commercial database management system (DBMS), such as MySQL® or Oracle, or whether you're writing your own DBMS in a language such as C or C⁺⁺. The point is that we must be able to take the logical data models and convert them into physical implementations that will minimize disk input/output (I/O) and provide the fastest possible throughput.

We need to be able to implement the DBMS in such fashion that performance will be fast while preserving the logical data structures. This book is dedicated to the premise that the database designer should be able to take logical data models and convert them into a series of data structures that allow for fast and easy, logical access to the data.

RELATIONAL DATABASES AND PHYSICAL DESIGN

Relational databases made the following improvements over hierarchical and network databases:

- Simplicity — the concept of tables with rows and columns is extremely simple and easy to understand. End users have a simple data model. Complex network diagrams used with the hierarchical and network databases are not used with a relational database.
- Data independence — data independence is the ability to modify data structures (in this case, tables) without affecting existing programs. Much of this is because tables are not hard-linked to one another. Columns can be added to tables, tables can be added to the database, and new data relationships can be added with little or no restructuring of the tables. A relational database provides a much higher degree of data independence than do hierarchical and network databases.
- Declarative data access — the Structured Query Language (SQL) users specify what data they want, then the embedded SQL (a procedural language) determines how to get the data. In relational database access, the user tells the system the conditions for the retrieval of data. The system then gets the data that meets the selection conditions in the SQL statements. The database navigation is hidden from the end user or programmer, unlike a Conference on Data Systems Languages (CODASYL) Data Manipulation Language (DML), where the programmer had to know the details of the access path.

The most important point about SQL is that it provided programmers and end users with a simple, easy way to add, change, and extract data from a relational database. Any two tables could be joined together on the fly at runtime using their primary or foreign keys. There are no pointers or hard links from one table to another.

SYSTEMS DEVELOPMENT AND PHYSICAL DESIGN

To understand all of the steps that occur during the physical database design, let's take a quick look at the overall phases of a database project:

1. Feasibility study — a feasibility study is a cost-benefit analysis for a proposed system, quantifying all tangible costs and benefits for the warehouse, as well as describing intangible costs and benefits. Essentially, the goal of this study is to provide a go/no-go decision about whether to proceed with the data warehouse project. Activities involve an analysis of technological and economical feasibility with a focus on understanding all of the costs and benefits that will accrue from the data warehouse.

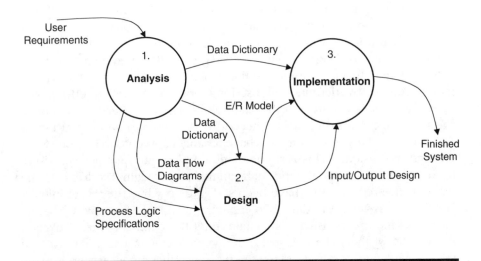

Figure 1.1   The System Development Life Cycle

2. Systems analysis — systems analysis is a logical description of the data sources for the warehouse, data extraction analysis, data cleansing analysis, and data loading analysis. Unlike a traditional system, the warehouse analysis is heavily data-centric and not concerned with defining the system interfaces.

3. Logical design — the systems design phase is the physical implementation of the logical data model that was developed in the systems analysis phase. This includes the design of the warehouse, specifications for data extraction tools, data loading processes, and warehouse access methods. In this phase, a working prototype should be created for the end user.

4. Physical design — the system design phase is also where the logical documentation is transformed into a physical structure. For database design, this involves the creation of the entity/relation (E/R) model and the determination of appropriate data storage techniques and index usage. This phase is where a thorough understanding of Oracle database architecture will pay off.

5. Implementation — the implementation phase is the phase in which the warehouse is constructed and the software is written and tested.

As shown in Figure 1.1, the implementation phase normally consumes as much effort as all of the other steps combined. Regardless of the reasons, it remains true that the implementation phase is by far the most time-consuming phase in the creation of any system.

If a development team has done a good job of analyzing, designing, and coding a new system, you might suspect that the programming team would disband immediately after coding is completed. But, this is seldom the case. The cost curve continues to grow after a system has been delivered: this can be attributed to the dynamic nature of systems requirements. Almost by definition, most long-term development efforts will deliver an obsolete system to their end users. The end users often lament, "You gave me the system that I needed two years ago when you began the project! Many requirements have changed, even while you were creating the system." This is a common complaint and it's not surprising to see that the programming staff immediately begins addressing the maintenance requests that have been stacking up while they were initially creating the system. A traditional computer system will continually become more and more expensive to maintain, until the cumulative costs exceed the benefits of the system. A goal of a savvy systems manager is to foresee this dilemma and to start rewriting the system so that a new system is ready to replace the aging system when the costs become too cumbersome.

SYSTEMS ANALYSIS AND PHYSICAL DATABASE DESIGN

Fundamentally, the purpose of any systems analysis is to logically identify the processes and the data moving between the processes and to describe the processing rules and data items. Only after these items are defined can design begin, regardless of the physical implementation of the system. To meet these goals, a data warehouse analysis should begin with the creation of a structured specification. A structured specification is a document that describes all of the data, data storage, external entities, and processes for a system. This document is then used in the design phase for the creation of the behaviors, E/R model, and class hierarchy.

The Structured Specification

Most of the system analysis methodologies provide a method for documenting logical processes, data items, and data stores. These components generally include:

- Data flow diagram (DFD) — the DFD is a set of top-down diagrams that depict all processes within a system, the data flow among the processes, and the data stores. Figure 1.2 depicts a sample DFD. The DFDs begin at a general level and become progressively more detailed. The lowest level of processing is called the functional primitive level, which has been traditionally used as the starting point for systems design.

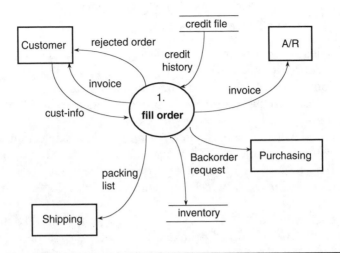

Figure 1.2   A Sample DFD

- Data dictionary — the data dictionary is a description of all of the logical data items, including all data flows and data stores (files). The data dictionary describes how all of the data items are stored and how they have been transformed by the processes. The data dictionary's file specifications also become the foundation for the relational tables that will comprise the Oracle warehouse.
- Process logic specifications (structured specifications) — these specifications describe all functional primitive processes. A process is defined as an operation that modifies a data flow. The tools used to describe processes include pseudocode, procedure flowcharts, decision trees, and decision tables.

In a traditional systems analysis, the DFD does not stand by itself. Rather, the DFD is augmented by a data dictionary that describes all of the data flows and files and a set of process logic specifications that describes how each process transforms data flows. A process logic specification (sometimes called a minispec) can be expressed as structured English, decision trees, or any of the many other techniques used to describe how data flows are being changed.

In traditional systems analysis, data dictionary definitions for all data items are normalized or grouped into database entities, which become E/R models in the database design phase. Eventually, the E/R models become relational tables during physical design. The identification and grouping of data items constitutes the entities that will establish the basic E/R model for the database engine.

THE ROLE OF FUNCTIONAL DECOMPOSITION IN PHYSICAL DATABASE DESIGN

The principles of top-down analysis tell us to begin our DFD at a general level. The entire system is viewed as a single process and this view is called a Context Level DFD. Next, the DFD is decomposed and levels of detail are added to the model. Any process that can be identified can probably be subdivided to smaller processes; it is possible to decompose a DFD to the level where each process represents a single statement. An extreme example of functional decomposition would be showing a statement such as add 1 to counter as a separate process on the DFD. The pivotal question is: At what point should the developer stop decomposing the processes?

Theoreticians such as Gane and Sarson tell us that a DFD should be decomposed to the functional primitive level, where each process bubble performs one granular function. Under this definition, one should departition the functional specs until each behavior performs a functional primitive process. For example, in Figure 1.2 we see a high-level specification for a process named fill_order. We can now take this process and departition it into sublevels (Figure 1.3).

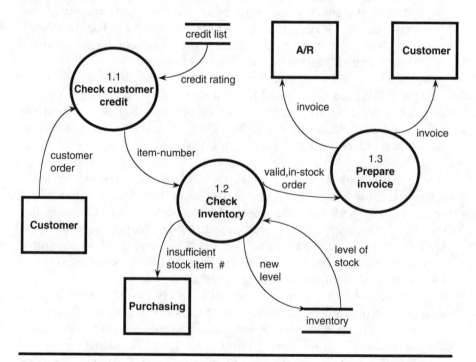

Figure 1.3 A Sample of Functional Decomposition

A good rule of thumb for database analysis is that a DFD should be decomposed to the level where each process corresponds to a SQL operation. This allows the use of triggers within a relational database and greatly simplifies the data physical database design.

As you are probably beginning to see, the level of partitioning is critical for a successful database systems analysis. While this level of decomposing is fine for traditional systems analysis, it is better to continue to decompose the behavior for effective relational database design.

There is still a great deal of controversy about the best way to approach database analysis for database systems. Architecturally, some theoreticians state that the relational model is better suited for use in an online transaction processing (OLTP) environment and multidimensional architectures are better suited to data warehouses. To address these data storage issues, Oracle has implemented physical constructs that are specific to data warehouse and object-oriented systems:

- Oracle data warehouse physical constructs:
  - Table value partitions
  - Table range partitions
  - Table hash partitioning
  - Oracle9*i*™ database multicolumn partitioning
  - Index partitioning
- Oracle object-oriented physical features:
  - Nested tables
  - Object tables
  - Abstract data types (ADTs)
  - Table member methods
  - Support for inheritance and polymorphism

Developers must remember that the main difference between traditional systems analysis and database analysis is the focus on the data sources and the data usage.

INTRODUCTION TO LOGICAL DATABASE DESIGN

Let's begin by briefly reviewing data modeling theory from a normalization perspective. It is interesting to note that Dr. Edgar F. Codd coined the term *normalization* in reference to current events of the day. At the time that Dr. Codd was developing his mathematical rules for data redundancy, President Nixon was normalizing relations with China. Because Nixon was normalizing relations, Dr. Codd decided that he would also normalize relations as he refined his rules.

As the decades progressed, disks became cheaper and the rules for normalization changed dramatically. Cheaper disks made redundancy acceptable and the deliberate introduction of redundancy is now a common physical design activity. All of logical database modeling techniques have a common goal in mind. Regardless of the methodology, we see the following goals of database modeling:

■ Manage redundancy — to control data redundancy was far more important during the 1970s and 1980s when disk devices work stream was expensive. Today in the 21st century, disk devices are far cheaper than they have been before, but that does not mean that we can throw away the principles of data normalization entirely. Rather, the Oracle database designer must take the logical database and introduce redundancy into the data model based on the cost of the redundancy. The cost of the redundancy or a function of the size of the redundant data item, and the frequency that the redundancy to items updated.

■ To correctly model data relationships — the proper modeling of data relationships is an important part of physical database design. Within any relational database, we find a wealth of choices that are available to us. For example, modeling a super type sub-type relationship can be done in about five different ways in an Oracle database. Each of these methods will allow proper storage of the data item, but with a radically different internal performance and ease of maintenance.

To see how logical modeling interfaces with physical design, let's look deeper into the logical database design. For database systems, a systems developer begins by taking raw, denormalized relations from a systems analysis data dictionary.

Then the developer takes the relations to 3NF and looks at the introduction of redundancy for improved performance. Of course, data redundancy becomes even more important for an Oracle warehouse developer than for a traditional OLTP designer, so we will carefully explore the options of table denormalization. We will also design a method for storing the precalculated data summaries that were defined in our systems analysis. Finally, we cannot always predict all the possible combinations of data attributes that will compose aggregate tables, so we must design a method for allowing our end users to dynamically define aggregation criteria and store the aggregate values into Oracle tables.

The process of normalization was originally intended to be a method for decomposing data structures into their smallest components. The process begins with the original data structures which are called unnormalized relations and progresses through 1NF to 3NF. At this stage, the data structures are completely free of redundancy and are at their most decomposed level. To fully appreciate the process, let's take a look at the successive process of normalization.

Unnormalized Form

Essentially, an unnormalized relation is a relation that contains repeating values. An unnormalized relation can also contain relations nested within other relations, as well as all kinds of transitive dependencies. Sometimes unnormalized relations are signified by 0NF, but an unnormalized relation is not to be confused with a denormalized relation. The unnormalized relation is any relation in its raw state and commonly contains repeating values and other characteristics that are not found in denormalized relations. The process of denormalization is a deliberate attempt to introduce controlled redundant items into an already normalized form.

Today, only á handful of DBMSs support repeating values, including Oracle, UniSQL® DBMS, and some other databases. The relational database model requires that each column within a table contains atomic values; and until Oracle8, there was no facility for indexing multiple occurrences of a data item within a table.

In any case, relations with repeating groups are supported by Oracle and the database designer must decide when to normalize the repeating groups into new relations or use Oracle constructs to leave the repeating group inside the entity. Oracle provides two constructs for allowing repeating groups within tables, the varying-array (VARRAY) table and the nested table. VARRAY tables (Figure 1.4) have the benefit of avoiding costly SQL joins and they can maintain the order of the VARRAY items based upon the sequence when they were stored. However, the longer row length of VARRAY tables causes full-table scans (FTSs) to run longer and the items inside the VARRAY cannot be indexed. More importantly, VARRAYs cannot be used when the number of repeating items is unknown or very large.

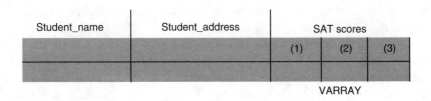

Figure 1.4   A VARRAY Table

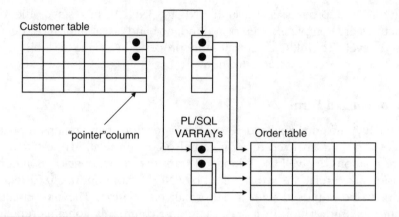

Figure 1.5   A Nested Table

NESTED TABLES

Using the Oracle nested table structure, subordinate data items can be directly linked to the base table by using Oracle's newest construct — object ID (OID). One of the remarkable extensions of the Oracle database is the ability to reference Oracle objects directly by using pointers as opposed to relational table joins (Figure 1.5). Proponents of the object-oriented database approach often criticize standard relational databases because of the requirement to reassemble an object every time it's referenced. They make statements such as, "It doesn't make sense to dismantle your car every time you are done driving it and rebuild the car each time you want to drive it."

Oracle has moved toward allowing complex objects to have a concrete existence. To support the concrete existence of complex objects, Oracle introduced the ability to build arrays of pointers with row references directly to Oracle tables. Just as a C++ program can use the char** data structure to have a pointer to an array of pointers, Oracle allows similar constructs whereby the components of the complex objects reside in real tables with pointers to the subordinate objects. At runtime, Oracle simply needs to dereference the pointers and the complex object can be quickly rebuilt from its component pieces.

Also, notice that sometimes repeating groups are derived from the sum of other values in the transaction relation. In those cases, we must make a conscious decision whether to redundantly store these summations or have Oracle compute them at runtime. Some shops even use nested tables as an adjunct to the 1NF representation of their data (Figure 1.6). Here we see that the student–grade relationship is accessible both with a

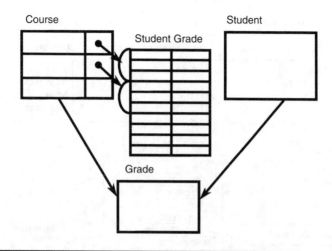

Figure 1.6   Concurrent 0NF and 1NF Data Representation

standard relational join into the grade table or by access via the nested table.

First Normal Form

In essence, any relation is in first normal form (1NF) if it does not contain any repeating values. Here, we have taken our relations with repeating values and moved them to separate relations. When the new relations are created, we carry the primary key of the original relation into the new relation.

From a physical design perspective, a 1NF relation implies that a table join will be required whenever the repeating groups are required in a SQL query. From a performance perspective, the table can be kept inside the base entity with VARRAY tables or nested tables. Another popular approach is to prejoin the tables using materialized views, thereby fetching the base data and the repeating groups in a single disk I/O.

For denormalization in data warehouses, 1NF tables are the most popular representation for fact tables (Figure 1.7).

This 1NF data representation is also popular for multidimensional data representation in data warehouse applications, where the end-user tools allow the end users to roll up data according to their specifications. In Oracle, the Oracle Express® engine provides multidimensional representation and the database must be sufficiently denormalized to quickly provide these views of the database. Figure 1.8 shows an Oracle9i external table mapped into a spreadsheet for multidimensional analysis as a Microsoft® Excel pivot table.

Star Query E/R Model

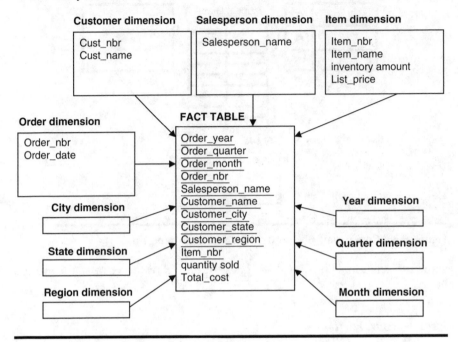

Figure 1.7   A 1NF Schema for a Data Warehouse

Second Normal Form

The purpose of the second normal form (2NF) test is to check for partial key dependencies. Partial key dependencies are created when we break off an unnormalized relation into 1NF by carrying the key, thereby creating a concatenated key with several data items. The formal definition of 2NF is described by Ted Codd and Chris Date:

> A relation is in second normal form if and only if the relation is in first normal form and each non-key attribute is fully functionally dependent on the entire concatenated key.

However, I prefer the following definition:

> A relation is in second normal form if each attribute depends on the key, the whole key, and nothing but the key, so help me Codd.

It should be apparent that the 2NF test only applies to relations that have more than one key field. A relation in 1NF that only has one key

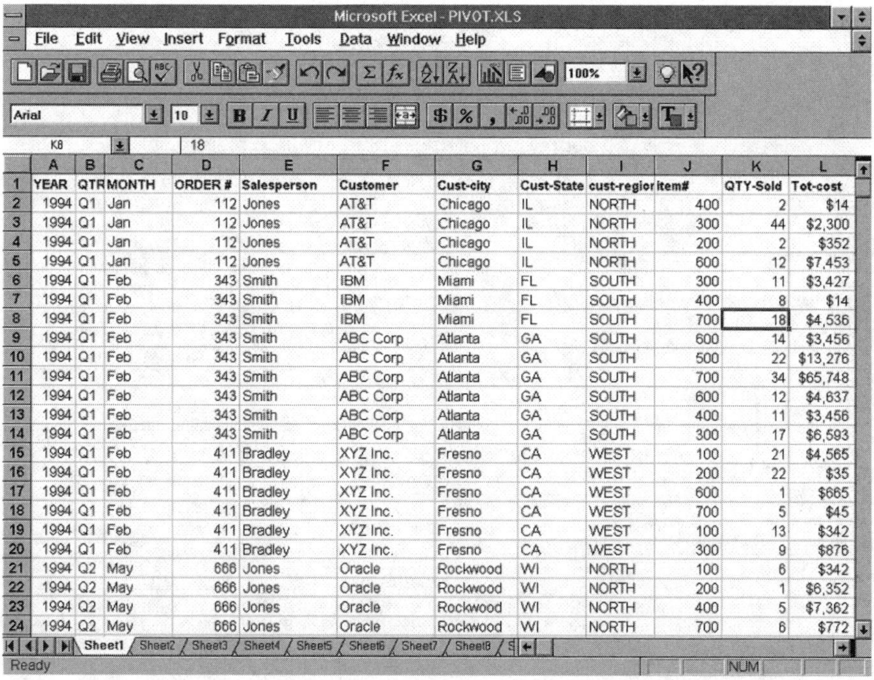

	A	B	C	D	E	F	G	H	I	J	K	L
1	YEAR	QTR	MONTH	ORDER #	Salesperson	Customer	Cust-city	Cust-State	cust-regior	item#	QTY-Sold	Tot-cost
2	1994	Q1	Jan	112	Jones	AT&T	Chicago	IL	NORTH	400	2	$14
3	1994	Q1	Jan	112	Jones	AT&T	Chicago	IL	NORTH	300	44	$2,300
4	1994	Q1	Jan	112	Jones	AT&T	Chicago	IL	NORTH	200	2	$352
5	1994	Q1	Jan	112	Jones	AT&T	Chicago	IL	NORTH	600	12	$7,453
6	1994	Q1	Feb	343	Smith	IBM	Miami	FL	SOUTH	300	11	$3,427
7	1994	Q1	Feb	343	Smith	IBM	Miami	FL	SOUTH	400	8	$14
8	1994	Q1	Feb	343	Smith	IBM	Miami	FL	SOUTH	700	18	$4,536
9	1994	Q1	Feb	343	Smith	ABC Corp	Atlanta	GA	SOUTH	600	14	$3,456
10	1994	Q1	Feb	343	Smith	ABC Corp	Atlanta	GA	SOUTH	500	22	$13,276
11	1994	Q1	Feb	343	Smith	ABC Corp	Atlanta	GA	SOUTH	700	34	$65,748
12	1994	Q1	Feb	343	Smith	ABC Corp	Atlanta	GA	SOUTH	600	12	$4,637
13	1994	Q1	Feb	343	Smith	ABC Corp	Atlanta	GA	SOUTH	400	11	$3,456
14	1994	Q1	Feb	343	Smith	ABC Corp	Atlanta	GA	SOUTH	300	17	$6,593
15	1994	Q1	Feb	411	Bradley	XYZ Inc.	Fresno	CA	WEST	100	21	$4,565
16	1994	Q1	Feb	411	Bradley	XYZ Inc.	Fresno	CA	WEST	200	22	$35
17	1994	Q1	Feb	411	Bradley	XYZ Inc.	Fresno	CA	WEST	600	1	$665
18	1994	Q1	Feb	411	Bradley	XYZ Inc.	Fresno	CA	WEST	700	5	$45
19	1994	Q1	Feb	411	Bradley	XYZ Inc.	Fresno	CA	WEST	100	13	$342
20	1994	Q1	Feb	411	Bradley	XYZ Inc.	Fresno	CA	WEST	300	9	$876
21	1994	Q2	May	666	Jones	Oracle	Rockwood	WI	NORTH	100	6	$342
22	1994	Q2	May	666	Jones	Oracle	Rockwood	WI	NORTH	200	1	$6,352
23	1994	Q2	May	666	Jones	Oracle	Rockwood	WI	NORTH	400	5	$7,362
24	1994	Q2	May	666	Jones	Oracle	Rockwood	WI	NORTH	700	6	$772

Figure 1.8 Using a Oracle9*i* External Table as a Spreadsheet for Data

is automatically in 2NF if each attribute is functionally dependent on the key.

Third Normal Form

The third normal form (3NF) test refers to transitive dependencies. A transitive dependency is a circumstance where one nonkey attribute is functionally dependent on another nonkey attribute. Whereas the 2NF test serves to check for dependencies between key fields and attribute fields, the 3NF test serves to check for dependencies between non-key attributes.

Next, let's examine the relationship between the logical database model and the database design.

E/R MODELING

If we have followed the process for normalization through 3NF, we will be able to derive an E/R model that is essentially free of redundant information. As a review, the E/R model was first introduced by Professor Emeritus Peter Chen from the University of Louisiana and it is sometimes

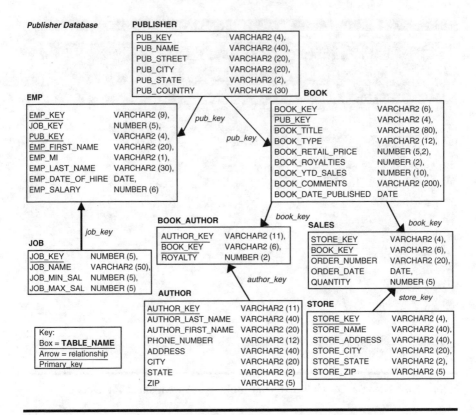

Figure 1.9   A 3NF E/R Model

called a Chen diagram. In the 25 years since the introduction of this model, many permutations have been created, but the basic principles of E/R modeling remain intact.

While an E/R model may be free of redundant information, it is impossible to implement the model in a relational database without introducing redundancy to support the data relationships. For example, if a data model was implemented using a pointer-based DBMS, such as IMS, pointers would be used to establish relationships between entities. For relational databases, data columns must be copied as foreign keys to establish data relationships, thereby introducing redundancy (Figure 1.9). Hence, the physical designer must implement tools to maintain the basic nature of the E/R model, while denormalizing the data structures for high-performance.

Oracle offers several denormalization tools and techniques, namely materialized views and manual preaggregation. This implies that we may have several relational models within the physical schema. The new Oracle9*i* data model extensions provide the following physical capabilities:

- Prejoining tables — this is achieved by deliberately introducing redundancy into the data model. Queries that required complex and time-consuming table joins can now be retrieved in a single disk I/O operation.
- Modeling real-world objects — it is no longer a requirement for the relational database designer to model complex objects in their most atomic components and rebuild them at runtime. Using Oracle's object-oriented constructs, real-world objects can have a concrete existence. Oracle can use arrays of pointers to represent these complex objects.
- Coupling of data and behavior — one of the important constructs of object orientation is the tight coupling of object behaviors with the objects themselves. In Oracle, member methods can be created upon the Oracle object. All processes that manipulate the object are encapsulated inside Oracle's data dictionary. This functionality has huge benefits for the development of all Oracle systems. Prior to the introduction of member methods, each Oracle developer was essentially a custom craftsman writing custom SQL to access Oracle information. By using member methods, all interfaces to the Oracle database are performed using pretested methods with known interfaces. Thus, the Oracle developer's role changes from custom craftsman to more of an assembly-line coder. You simply choose from a list of prewritten member methods to access Oracle information.

These physical constructs allow us to create many levels of data aggregation and enjoy the benefits of a 3NF and a denormalized data structure (Figure 1.10).

BRIDGING BETWEEN LOGICAL AND PHYSICAL MODELS

To bridge the gap between the logical data model in the physical database design, the database designer must start by taking a survey all the different kinds of constructs that are available within their DBMS. In this example, we will use the Oracle databases as an example and look at the different constructs that are available for our use in physical design:

- Data files — data files may be created with different block sizes, spanned upon different disks, and use different rate levels.
- Tablespaces — tablespaces may be created with automatic segments space management (ASSM), dictionary-managed or locally managed tablespaces (LMTs), and a host of other tablespace options that affect the physical design of the system.

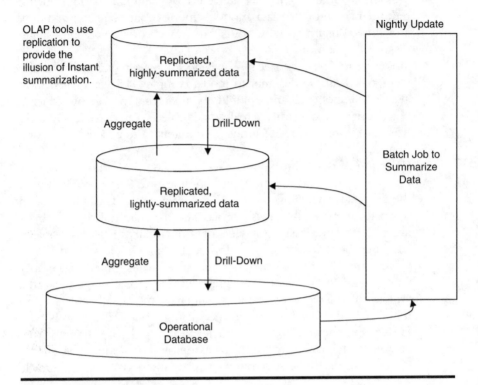

Figure 1.10 A Multilevel Physical Data Representation

- Instance — the physical design of the database instance is critical to the database. In Oracle, the instance region is composed of over a dozen background processes and a random-access memory (RAM) region called the System Global Area (SGA).
- Table structures — the Oracle database offers a host of different table structures, including standard relational tables, the array tables, (non-1NF tables), nested tables, index-organized tables (IOT), as well as table storage for the objects such as video and other images.
- Column structures — the Oracle database allows for a variety of different ways to define columns within the table, most notably the object-oriented concept of ADTs (user-defined data types). ADTs allow the nesting of all data types with other data types to more accurately model the real world.
- Indexing structures — an important part of physical database design is building indexes and other access structures with the sole intent of improving the performance of the database system. Within

Oracle, these index structures can take a variety of forms including standard B-tree indexes, bitmapped indexes, function-based indexes (FBIs), and partitioned indexes. It's up to the database designer to create the appropriate indexes on the Oracle tables to ensure the fastest performance for all SQL that runs against these tables.

Again, the primary goal of physical database design is to translate the logical data model into a suitable physical database model. Next, we will move on and look at how specific data relationships are transformed from a logical model into a physical Oracle database design.

Activities of Oracle Physical Design

During the physical design phase, Oracle professionals apply the specific constructs of Oracle to their logical data models. In addition to the tasks listed above, we also see important physical design tasks:

- Estimate initial size and growth — proper sizing and disk planning help ensure unlimited growth and reduced fragmentation. In Oracle Database 10g, a common approach is to implement automatic storage management (ASM). With ASM, all internal components (files, tablespaces, object sizing) are internalized and managed by Oracle.
- Create data purging/archiving — this task has become less important as Oracle has grown in the ability to support large volumes of data, but in multiterabyte systems, archiving is still an important design issue.
- Planning access keys — in dynamic Oracle systems, frequently changing keys can cause a huge problem, because shifts in keys can cause massive row movement and out-of-balance indexes. The use of sequence-based keys is essential for these types of systems.
- Proper indexing — failure to add appropriate indexes (especially FBIs, bitmap indexes, and IOTs) can impede system performance by causing suboptimal index access and unnecessary large-table, FTSs.

In summary, Oracle physical design involves the mapping of specific Oracle physical constructs to the logical database model. Now that we have covered the basics, we are ready to explore the use of specific Oracle entities (e.g., tables, indexes, IOTs) and see how they map to your logical database design.

PHYSICAL DESIGN REQUIREMENTS VALIDATION

The requirements validation is performed to ensure that the system meets the infrastructure requirements of the end user. A requirements evaluation is a simple assessment and mapping of the components of all inputs, data storage, and outputs to ensure that all data items are present. The requirements analysis does not attempt to validate the functionality of the system and is commonly performed after the nonfunctional prototype is completed. For most database systems development, the nonworking prototype screens, prototype Oracle table and index design, and the output design (mockup screens and reports) can be done quickly.

Working from the use-case documents and functional analysis documents (DFD, process logic specifications), the designer can create dummy screens in a matter of minutes. For an online system with 100 tables and 200 screens, a nonworking prototype can be created in a few weeks by a single designer.

This nonworking prototype is shown to the end-user representative to ensure that the infrastructure requirements have been met. Once approved by the end-user community, the development team begins the process of fleshing out the prototype and turning it into a working system. This is the bulk of the development process and commonly takes more effort than all of the other development areas combined.

In summary, the requirements evaluation has the following tasks:

- End-user interface (EUI) requirements validation — do the online screens and output reports contain the stated data items?
- Input requirements validation— do each of the input screens properly validate the data? In the information technology (IT) industry, this is called chimpanzee testing because the validation involves randomly pressing keys and filling-in inputs in an attempt to confuse the input screen.
- Database requirements validation — do the data structures meet the requirements specified in the EUI?
- Requirements data mapping— each of the data inputs are mapped to the database and to the output screens and reports. Again, this is a simple mapping and it says nothing about the functionality (or lack thereof) of the existing system.

Again, the requirements evaluation is nothing more than the identification of input, storage, and output data items and the mapping of the data items to and from the database. It says nothing about the whether the system actually does anything.

It is also sad that many academicians (and others without real-world experience) fail to understand that the requirements validation is so simple that it is almost trivial. In a dynamic analysis project, screens, reports, and Oracle tables can be created in minutes using wizards, Hypertext Markup Language (HTML) generators, Oracle Enterprise Manager, etc. Even a complex system with 500 screens can be prototyped by a single analyst in just a few weeks.

Once we've confirmed that the system components (input screens, database objects, output screens, and reports) contain the proper data elements and mappings, we're ready for the true validation of the system — the functional validation.

How to Identify a Poor Requirements Evaluation

The experienced Oracle professional can quickly identify an inept requirements validation. Sadly, it is not uncommon for companies to hire inept academicians. These PhD fools are so common that IT professionals have special names for them, the most common being the Educated Idiot or EI for short.

The EI usually has an impressive resume with PhD degrees and dozens of citations to research projects with no practical application and publications in obscure academic journals that few people ever read. They may site books that they have written, but fail to tell you that their books were so obtuse and unpopular that they only sold a thousand copies.

The EI is dangerous because nontechnical, non-IT managers may give the EI more credit than she deserves. The EI commonly does not possess any real-world development experience and lacks the necessary technical skills to perform a complete requirements analysis. She may be able to view the input and output screens and look at the reports, but does not have enough skill to examine the critical requirements component of the structure of the underlying database.

Functional Validation

The most important part of any systems design is evaluating the functionality of the existing system. A functional analysis of the existing system gives the designer insights into the three major areas of functional evaluation, inputs, processes, and outputs. All systems, regardless of size, complexity, or implementation, have the following functional characteristics:

- Input functional validation — end-user interfaces via online screens or batch interfaces (File Transfer Protocol, document submission) are validated to ensure that they accept the correct datatypes and conform to all required check constraints (as defined in the Oracle dba_constraints view).

- Processing functional validation — this step examines how the inputs are transformed and stored in the database. This is the most critical area of functional evaluation because the data transformations are the core of the system. Without meaningful processes, the system is nothing more than an empty shell of prototype screens.
- Output functional validation — all systems provide output. The output may be in the form of EUI display (both online and batch) or stored in the database.

To properly conduct a functional evaluation, we must carefully look under the covers. The analyst must hand-execute all of the code within the system to ensure that the internal data transformations match the requirements.

Remember, only the functional evaluation can tell you anything about the functional quality of the existing system. Relying solely on the requirements validation is insanity, because a system has no use without process logic to transform the data.

A legitimate functional validation must include a complete description of all process logic and validation data. In plain English, the existing system must be exercised to ensure that expected inputs produce the proper outputs.

How to Spot a Poor Functional Analysis

Because the work of specifying and validating the functional requirements is commonly the task of a nontechnical or semitechnical person, there are many opportunities for serious misunderstandings and errors.

The most common hallmark of a poor functional analysis is a misunderstanding of the purpose of functional analysis. The EIs are noted for this type of error. In their quest to appear erudite, EIs will commonly attempt to cloud the issue with wordy, verbose, and redundant jargon, replete with *non sequiturs* and inaccurate conclusions. I once heard an alleged expert claim that it was not necessary to test the system or inspect the database to perform a valid functional analysis! (I swear, I'm not making this up.)

Next, let's examine how to estimate the costs for the existing system.

Evaluating the Worth of an Existing System

As an Oracle professional you may be asked to evaluate an existing system and estimate the amount of money that was (or should have been) expended on the development effort for the system. Estimating the costs of an existing system is always problematic because of the following issues:

■ Technology factors — the type of technology has a huge influence on the costs. A system developed in an older technology (i.e., DC Common Business-Oriented Language [COBOL] system with CICS BMS screens) may cost ten times more than a state-of-the-art Java™ system with reusable components and HTML screens that are generated quickly with a HTML generator software (FrontPage®, Cold Fusion®, Dreamweaver®, etc).

■ Productivity factors — it has long been recognized that IT develops have a nonlinear relationship between productivity and costs. On the low end, a $30-an-hour beginner has a cost/productivity factor far less than the $200-an-hour guru. This is because IT developers with more than a decade of full-time development experience know exactly how to solve a problem. Further, experienced IT developers usually have a personal library of reusable code that performs common business functions. These libraries allow the experienced developer to be far cheaper than the less expensive, inept beginner.

■ Cost factors — the widespread difference in costs between U.S. and overseas IT consulting can differ by an order of magnitude. In today's virtual world, many companies abandon the U.S. resources and outsource their IT development efforts where experienced programmers can be acquired for less than $500 per month. As of 2003, Bangalore, India; Moscow, Russia; and Eastern Europe are all courting U.S. customers.

Before we see the problems that these variables introduce into any attempt to place an estimated cost on a system, let's examine the different methods that are employed to estimate the costs for an existing system. The following approaches have been tried in attempts to estimate the worth of an existing system:

■ Compare your system with a known, similar system — in this approach, common metrics are gathered for the existing system and then compared to a similar system. The common metrics might include the programming language, a subjective complexity rating for each function, and estimated productivity rates for the developers. Of course, this approach is fraught with problems, the foremost being the subjective nature of the estimates and the problem of finding a truly similar system. The subjective nature of the inputs allows you to rig the result to say anything that you desire.

■ Use mathematical models — there are numerous numerical tools that have been designed to attempt to determine how much money a system may have cost. These tools include Constructive Cost Model (COCOMO) and many others, none of which are recognized as statistically valid. All of these tools have a fatal flaw that makes them useless as a *post hoc* cost estimation tool. The major flaw is the subjective nature of the estimation parameters. For example, the COCOMO tool allows the analyst to specify the following nonquantifiable and subjective factors:

– Module size — this is flawed because of the widespread use of object-oriented languages such as Java. The hallmark of an object-oriented language is the ability to reuse components to greatly reduce development time. It is invalid for any tool (like COCCOMO) to assume that a Java method of a given size required any specific amount of effort to produce.

– Labor rates — as we have noted, this is an invalid parameter because it does not consider the nonlinear relationship between experience and productivity.

– Effort multipliers — if the analyst does not like the resulting numbers, they need only adjust one of the subjective multipliers to receive any cost they desire.

■ Accept external bids — using this approach, the IT analyst presents a requirements document (or maybe a functional prototype with process logic specification) to a series of vendors for an estimate. To avoid the immoral act of asking for an estimate under false pretenses (because you have no intention of actually accepting the estimate), the analyst engages the third party consultancy with the promise to pay the fair market price for all estimation services if they fail to engage the consultancy to develop the system. To ensure that the external bid is accurate, the bidder is only provided with the functional analysis document and they have no access whatsoever to the existing system.

As we can see, both the comparison approach and math model approach have a problem with current-value dollars. The costs of developing a system three years ago might be quite different than the costs today. In summary, the only valid way to determine the real costs for an existing system is to commission a consultancy to bid on the system, seeing only the functional specifications. Offering up front to pay for the estimate removes the moral issue of asking for a bid when you do not intend to accept the bid. Also, not telling the consultancy that you have no intention of using the bid ensures that you receive a competitive bid.

LOCATING ORACLE PHYSICAL DESIGN FLAWS

Once you have your database design arsenal in place, you can begin the work of building correct physical designs from scratch and managing the physical design lifecycle once a system goes into production. But, how do you quickly spot physical design flaws in an up-and-running database?

It definitely takes a trained eye to uncover the root cause of identified performance problems, but Table 1.1 will help get you started. It lists just a few of the most common database performance problems and the possible physical design gremlins that could be the culprit in an Oracle database.

Using a quality performance monitor, you can be quickly led to the performance headaches in your database. Then, using either your intelligent data-modeling tool or the combination of your database administration and change control product, you can remedy the situation.

Fixing foundational flaws in a database is never easy, but perhaps one day the DBA community will be treated to software that gets things right, before the situation turns ugly.

Table 1.1   Performance Problems and Possible Causes

Performance Category	Performance Problem	Possible Design Cause
Memory	Poor data buffer cache hit ratio	Too many long table scans — invalid indexing scheme
		Not enough RAM devoted to buffer cache memory area
		Invalid object placement using Oracle's KEEP and RECYCLE buffer caches
		Not keeping small lookup tables in cache using CACHE table parameter
	Poor memory/disk sort ratio	Not presorting data when possible
Contention	Redo log waits	Incorrect sizing of Oracle redo logs
		Insufficient memory allocated to log buffer area
	Free list waits	Not enough free lists assigned to tables
		Not using Oracle9i's auto segment management
	Rollback waits	Insufficient number of rollback segments
		Not using Oracle9i's auto-UNDO management

Table 1.1 Performance Problems and Possible Causes (Continued)

Performance Category	Performance Problem	Possible Design Cause
I/O	Identified disk contention	Not separating tables and accompanying indexes into different tablespaces on different physical drives
	Slow access to system information	Not placing SYSTEM tablespace on little accessed physical drive
	Slow disk sorts	Placing tablespace used for disk sort activity on RAID5 drive or heavily accessed physical volume
	Abnormally high physical I/O	Too many long table scans — invalid indexing scheme Not enough RAM devoted to buffer cache memory area Invalid object placement using Oracle8's KEEP and RECYCLE buffer caches Not keeping small lookup tables in cache using CACHE table parameter
Space	Out of space conditions (storage structures)	Poorly forecasted data volumes in physical design
	Tablespace fragmentation	Invalid settings for either object space sizes or tablespace object settings (e.g., PCTINCREASE) Not using locally managed tablespaces in Oracle8 and above
SQL	Large JOIN queries	Overnormalized database design
Object activity	Chaining in tables	Incorrect amount of PCTFREE, PCTUSED settings for objects Too small database block size
	Rollback extension	Incorrect sizing of rollback segments for given application transaction Not using Oracle9i's auto-UNDO management
	Many large table scans	Incorrect indexing scheme
	Object fragmentation	Incorrect initial sizing Not using LMTs

2

PHYSICAL ENTITY DESIGN
FOR ORACLE

INTRODUCTION

This chapter deals with the conversion of a logical schema into a physical design. As we noted in Chapter 1, Oracle provides a wealth of options for modeling data relationships. It's up to the physical designers to choose the most appropriate physical construct to represent their data.

This chapter addresses the following topics and discusses how the logical data model can be converted into an Oracle physical design:

- Data relationship and physical design
- Hierarchical attribute design
- Object-oriented design for Oracle
- Using referential integrity (RI)

Let's begin by looking at the different physical options for modeling logical data relationships.

DATA RELATIONSHIPS AND PHYSICAL DESIGN

As we know, five types of data relationships must be considered when converting a logical model into a physical design:

1. One-to-one relationships
2. One-to-many relationships
3. Many-to-many relationships
4. Recursive many-to-many relationships
5. The IS-A (pronounced "is a") relationship (class hierarchies)

The effective database designer's job is to represent these types of relationships in a sensible way and ensure acceptable warehouse performance.

Redundancy and Physical Design

An Oracle database with either one-to-many or many-to-many relationships must have redundant foreign keys embedded in the tables to establish logical relationships. Redundant foreign keys in the subordinate tables create the data relationships, making it possible to join tables together and relate the contents of the data items in the tables. While 3NF designs were very popular in the 1980s when disks were expensive, today's database designers deliberately introduce redundancy into the physical model to improve performance.

As the size of the database increases, redundancy can become a major problem. Today, many users create large databases, many of which contain trillions of bytes. For databases of this size, a single table can contain more than a billion rows, and the introduction of a single new column to a table can represent thousands of dollars in additional disk expense. Data redundancy is detrimental for two reasons:

1. Duplicating the redundant material consumes disk storage space
2. Updating redundant data requires extra processing

Redundant duplication of very large and highly volatile data items can cause huge processing bottlenecks.

However, this does not imply that redundancy is always undesirable. Performance is still an overriding factor in most systems. Proper control of redundant information implies that redundant information may be introduced into any structure as long as the performance improvements outweigh the additional disk costs and update problems.

Since the first publication of Dr. Edgar F. Codd's 1993 research paper, "Providing OLAP (Online Analytical Processing) To User-Analysts: An IT Mandate," database designers have attempted to find an optimum way of structuring tables for low data redundancy. Codd's rules of normalization guide designers to create logically correct table structures with no redundancy, but performance rules often dictate the introduction of duplicated data to improve performance.

This is especially true for distributed Oracle databases. Any node in a distributed database might want to browse a list of customers at other nodes without establishing a connection to that node. The technological problems inherent in the two-phase commit necessitate widespread replication of entire tables or selected columns from tables. However, the

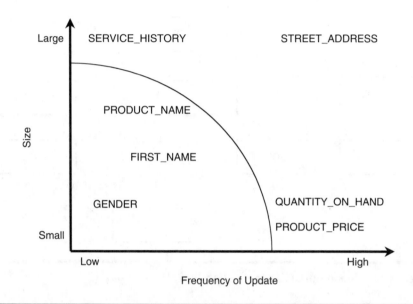

Figure 2.1 The Data Redundancy Boundary

distributed database designer does not have free reign to introduce redundancy anywhere in the enterprise. Redundancy always carries a price, whether it is the cost of the disk storage or the cost of maintaining a parallel update scheme. Figure 2.1 shows a strategy for analyzing the consequences of data redundancy.

In Figure 2.1, a boundary line lies within a range between the size of a redundant data item and the update frequency of the data item. The size of the data item relates to the disk costs associated with storing the item. The update frequency is associated with the cost of keeping the redundant data current, whether by replication techniques or by materialized views.

Because the relative costs are different for each hardware configuration and for each application, this boundary may be quite different depending on the type of application. The rapid decrease in the disk storage costs designates that the size boundary is only important for large-scale redundancy. A large, frequently changing item is not a good candidate for redundancy. But large static items or small, frequently changing items are acceptable for redundancy. Small static items (e.g., gender) represent ideal candidates for redundant duplication.

As we have noted, Oracle provides a wealth of options for modeling data relationships and we must understand the ramifications of each option. Let's begin with a review of one-to-many data relationships.

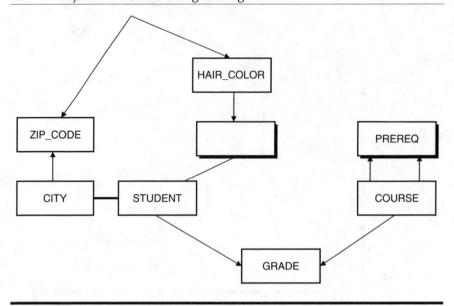

Figure 2.2 Inappropriate Data Relationships

The Dangers of Overnormalization

When creating an E/R model, it is often tempting to look at the data model from a purely logical perspective without any regard for the physical implementation, specifically, the overhead from SQL table joins.

The savvy database designer strives to identify all of the logical relationships in the data model, but does not fall into the trap of overnormalization. For example, a common mistake is pseudorelationships. A pseudorelationship is when the one-to-many relationship actually exists, but the application has no need to reference this relationship. To illustrate, consider the E/R model in Figure 2.2.

From a purely theoretical perspective, this is a correct 3NF data representation:

■ A many-to-many data relationship exists between the HAIR_COLOR and STUDENT entities. Many students have blonde hair and blonde hair is common to many students. Hence, we create a many-to-many relationship between these entities.
■ A one-to-many relationship (or possibly a many-to-many relationship) exists between CITY and ZIP_CODE. Each city has many zip codes and a zip code is for one and only one city.

So, does this logical model imply the physical creation of a ZIP_CODE and HAIR_COLOR table? The solution depends upon whether any other nonkey data items exist within the HAIR_COLOR entity.

Remember, the overhead of a relational database is the requirement that actual column values be repeated to establish the data relationship. Hence, if many other data items relating to hair color are required, then it is perfectly appropriate to create another entity called HAIR_COLOR. But in this case, even though a many-to-many relationship exists between HAIR_COLOR and STUDENT, HAIR_COLOR is a stand-alone data attribute, so it is unnecessary to create an additional data structure.

Another example is the ZIP_CODE attribute in the STUDENT entity. At first glance, it appears that a violation of 3NF (i.e., a transitive dependency) has occurred between CITY and ZIP_CODE. In other words, it appears that a ZIP_CODE is paired with the CITY of residence for the STUDENT. If each city has many zip codes, while each zip code refers only to one city, it makes sense to model this as a one-to-many data relationship and theory demands creating a separate entity called ZIP. However, this is another case where the ZIP entity lacks key attributes, making it impractical to create the ZIP entity. In other words, ZIP_CODE has no associated data items. Creating a database table with only one data column would be nonsense.

This example demonstrates that it is not enough to group together like items and then identify the data relationships. A practical test must be made regarding the presence of nonkey attributes within an entity class. If an entity has no attributes (i.e., the table has only one field), the presence of the entity is nothing more than an index to the foreign key in the member entity.

Therefore, both of these pseudorelationships can be removed from the E/R model. This technique not only simplifies the number of entities, but it creates a better environment for an architecture. More data is logically grouped together, resulting in less SQL join overhead.

Now, let's take a look at another example of overnormalization. The goal of these examples is to give you a feel for the judgments required for proper physical design techniques.

Denormalizing One-to-Many Data Relationships

One-to-many relationships exist in many real-world situations. Many entities that possess one-to-many relationships can be removed from the data model, eliminating some join operations. The basic principle here is simple: redundant information avoids expensive SQL joins and yields faster processing. But remember, designers must deal with the issue of additional disk storage and the problems associated with updating the redundant data. For example, consider the E/R model shown in Figure 2.3, where the structure is in pure 3NF with no redundancy.

Note the separate tables for CITY and STATE. These tables exist because each state has many cities and each city belongs to one and only one state.

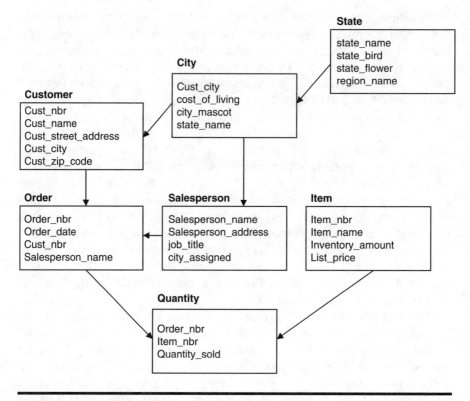

Figure 2.3 An Overnormalized Design

This model works for most transactions on an OLTP system. However, this high degree of normalization would require the joining of the CITY and STATE tables every time that address information is requested.

Consider a query to display the STATE_BIRD for all orders that have been placed for birdseed. This is a cumbersome query that requires the joining of six tables. From a schema perspective, this is because the ITEM_NAME (birdseed) is separated from STATE (STATE_BIRD) by six tables:

```
select
    state_bird
from
    state
natural join
    city
natural join
    customer
```

```
natural join
    order
natural join
    quantity
natural join
    item
where
    item_name = 'birdseed'
;
```

Note in the example above that we are using the Oracle9*i* natural join feature, which allows us to remove the join criteria from the WHERE clause.

What if your goal is to simplify the data structure by removing several of the one-to-many relationships? Adding redundancy poses two problems:

1. You need additional disk space for the redundant item.
2. You need a technique to update the redundant items if they are changed.

Here is a proposed solution that removes the STATE and CITY tables (Figure 2.4).

Now that we have denormalized the STATE and CITY relations, we will have widespread duplication of several data items in the CUSTOMER tables, namely COST_OF_LIVING, STATE_BIRD, and so on. Of course, these data items are static, so updates are not an issue.

The real benefit of this denormalization is on the speed of the query. Using this same STATE_BIRD query as before, you can see how it is simplified by removing the extra tables. This removes two table joins and speeds up the whole query:

```
select
    state_bird
from
    customer
natural join
    order
natural join
    quantity
natural join
    item
```

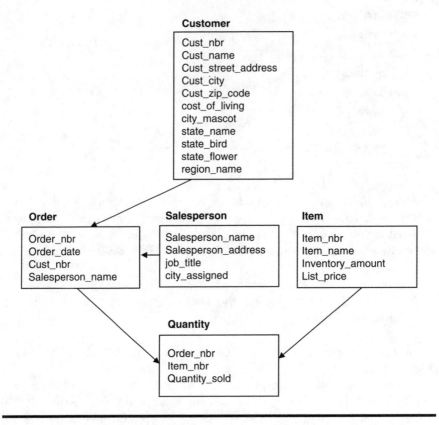

Figure 2.4   A Denormalized Schema

```
where
     item_name = 'birdseed'
;
```

It is still necessary to join three tables, but this query results in a much faster, simpler query than the original five-way table join. Of course, there are limits to massive denormalization. If you carry the denormalization concept to the extreme, you could prejoin every entity in the schema together into a single, highly redundant table. Such a table would be impossible to manage because of the high degree of redundancy.

Denormalizing Many-to-Many Data Relationships

In many cases, a many-to-many relationship can be condensed into a more efficient structure to improve the speed of data retrieval. After all, fewer tables need to be joined to get the desired information. To understand how

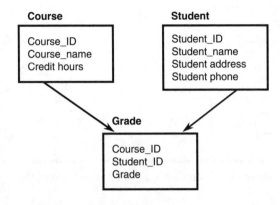

Figure 2.5 A Many-to-Many Relationship

a many-to-many relationship can be collapsed into a more compact structure, consider the relationship between a course and a student.

We can assume that a student takes many courses and each course has many students. This is a classical many-to-many relationship and requires that we define a junction table (Figure 2.5) between the base entities to establish the necessary foreign keys. Note that the junction table is called GRADE with the following contents:

- COURSE_ID — the primary key for the COURSE table
- STUDENT_ID — the primary key for the STUDENT table
- GRADE — a single, nonkey attribute for both foreign keys

Next, consider the question: In what context does a grade have meaning? Stating that "the grade was A in CS-101" is insufficient and stating, "Joe earned an A" makes no sense. Only when both the student number and the course number are associated does the grade column have meaning. Stating that "Joe earned an A in CS-101" makes sense. In summary, the grade only makes sense in the context of both the student and course.

So, how could we denormalize such a relationship? The answer is that we could join all three tables together and create a single, highly redundant table. The advantage to this denormalization would be that all STUDENT, COURSE, and GRADE information would be available in a single disk I/O, but the downside would be the increase volume of update overhead for DML statements. In practice, this type of many-to-many relationship would be ideal for an Oracle materialized view.

Next, let's examine recursive many-to-many relationships.

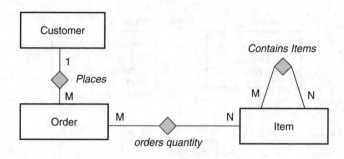

Figure 2.6   Examples of a Recursive Many-to-Many Relationship

Recursive Data Relationships

Recursive many-to-many relationships contain an object that also has a many-to-many relationship with other occurrences of the same object. These relationships are often termed Bill-of-Materials (BOM) relationships and the graphical representation of the recursive relationship is sometimes termed a BOM explosion. These relationships are recursive because a single query makes many subpasses through the tables to arrive at the solution (see Figure 2.6).

BOM relationships denote an object with a many-to-many relationship with another object in the same class. In other words, a part may consist of other parts, but at the same time, it is a component in a larger assembly. For example, a class at a university may have many prerequisites, but at the same time, it is a prerequisite for another class. Figure 2.7 depicts a course–prerequisite hierarchy for a university. Note that the IS-A prerequisite relationships are relatively straightforward, indicating which courses are required before taking another course. For example, the prerequisites for Linear Equations 445 are Business 400, Accounting 305, and Multivariate Statistics 450. These courses all have prerequisites of their own, which may also have prerequisites, and so on.

Each occurrence of a COURSE object has different topics and a complete implementation must iterate through all courses until reaching terminus, the point where the course has no further prerequisites. Unfortunately, the recursive many-to-many relationship is confusing and almost impossible to understand without the aid of a graphical representation. Visualize the recursive many-to-many relationship as an ordinary many-to-many relationship with the Part entity pulled apart into Part' and Part" (Figure 2.8).

There are many real-world examples of recursive many-to-many data relationships (Figure 2.9). For example, parts and components are recursive.

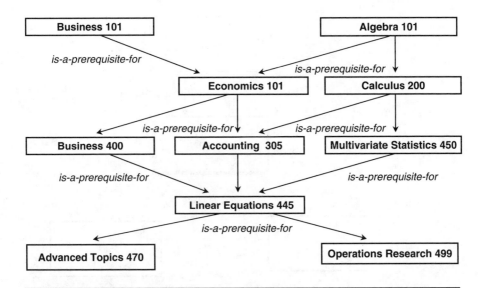

Figure 2.7   Expanding a Recursive Many-to-Many Relationship

Each part has many parts and at the same time, a part may be a subpart of a larger part.

With an understanding of the nature of recursive relationships, the question becomes one of implementation: What is the best way to represent a recursive relationship in Oracle and navigate the structure?

The following Oracle table definitions describe the tables for the part–component example:

```
CREATE TABLE PART(
part_nbr      number,
part_name     varchar2(10),
part_desc     varchar2(10),
qty_on_hand   number);

CREATE TABLE COMPONENT (
has_part      number,
is_a_part     number,
qty           number);
```

Look closely at the COMPONENT example. Both the has_part and is_a_part fields are foreign keys for the part_nbr field in the PART table. Therefore, the COMPONENT table is all keyed except for the qty

The relationship:

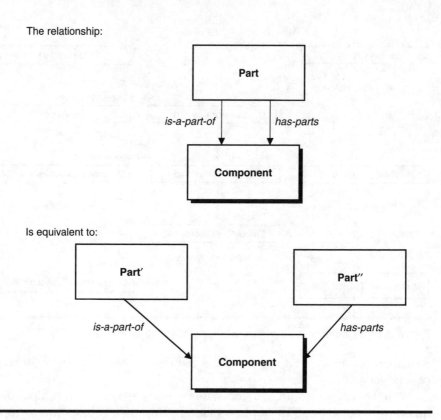

Figure 2.8   A Junction Table Establishes the Relationship

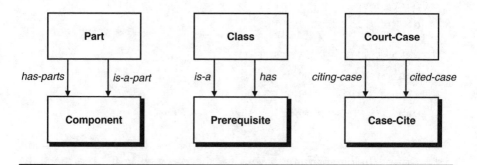

Figure 2.9   Examples of Recursive Relationships

field, which tells how many parts belong in an assembly. Look at the following SQL code required to display all components in a `Happy_Meal`:

```
select
    part_name
from
    part,
    component
where
    has_part = 'happy meal'
and
    part.part_nbr = component.has_part;
```

This type of Oracle SQL query requires joining the table against itself. Unfortunately, because all items are of the same type (e.g., PART), no real substitute exists for this type of data relationship.

MASSIVE DENORMALIZATION: STAR SCHEMA DESIGN

Dr. Ralph Kimball first introduced the star schema design as an alternative database design for data warehouses. The name *star* comes directly from the design form, where a large fact table resides at the center of the model surrounded by various points or reference tables. The basic principle behind the star query schema is the introduction of highly redundant data for high performance. With a star schema, the designer can simulate the functions of a multidimensional database without having to purchase expensive third-party software. Kimball describes denormalization as the prejoining of tables, such that the runtime application does not have to join tables. At the heart of the star schema, the fact table is usually composed entirely of key values and raw data. A fact table may have millions of rows.

Surrounding the fact table is a series of dimension tables that add value to the base information in the fact table. For example, consider the E/R model for the sales database shown in Figure 2.10.

Remember, the rules of database design have changed. In the 1980s, normalization theory emphasized the need to control redundancy and touted the benefits of a structure that was free of redundant data. Today, with disk prices at an all-time low, the attitude toward redundancy has changed radically. The relational vendors are offering a plethora of tools to allow snapshots and other methods for replicating data. Other vendors are offering database products such as UniSQL that allow for non-1NF implementations. Today, it is perfectly acceptable to create 1NF implementations

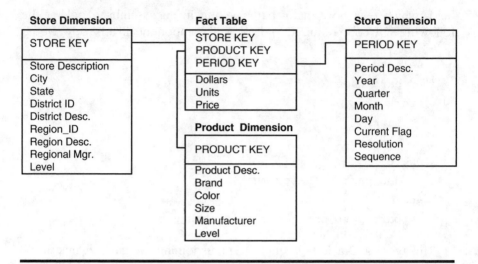

Figure 2.10   A Sample Star Schema

of normalized databases, which means prejoining tables to avoid the high performance costs of runtime SQL joins.

In summary, the basic principle behind the star query schema is to introduce highly redundant data for performance reasons.

OBJECT-ORIENTED DATABASE DESIGN

Rather than rebuild the Oracle engine as an object-oriented architecture, Oracle decided to keep the base relational engine and add object-oriented functionality on top of the standard relational architecture. Critics of the relational database model cite the shortcomings of relational databases:

- No modeling of real-world objects — unlike pure object-oriented languages that support collections of pointers, relational databases require real-time table joins to build complex objects. Figure 2.11 shows the mapping between real objects and a relational database schema.
- No support for object-oriented constructs such as inheritance and polymorphism.
- No methods — objects cannot behave according to predefined methods.
- Low code reusability — all SQL and Procedural Language/Structured Query Language (PL/SQL) is stored externally and is hard to locate and reuse.

The object layer of Oracle9*i* has implemented a number of new features. In this chapter, we'll limit our discussion to the following object-oriented issues:

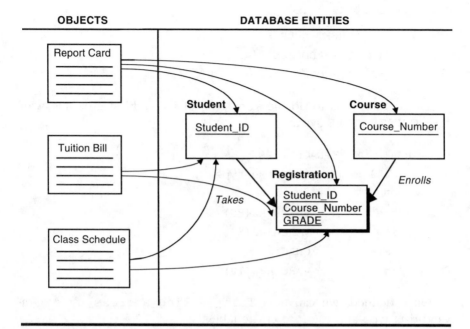

Figure 2.11   Complex Objects and Relational Schema

- ADTs
- Modeling class hierarchies (IS-A relationships)

In Chapter 7, we'll examine object tables in more detail, but for now we will limit our discussion to schema-level modeling with objects. Let's take a quick look at each of these features and see how they influence the physical design of the database.

Abstract Data Types

Rather than being constrained to the basic relational data types of INT, VARCHAR, and FLOAT, Oracle9*i* allows the definition of data types to be composed of many subtypes. For example, the following hierarchical COBOL data definition could be implemented in Oracle as an ADDRESS data type:

```
02 CUSTOMER_STUFF

05 CUSTOMER_FULL_NAME

      07 FIRST_NAME         PIC X(80).
      07 MIDDLE_NAME        PIC X(80).
      07 LAST_NAME          PIC X(80).
```

```
05  CUSTOMER-ADDRESS.
      07 STREET-ADDRESS          PIC X(80).
      07 CITY-ADDRESS            PIC X(80).
      07 ZIP-CODE                PIC X(5).
```

Oracle allows us to do the same type of hierarchical grouping with their CREATE TYPE syntax.

```
CREATE OR REPLACE TYPE
    full_mailing_address_type
AS OBJECT
( Street        VARCHAR2(80),
  City          VARCHAR2(80),
  State         CHAR(2),
  Zip           VARCHAR2(10) );
```

Once defined, we can treat full_mailing_address_type as a valid data type and use it to create tables.

```
CREATE TABLE
    customer
    (
      full_name              full_name_type,
      full_address           full_mailing_address_type,
    );
```

Now that the Oracle table is defined, we can reference full_mailing_address_type in our SQL just as if it were a primitive data type:

```
insert into
    customer
values (
    full_name_type('ANDREW','S.','BURLESON'),
    full_mailing_address_type
        ('123 1st st','Minot','ND','74635');
```

Next, let's select from this table. Below, we see a different output than from an ordinary SELECT statement.

```
SQL> select * from customer;


FULL_NAME(FIRST_NAME, MI, LAST_NAME)
-----------------------------------------
FULL_ADDRESS(STREET, CITY, STATE, ZIP)
---------------------------------------------------
-----------
FULL_NAME_TYPE('Andrew', 'S', 'Burleson')
FULL_MAILING_ADDRESS_TYPE('123 1st st', 'Minot', '
ND', '74635')
```

As we can see, using ADTs allows for the physical representation of hierarchical data relationships, but this ability is not always used in relational design because of the obtuse SQL syntax that is required to access the data.

Next, let's examine the modeling of class hierarchies in physical database design.

DESIGNING CLASS HIERARCHIES

The IS-A relationship is a data relationship that indicates a type/subtype data relationship. While traditional E/R modeling deals only with single entities, the IS-A approach recognizes that many types or classes of an individual entity can exist. In fact, the IS-A relationship is the foundation of object-oriented programming, which allows the designer to create hierarchies of related classes and then use inheritance and polymorphism to control which data items will participate in the low-level objects.

After establishing a class hierarchy with the E/R model, the object-oriented principle of generalization is used to identify the class hierarchy and the level of abstraction associated with each class. Generalization implies a successive refinement of a class, allowing the superclasses of objects to inherit data attributes and behaviors that apply to the lower levels of a class. Generalization establishes taxonomy hierarchies. Taxonomy hierarchies organize classes according to their characteristics in increasing levels of detail. These hierarchies begin at a general level and then proceed to a specific level, with each sublevel having its own unique data attributes and behaviors.

In Figure 2.12, the IS-A relationship is used to create a hierarchy within the EMPLOYEE class. The base class for an employee has the basic data items such as name, address, and phone number. However, there are subclasses of employees, executives, and hourly employees, each with their own special data items and methods.

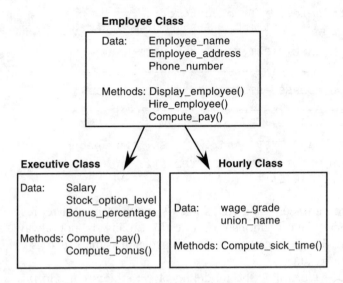

Figure 2.12 An E/R Model with Added IS-A Relationships

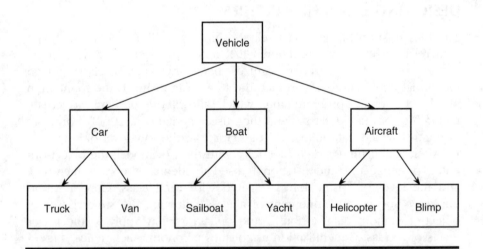

Figure 2.13 A Class Hierarchy for a Vehicle Rental Company

Let's look at another example. Consider the application of the IS-A relationship for a vehicle dealership, as shown in Figure 2.13. As you can see, the highest level in the hierarchy is VEHICLE. Beneath the VEHICLE class, you might find CAR and BOAT subclasses. Within the CAR class, the classes could be further partitioned into classes for TRUCK and VAN. The VEHICLE class would contain the data items unique to vehicles, including the vehicle ID and the year of manufacture. The CAR class, because it

IS-A VEHICLE, would inherit the data items of the VEHICLE class. The CAR class might contain data items such as the number of axles and the gross weight of the vehicle. Because the VAN class IS-A CAR, which in turn IS-A VEHICLE, objects of the VAN class inherit all data items and behaviors relating to the CAR and VEHICLE classes.

These types of IS-A relationships, while valid from a data modeling viewpoint, do not have a simple implementation in Oracle. Because Oracle does not support hierarchical relationships, it is impossible to directly represent the fact that a database entity has subentities. However, this type of relationship can be modeled in a relational database in two ways.

The first technique is to create subtables for car, boat, sedan, and so on. This encapsulates the data items within their respective tables, but it also creates the complication of doing unnecessary joins when retrieving a high-level item in the hierarchy. For example, the following SQL would be required to retrieve all the data items for a luxury sedan:

```
select
    vehicle.vehicle_number,
    car.registration_number,
    sedan.number_of_doors,
    luxury.type_of_leather_upholstery
from
    vehicle,
    car,
    sedan,
    luxury
where
    vehicle.key = car.key
and
    car.key = sedan.key
and
    sedan.key = luxury.key;
```

The second approach is to create a megatable, with each data item represented as a column (regardless of whether it is needed by the individual row). A TYPE column could identify whether a row represents a car, van, or sailboat. In addition, the application must have intelligence to access only those columns applicable to a row. For example, the SAIL-SIZE column would have meaning for a sailboat row, but would be irrelevant to a sedan row.

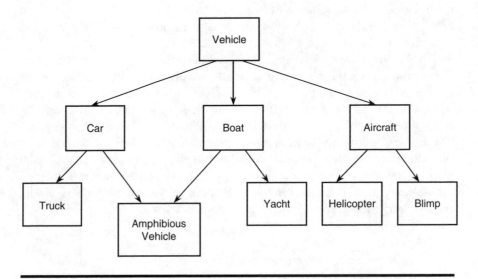

Figure 2.14 An Example of Multiple Inheritance

The IS-A relationship is best suited to the object-oriented data model, where each level in the hierarchy has associated data items and methods and inheritance and polymorphism can be used to complete the picture. It is important to note that not all classes within a generalization hierarchy will be associated with objects. These noninstantiated classes only serve the purpose of passing data definitions to the lower-level classes. The object-oriented paradigm allows for abstraction, which means that a class can exist only for the purpose of passing inherited data and behaviors to the lower-level entities. The classes VEHICLE and CAR probably would not have any concrete objects, while objects within the VAN class would inherit from the abstract VEHICLE and CAR classes.

Multiple inheritance can be illustrated by the AMPHIBIOUS_VEHICLE class. Instances of this class probably would inherit data and behaviors from both the CAR and the BOAT classes (Figure 2.14).

It is important to note one very big difference between one-to-many relationships and IS-A relationships. The IS-A construct does not imply any type of recurring association, while the one-to-many and many-to-many relationships imply multiple occurrences of the subclasses. In the previous example, the entire class hierarchy describes vehicles associated with the ITEM entity in the overall database. The fact that a class hierarchy exists does not imply any data relationships between the classes. While one customer can place many orders, it is not true that one car can have many sedans.

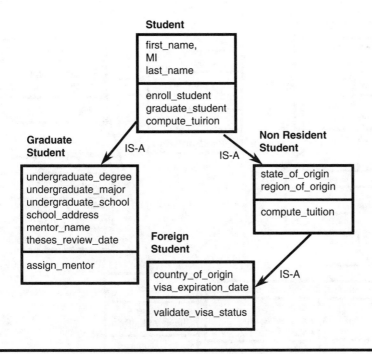

Figure 2.15   A Multilevel Class Hierarchy

Representing Class Hierarchies

In the real world, we see many instances of class hierarchies. It is not uncommon to see multilevel class hierarchies (Figure 2.15) and this data construct can wreak havoc with a database design.

When depicting a class hierarchy, it is important to distinguish between relationships and IS-A attributes. In Figure 2.16, we see that the standard E/R notation is used for entities and relationships and the IS-A relationships are attached to the E/R diagram.

Now that you have a general understanding of object-oriented design principles, let's see how the principles are implemented within Oracle9*i*.

MATERIALIZED VIEWS AND DENORMALIZATION

Materialized views allow subsecond response times by precomputing aggregate information and prejoining tables for complex queries. Oracle dynamically rewrites SQL queries to reference existing materialized views.

Materialized views are an introduction of redundancy, along the same lines as Oracle snapshots. When an Oracle materialized view is created, Oracle treats the materialized view just as it would an Oracle snapshot. In other words, the data is replicated and Oracle requires you to specify

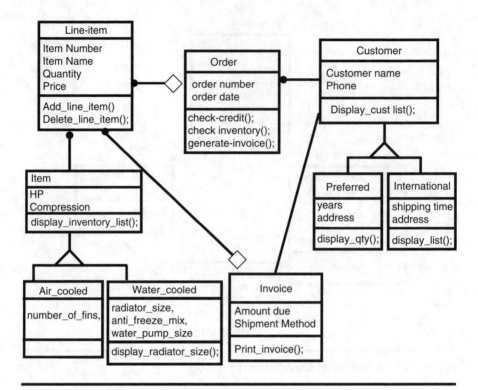

Figure 2.16 Extension of an E/R Model for Class Hierarchies

a schedule for periodic updates. Updates are accomplished by way of a refresh interval, which can range from instantaneous rebuilding of the materialized view to a hot refresh that occurs weekly.

Oracle materialized views are quite complex in nature and require a significant understanding to be used effectively. Let's now cover the required setup methods and the steps for creating materialized views and appropriate refresh intervals.

In the world of database architecture, the need to dynamically create complex objects conflicts with the demand for subsecond response time. Oracle's answer to this dilemma is the materialized view. Database designers can use materialized views to prejoin tables, presort solution sets, and presummarize complex data warehouse information. Because this work is completed in advance, it gives end users the illusion of instantaneous response time. Materialized views are especially useful for Oracle data warehouses, where cross-tabulations often take hours to perform. This chapter explores the internals of materialized views and demonstrates how to precompute complex aggregates — having Oracle dynamically rewrite SQL to reference precomputed aggregate information. This is the first of two chapters concentrating on Oracle materialized views.

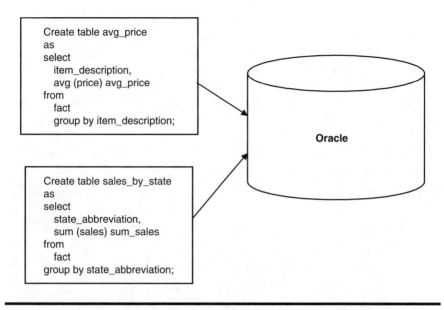

```
Create table avg_price
as
select
    item_description,
    avg (price) avg_price
from
    fact
    group by item_description;
```

```
Create table sales_by_state
as
select
    state_abbreviation,
    sum (sales) sum_sales
from
    fact
group by state_abbreviation;
```

Oracle

Figure 2.17 Preaggregation for High Performance

Prior to materialized views, DBAs using summaries spent a significant amount of time manually identifying which ones to create; then creating, indexing, and updating them; and then advising their users about which ones to use. Figure 2.17 illustrates the process of preaggregation.

The problem with manually creating summary tables is that you have to tell the end user to go to the new table. There was no Oracle mechanism to automatically rewrite the SQL to go to the precreated summary. Materialized views provide an alternate approach. Materialized views are popular in Oracle systems where performance is critical and complex SQL queries exist against large tables. Generally, we see materialized views used in two areas:

1. Aggregation
2. Replication

In terms of aggregation, materialized views improve query speed by rewriting a query against the base table with a query against the pre-aggregated summary table via the following:

- Precalculated summaries — the `rollup`, `cube`, `sum`, `avg`, `min`, `max`, `count(*)`, `count(distinct  x)` functions can now be used to presummarize data.
- Prejoined tables — tables can be prejoined to substantially improve performance.

It is important to note that a materialized view is a form of replication. From the moment that the materialized view is created, it can become stale if any of the base tables data is changed. Hence, Oracle has incorporated their snapshot concept with materialized view technology, such that all forms of replication are considered materialized views.

Below we see the Oracle `create snapshot` syntax. Note that we get a reply from Oracle stating "`Materialized View Created.`"

```
create snapshot
   cust_snap
on
   customer
refresh fast
   start with sysdate
   next sysdate + 1/1440
as
select * from customer@remote;
```

Automatic SQL Query Rewrite

One of the greatest features of the materialized view is the automatic SQL rewrite facility. When we create a materialized view, none of the SQL has to be changed to reference the new view. Oracle does this automatically.

The query optimizer automatically recognizes when an existing materialized view can be used to satisfy a request. Next, it transparently rewrites the request to use the materialized view. Queries can then be directed to the materialized view and not to the underlying detail tables, resulting in a significant performance gain.

Figure 2.18 shows how the Oracle SQL optimizer checks the Oracle data dictionary for the presence of a materialized view whenever a new SQL statement enters the Oracle library cache.

In the next example, we create a materialized view that determines the average salary for each job in the database. Once the materialized view is created, we can run queries against the base table and use an Oracle hint to direct the SQL optimizer to fetch the average salary from the materialized view rather than performing an expensive and time-consuming scan against the emp table as shown below:

```
create materialized view
    job_avg_sal
enable query rewrite
as
```

```
select
   job,
   avg(sal)avg_sal
from
   emp
group by
   job;


select /*+ rewrite(job_avg_sal) */
   avg(sal)
from
   emp
where
   job = 'CLERK';
```

In the above example, we used an Oracle hint to ensure that the materialized view is referenced.

When Is SQL Query Rewrite Used?

Oracle has a sophisticated SQL query rewrite capability. The Oracle DBA can control the propensity of the SQL optimizer to go to the materialized views to service the query. The options are as follows:

- Full SQL text match — in this method, the SQL text of the query's select statement clause is compared to the SQL text of the select clause in the materialized view's defining query.
- Partial text match — if a full SQL test match fails, the optimizer will attempt a partial SQL text match. The optimizer compares the remaining SQL text of the query (beginning with the FROM clause) to the remaining SQL text of the materialized view's defining query.
- No match — if the full and partial SQL text matches both fail, the optimizer uses general query rewrite methods that enable the use of a materialized view even if it contains only part of the data, more than the data, or data that can be converted.

REFERENTIAL INTEGRITY

Oracle databases allow for the control of business rules with constraints. These RI rules ensure that one-to-many and many-to-many relationships are enforced within the distributed relational schema. For example, a

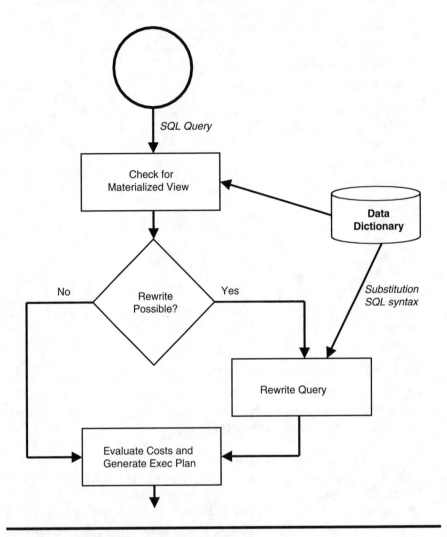

Figure 2.18   Materialized View Query Rewrite

constraint could be used to ensure that orders are not placed for nonexistent customers or to ensure that a customer is not deleted until all of their orders have been filled.

Relational systems allow control of business rules with constraints and RI rules form the backbone of relational tables. For example, in Figure 2.19, RI ensures that a row in the CUSTOMER table is not deleted if the ORDER table contains orders for that customer.

It is clear that enforcing the business rule in Figure 2.19 is a real challenge. While it's relatively simple to tell an Oracle system not to delete a row from its CUSTOMER table if rows for that customer exist in the

RI Rule = ORDER.CUST_NAME references CUSTOMER.CUST_NAME

Two Options:
ON DELETE RESTRICT   Customers may be deleted if they have orders in the order table
ON DELETE CASCADE   Customers' deletion will cause all orders for the customer to delete

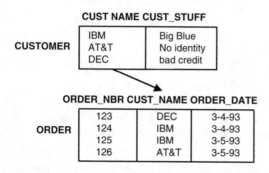

CUST NAME CUST_STUFF

	CUST NAME	CUST_STUFF
CUSTOMER	IBM	Big Blue
	AT&T	No identity
	DEC	bad credit

ORDER_NBR CUST_NAME ORDER_DATE

	ORDER_NBR	CUST_NAME	ORDER_DATE
ORDER	123	DEC	3-4-93
	124	IBM	3-4-93
	125	IBM	3-5-93
	126	AT&T	3-5-93

Figure 2.19   Foreign Key RI

ORDER table, it's not simple to enforce this rule when the CUSTOMER table resides in a Sybase™ database and the ORDER table resides within Oracle.

Before most relational database-supported RI, it was the responsibility of the programmer to guarantee the maintenance of data relationships and business rules. While this was fine for the applications, the risk came into play when *ad hoc* updated SQL commands were issued using Oracle's SQL*Plus® software. With these *ad hoc* update tools, the programmatic SQL could be easily bypassed, skipping the business rules and creating logical corruption.

RI has earned a bad reputation in Oracle because of the overhead that is created when enforcing the business rules. In almost every case, it will be faster and more efficient to write your own rules to enforce RI instead of having Oracle do it for you. Provided that your application doesn't allow *ad hoc* query, it's relatively easy to attach a trigger with a PL/SQL routine to enforce the RI on your behalf. In fact, this is one of the best uses of a trigger, since the DML DELETE event will not take place if the RI rules are invalid. For example, consider the foreign key constraint that protects a customer from being deleted if they have outstanding orders:

```
create table customer (
    cust_id                number,
    cust_name              varchar(30),
    cust_address           varchar(30);
```

```
create table order (
    order_id                    number,
    order_date                  date,
    cust_id                     number
    CONSTRAINT cust_fk REFERENCES CUSTOMER ON DELE
TE RESTRICT,
);
```

Several types of constraints can be applied to Oracle tables to enforce RI, including the following constraints:

- CHECK constraint — this constraint validates incoming columns at row insert time. For example, rather than having an application verify that all occurrences of REGION are north, south, east, or west, a CHECK constraint can be added to the table definition to ensure the validity of the region column.
- NOT NULL constraint — this constraint is used to specify that a column may never contain a NULL value. This is enforced at SQL INSERT and UPDATE time.
- PRIMARY KEY constraint — this constraint is used to identify the primary key for a table. This operation requires that the primary column is unique. Oracle will create a unique index on the target primary key.
- FOREIGN KEY constraint — this is the foreign key constraint as implemented by Oracle. A foreign key constraint is only applied at SQL INSERT and DELETE times. For example, assume a one-to-many relationship between the CUSTOMER and ORDER tables, such that each CUSTOMER may place many ORDERs, yet each ORDER belongs to only one CUSTOMER. The REFERENCES constraint tells Oracle at INSERT time that the value in ORDER.CUST_NUM must match the CUSTOMER.CUST_NUM in the customer row, thereby ensuring that a valid customer exists before the order row is added. At SQL DELETE time, the REFERENCES constraint can be used to ensure that a CUSTOMER is not deleted if rows still exist in the ORDER table.
- UNIQUE constraint — this constraint is used to ensure that all column values within a table never contain a duplicate entry.

Note the distinction between the UNIQUE and PRIMARY KEY constraint. While both of these constraints create a unique index, a table may only contain one PRIMARY KEY constraint column, but it may have many UNIQUE constraints on other columns.

Note: It is a critical point that the RI cannot be maintained in a denormalized schema unless materialized views are built against the 3NF representation of the data.

CONCLUSION

This chapter has dealt with schema-level physical design for Oracle databases and looked into the issues relating to the physical modeling of data relationships. We explored one-to-many, many-to-many, and recursive relationships and object-oriented constructs.

The main points of this chapter include:

- Normalization is key — proper denormalization (prejoining tables) is critical to high-speed Oracle performance.
- Multiple representations are available — for cases where the data must appear in both denormalized and normalized forms, materialized views can be used to synchronize the data.
- Use object-oriented constructs when appropriate — Oracle provides a wealth of object-oriented database constructs, such as ADTs, that can be used to simplify implementation.

We are now ready to explore the physical design issues relating to hardware and see how the physical database designer must consider the environment for the database.

3

ORACLE HARDWARE DESIGN

INTRODUCTION

This chapter is devoted to some of the hardware design issues associated with implementing a successful Oracle database. The discussion will focus on the physical design of the database and how it relates to available hardware. Oracle9*i* provides a wealth of features and tools that allow the designer to tailor database response for the needs of a particular application. These are also explored.

The main topics of this chapter include:

- Planning the server architecture
- Hardware design and central processing unit (CPU) issues
- Hardware design and RAM issues
- Oracle network design
- Server design and disk allocation

Designing a server environment entails making decisions about the basic hardware requirements, as well as selecting the more advanced database configuration methods necessary to effectively interact with the available hardware. The designer needs to understand the demands that the server places on CPU resources, which is discussed in detail in this chapter. The discussion then moves to a consideration of the demands that the server places on RAM resources. The focus then shifts to server design as it relates to general memory issues. The chapter concludes with a detailed look at designing the overall network, including connectivity concerns.

Although Oracle offers many performance-tuning techniques, you can't tune away a poor database design — especially a poor architectural design. So, it is imperative that the Oracle database designer understand (from the inception of the project) how to create robust Oracle data architectures that can retrieve information as rapidly as possible while preserving maintainability and extensibility.

If you strip away all the complex methodology and jargon surrounding the Oracle database, one simple factor remains — disk I/O. Disk I/O is the most expensive Oracle database operation. Oracle design professionals should always remember to design with data architectures to retrieve the desired information with a minimal amount of disk access.

This section shares some of the tricks I use to ensure Oracle hardware architecture designs perform at optimal levels while making a design that is easy to maintain and extend:

- Use RAM data caching — you must be aware that Oracle9*i* allows large memory regions to cache frequently referenced row information. The caching of frequently referenced information should be a major design goal primarily because RAM access is two orders of magnitude (more than 10,000 times) faster than row access from disk. The larger the Oracle data block buffer cache, the faster the SQL queries will execute. The size of the RAM data buffers will have a direct impact on Oracle performance and all systems run fastest when fully cached in the data buffers.
- Buy fast processors — the CPU speed of the Oracle database server has a direct impact on performance. High-performance 64-bit CPUs will often perform 10 times faster than 32-bit processors. The 64-bit processors are available on all major platforms and include:
  - Windows® operating system (OS) — Intel® Itanium® processor
  - HP/UX PA-8000 processor
  - Solaris™ operating environment — 500-MHz Ultrasparc-iie processor
  - IBM® AIX® OS — RS/6000® PowerPC® processor
- Use a 64-bit version of Oracle — it is highly recommended that Oracle systems exist on a dedicated database server with a 64-bit CPU architecture and a 64-bit version of Oracle. The 64-bit version of Oracle lets you create large SGA regions and large projects commonly require more than 20 gigabytes (GB) of RAM data buffers. A serious shortcoming of 32-bit Oracle is the 1.7 GB size limitation for the SGA.
- Design for faster SGA access — one of the foremost reasons stored procedures and triggers function faster than traditional code is related to the Oracle SGA. After a procedure has been loaded into the shared pool of the SGA, it remains until it is paged out of memory to make room for other stored procedures. Items are paged out based on a least recently used (LRU) algorithm. Once loaded into the RAM memory of the shared pool, procedures will

execute quickly — the trick is to prevent pool thrashing, as many procedures compete for a limited amount of shared-pool memory. Stored procedures load once into the shared pool and remain there unless they become paged out. Subsequent executions of the stored procedure are far faster than executions of external code.

One of the trademarks of a superior Oracle designer is the ability to create an overall architecture that is robust, maintainable, and efficient. Today's Oracle design professionals are required to design systems that may support thousands of transactions per second while at the same time delivering subsecond response time, easy maintenance, and extensibility. With a thorough understanding of Oracle9*i* database features and the help of the tips presented in this chapter, you can build an appropriate data model architecture that supports the requirements of end users.

Let's start with a review of important issues for planning the Oracle server environment.

PLANNING THE SERVER ENVIRONMENT

The minimum hardware requirements for the Oracle server environment are determined by three factors:

1. Type of application (OLTP, decision support system [DSS], data warehouse)
2. Expected maximum transactions per second
3. Number of users

   Note: The size of the database should not be one of the factors used to select a hardware or OS configuration. The disk I/O subsystem determines database size. This will be discussed further in the next chapter, along with other database issues.

Let's explore than main areas of Oracle server design, CPU, and RAM memory usage.

Design for Oracle Server CPU

CPU transactions are managed automatically by the server. The internal machine code of the server assigns processors to active tasks and ensures that the maximum amount of processing power is directed to each task. Servers are configured to use CPU cycles as they are needed and the Oracle database uses CPU resources freely. It's important to monitor possible CPU shortages.

UNIX® servers handle tasks according to their internal dispatching priority. UNIX OS tasks will obviously have a higher dispatching priority. CPU overload is typically indicated by high values in the vmstat run queue column. If the run queue value exceeds the number of CPUs available to the server, some tasks may await completion.

There are several options available for managing CPU shortages:

- Add additional processors.
- Reduce server load.
- Turn off Oracle parallel query.
- Replace the standard Oracle listener with the multi-threaded server (MTS).
- Alter task dispatching priorities.
- Upgrade the server.

Symmetric multiprocessor configurations for Oracle database servers are usually expandable. Additional processors can be added at any time. The new CPUs are immediately made available to the Oracle database by the processor architecture.

The disadvantage of adding processors is the high cost, which is often greater than the cost of a new server. Reduced productivity due to increased response time can be compared with the cost of additional processors by performing a cost-benefit analysis to determine the feasibility of adding more processors.

CPU overloads can be sporadic and complicate justifying additional processors. Overloads are often transient or momentary. These types of overloads heavily burden the server at certain times while leaving processing resources only partially utilized at other times. A load balancing analysis can be performed to ensure that batch-oriented tasks are sent to the server at nonpeak hours. The nature of the individual business is a factor here. For example, if the business is conducted primarily online, the response time when the online users are active is the only important one. The fact that the server may be idle late at night has no bearing on the decision to add CPUs.

Designing Task Load Balancing Mechanisms

Task load balancing may be the remedy if CPU overload is intermittent. A server typically overloads during peak work hours, while in the evenings it may run at only 20 percent of capacity. Batch tasks can simply be rescheduled in cases such as these. After the CPU overload times have been identified, Statspack should be used to examine the activity during overload. Statspack will help determine which tasks can be scheduled for off-peak hours. Task schedules can be implemented using:

- The dbms_job utility
- The UNIX cron utility
- A transaction processing monitor such as the Tuxedo® application
- Oracle Concurrent Manager (for Oracle Applications)

Most OSs allow the root user to change the task dispatching priority. In general, the online database background tasks are given greater priority (a smaller priority value), while less critical batch processes are assigned less priority (a higher priority value).

> **Note:** In the long run, it's not a satisfactory solution to alter the default dispatching priorities. The default priorities should be changed only in emergency situations.

Design for Oracle Server RAM

The first step in tuning server memory is to review the kernel settings that relate to available memory. The settings that relate to memory usage (i.e., SHMMAX, SHMMNI, db_max_pct) should be double-checked to make sure they are configured properly. The configuration of the swap disk should also be verified. Most servers recommend that the swap disk be set to twice the amount of physical RAM.

Some servers do not have the ability to address high memory. For example, memory greater than 1.7 GB cannot be accessed in many 32-bit Oracle versions, regardless of the amount of RAM available to the server. The bit-size of the application physically determines the high memory boundary. The only way to utilize high memory is through special OS techniques. The administrator who is unaware of this could be quite perplexed upon seeing page-in operations on the database server, while top and glance utilities continue to indicate that the server has excess memory. Some UNIX systems, such as Solaris, allow the DBA to create SGA regions over 2 GB by applying a special patch on the 32-bit server. This technique is called memory windows in HP/UX; it routes applications to high memory areas using a SHARED_MAGIC executable.

Memory management is further enhanced in Oracle9i by creating a pga_aggregate_target parameter. This parameter holds all Program Global Area (PGA) RAM regions inside the Oracle SGA. Within the Oracle9i architecture, 80 percent of all RAM memory on a dedicated database server can be allocated directly to the SGA. (This leaves 20 percent of RAM for the UNIX kernel.) This configuration should preclude any UNIX RAM swapping or paging. Fortunately, all 64-bit Oracle versions have the ability to address high memory. However, the administrator must make sure that the Oracle database and other applications are capable of accessing the

Table 3.1 Overloaded RAM

TO_CHAR(START_DA	RUNQUE_WAITS	PAGE_IN	SYSTEM_CPU	USER_CPU	IDLE_CPU
06/02/2001 05:01	2	85	1	0	99
06/02/2001 13:47	2	193	0	0	99
06/03/2001 05:04	0	114	2	3	95
06/03/2001 22:31	1	216	0	1	99
06/04/2001 05:02	0	146	1	1	99
06/04/2001 22:34	1	71	1	8	90
06/05/2001 06:57	1	213	0	0	99
06/05/2001 07:25	1	113	0	0	99
06/05/2001 07:35	1	72	0	0	99
06/05/2001 11:06	1	238	0	1	99

available memory. For example, even though the CPU seems to be 99 percent idle, the RAM is clearly overloaded in Table 3.1.

Making Oracle Memory Nonswappable

In the final analysis, the best solution to a RAM problem is to add RAM to the server. However, there are some short-term techniques to prevent the Oracle SGA memory from paging. It is possible to use a memory-fencing technique on some OSs to guarantee that the Oracle SGA is not paged-out to the swap disk.

Design for the Oracle Server Swap Disk

It can be difficult to know whether server RAM is overstressed and swapping while RAM pi and po values remain within an acceptable range. One method correlates the UNIX scan rate with page-in operations. UNIX treats RAM memory as a sharable resource whenever an Oracle server begins to run low on memory. The paging process begins moving memory frames to the swap disk. Paging escalates as RAM shortages increase. If the demands continue to increase, entire RAM regions may be paged-out. When memory shortages are not critical, paging will only take small chunks of the least current RAM from a program. To know whether page-in operations are normal housekeeping or a serious memory shortage, we must correlate the amount of paging with the page-in output.

The memory page scan rate is designated by the sr column in the vmstat utility. If the scan rate rises steadily, the first threshold of the paging operation has been reached. This is an indication that whole regions of RAM memory are being paged-out to the swap disk. As this continues, pi values begin to correlate with the high po values as pages are swapped back into RAM memory.

The HP/UX vmstat list below should be carefully reviewed. The scan rate is the far right-hand column. We can see the value of sr rising steadily as the paging operation prepares to page-in. RAM on the Oracle server is exceeded as the sr value peaks and the page-in operation begins.

```
root> vmstat 2
     procs                memory                       page
  r   b   w      avm     free    re  .at   pi   po     fr   de   sr
  3   0   0   144020    12778    17    9    0   14     29    0    3
  3   0   0   144020    12737    15    0    1   34      4    0    8
  3   0   0   144020    12360     9    0    1   46      2    0   13
  1   0   0   142084    12360     5    0    3   17      0    0   21
  1   0   0   142084    12360     3    0    8    0      0    0    8
  1   0   0   140900    12360     1    0   10    0      0    0    0
  1   0   0   140900    12360     0    0    9    0      0    0    0
  1   0   0   140900    12204     0    0    3    0      0    0    0
  1   0   0   137654    12204     0    0    0    0      0    0    0
```

The most important columns in this report are:

- r = the runqueue value showing the number of processes in the CPU dispatcher
- pi = the page-in values showing OS page-in operations from the swap disk
- po = the number of page-out operations of the OS to swap disk, in anticipation of a possible page-in

Before looking further into excess memory demands on the server, we need to determine how much memory is available on the server.

Once we know the amount of RAM on our server, we can investigate the Oracle server's RAM and swap disk usage. Whenever the memory demands of the server exceed the amount of RAM, the virtual memory facility is invoked. Virtual memory moves segments of RAM onto the special swap disk. The swap disk holds excess RAM memory contents. Its parameters are defined by the system administrator. It is common practice for the virtual memory system to page-out memory segments and this does not indicate a memory problem. However, a page-in operation does indicate that the server has exceeded the amount of available RAM and that memory segments are being recalled from the swap disk.

During swapping (page-in), data usually stored in RAM memory is read from the swap disk back into memory. This slows down a server. The solution to a page-in problem on an Oracle database server involves:

- Smaller SGA — the demand for RAM is reduced by making the SGA smaller. The size of the SGA was decreased in Oracle8i and earlier versions by reducing the `db_block_buffers`. Oracle9*i* reduces it by `db_cache_size`, `sga_max_size`, `db_xK_cache_size`, `shared_pool_size`, or `java_pool_size` init.ora parameters. This results in more RAM memory and adds additional RAM memory to the server. (Remember that some 32-bit versions of Oracle cannot use more than 1.7 GB of RAM.)

■ Reduce RAM demand — the amount of RAM consumed by a database server can be decreased by reducing the demands on PGA. The amount of RAM allocated to each user's PGA can be greatly increased by Oracle parameters such as `sort_area_size`.

A memory-bound database server is always subject to paging from the swap disk. The `vmstat` utility displays paging as the `po` and `pi` columns of `vmstat`. The following diagram indicates that the database server is burdened by nine page-out and five page-in operations. The page-in operations show that the server is suffering excessive memory requests.

```
root> vmstat 1 2
```

kthr		memory		page						faults			cpu			
r	b	avm	fre	re	pi	po	fr	sr	cy	in	sy	cs	us	sy	id	wa
0	0	218094	166	0	4	0	4	16	0	202	301	211	14	19	45	22
0	0	218094	166	0	5	9	4	14	0	202	301	211	14	19	45	22

To summarize, page-out operations are normal within virtual memory, but page-in operations indicate excessive RAM demands on the server.

To derive optimum performance for a database application, the designer must carefully weigh the issues of server CPU demand and server demand on RAM resources. We have focused on the techniques and tools that the designer must employ to effectively integrate server design with actual memory consumption. The remainder of the chapter considers how to design the network for seamless interaction with the user, as well as how to design the network for the best possible level of performance.

Now that we understand the basics of server design for RAM, let's explore network design issues for Oracle databases.

DESIGNING THE NETWORK INFRASTRUCTURE FOR ORACLE

It is commonly thought that Oracle Net can be used to realize performance gains across a network by tuning network parameters. However, Oracle Net merely passes data to the protocol stack. For example, Oracle Net will retrieve the information from a data request and send it to the protocol stack for transmission. The protocol stack in turn creates a packet and sends it over the network. In reality, Oracle Net can do little to improve performance, with a few minor exceptions since network traffic and tuning is addressed outside of the Oracle environment.

Oracle DBAs do have control over the size and frequency of network packets. Many tools are available to change the packet size and the frequency that packets are sent over the network. For example, larger amounts of data can be sent over the network less often by changing the refresh interval for a snapshot.

The remainder of the section is devoted to the issues involved with successful network design. The tools available to the designer to tune performance are emphasized. Understanding the use of these tools will facilitate the optimum design of the desired configuration. The following material is divided into two major sections:

1. Optimizing Oracle Net configuration
2. Other Oracle features that affect network performance

The first section discusses the tuning parameters that are used with the Oracle Net layer. The second explores some salient Oracle features that can be used to fine-tune network performance.

ORACLE NETWORK DESIGN

Several tuning parameters that affect the performance of Oracle Net connections between servers are considered below. These tuning parameters only affect the performance of the Oracle Net layer. To tune the entire network, a network administrator should be consulted.

The parameter files listed below contain settings that change the size and frequency of packet shipping across the network:

- `protocol.ora`
- `sqlnet.ora`
- `tnsnames.ora` file — SDU, TDU
- `listener.ora` file — SDU, TDU

Let's take a closer look at these parameters and see how they affect the network.

The `tcp.nodelay` parameter

Oracle Net will wait to transmit a request until the buffer is full in its default setting. This could potentially cause a request to be deferred while

Oracle Net waits for the buffer to fill. A `protocol.ora` file that specifies `tcp.nodelay` will end delays in the buffer flushing process for all Transmission Control Protocol/Internet Protocol (TCP/IP) implementations. This parameter may be applied to both the client and the server.

The `protocol.ora` statement is:

```
tcp.nodelay = yes
```

All requests are sent immediately when this parameter is specified. This parameter can cause the network to run slower in some cases. For this reason, Oracle recommends that `tcp.nodelay` be used only when encountering TCP timeouts. Because network packets will be transmitted more frequently between the client and server, network traffic can increase. Nevertheless, using `tcp.nodelay` can offer a huge performance improvement between database servers during times of high-volume traffic.

The `automatic_ipc` parameter

Local connections to a database are more rapid with the `automatic_ipc` parameter because the network layer is bypassed. The network layer will be bypassed and the connection transmitted to a local interprocess communication (IPC) if a local database with the same alias definition is used. This is useful only on database servers.

The statement in `sqlnet.ora` is:

```
automatic_ipc = on
```

The `automatic_ipc` parameter should only be used on the database server when an Oracle Net connection must be established with the local database. The parameter should be set to `off` if no local database connections are needed. All Oracle Net clients should take advantage of this setting to improve performance.

The `break_poll_skip` parameter

This parameter reduces polling overhead on the system. Here is the syntax:

```
BREAK_POLL_SKIP=n   (where n = the number of packets to skip
between checking for breaks - the default is 4)
```

This parameter affects the amount of CPU consumed on the Oracle Net client. It is a client-only parameter. Some general rules for using this parameter are:

- The higher the value of break_poll_skip, the less frequently Ctrl-C is checked and the less CPU overhead used.
- Conversely, the lower the value of break_poll_skip, the more frequently Ctrl-C is checked and the more CPU overhead used.
- This parameter only functions on servers that support inband breaks and is only useful on an Oracle Net client sqlnet.ora file.

The disable_oob parameter

A data exception or break is a function in Oracle Net that allows a transaction to be interrupted before it is completed. It returns both the client and the server to a condition from which they can continue. A break such as Ctrl-C can be sent as part of the normal data stream (inband) or as a separate asynchronous message (outband). An outband break is much faster and interrupts the flow of data.

Out of Bound Breaks (OOB) are enabled by default. To disable the OOB, use the following syntax in the SQLNET.ORA file:

```
DISABLE_OOB=on
```

The SDU and TDU parameters

The session data unit (SDU) specifies the size of the packets to be sent over the network. If none is specified, Oracle Net defaults to the transport data unit (TDU) packet size to group data together. Both parameters were fixed at two kilobytes (K) prior to release 7.3.3 and could not be changed. These parameters are placed in the tnsnames.ora and listener.ora files.

The SDU should not be greater than the maximum transmission unit (MTU). The MTU depends on the particular network implementation used and is fixed. Oracle recommends that the SDU be set to equal the MTU. Also, the TDU parameter should be some multiple of the SDU. The default values for both are 2048 bytes (B) and the maximum value is 32,767 B.

The following guidelines may be used to determine the values for SDU and TDU:

- The SDU and TDU should be set to equal the MTU of the network for a fast network connection such as a T1 or T3 connection. SDU=TDU=MTU. Standard Ethernet networks default the MTU size at 1514 B. Standard Token Ring networks default the MTU size at 4202 B.
- Setting the SDU greater than the TDU wastes network resources because each packet sends wasted space.

- The SDU and TDU parameters may be set to smaller values for users who connect over modem lines because of the frequent resends that can occur over dial-up connections.
- If the MTS is used, the `mts_dispatchers` must also be set with the proper MTU and TDU configuration.

An example of the parameters on a Token Ring network with a MTU of 4202 B is:

`listener.ora`

```
    SID_LIST_LISTENER =
        (SID_LIST =
            (SID_DESC =
                (SDU = 4202)
                (TDU = 4202)
                (SID_NAME = ORCL)
                (GLOBAL_DBNAME = ORCL.WORLD)
            )
        )
```

`tnsnames.ora`

```
    ORCL.WORLD =
        (DESCRIPTION =
            (SDU=4202)
            (TDU=4202)
            (ADDRESS =
                (PROTOCOL = TCP)
                (HOST = fu.bar)
                (PORT = 1521)
            )
            (CONNECT_DATA = (SID = ORCL))
        )
```

The Oracle8*i* database automatically registers instances in the `listener.ora` file unless one of the following is done:

- Implement the MTS and define the `mts_dispatchers` in your `init.ora` file:

```
MTS_DISPATCHERS="(DESCRIPTION=(SDU=8192)(TDU=8192)\
ADDRESS=(PARTIAL=TRUE)(PROTOCOL=TCP)(HOST=supsund3)))\
                    (DISPATCHERS=1)"
```

- Use `service_name=global_dbname` in the `Connect_Data` section of the `tnsnames.ora` file, where `global_dbname` is configured in `listener.ora`.

Note: `Global_dbname` disables Transparent Application Failover (TAF) because it does not support it. The Oracle Net Administrator's Guide provides more information under "Configuring Transparent Application Failover."

- Do not use automatic service registration. Set the `init.ora` parameter — `local_listener` — to use a different TCP port than the one defined in your `listener.ora` file.

The `queuesize` Parameter in `listener.ora`

If it is expected that the listener will receive large numbers of requests for connection, a queue may be specified for the process. This enables the listener to handle larger numbers of simultaneous connection requests. The number of requests the listener can store while Oracle works to establish a connection is specified by the `queuesize` parameter. The value of this parameter should be equivalent to the number of expected simultaneous connections. Below is an example of the `queuesize` parameter in the `listener.ora` file:

```
LISTENER =
  (ADDRESS_LIST =
      (ADDRESS =
         (PROTOCOL = TCP)
         (HOST = marvin)
         (PORT = 1521)
         (QUEUESIZE = 32)
      )
  )
```

Use of `queuesize` can be disadvantageous since more resources and memory is used. The parameter preallocates resources for anticipated connection requests. For this reason, if high-volume connections into a dedicated listener are anticipated, it may be beneficial to implement the MTS and use prespawned Oracle connections.

Connection Pooling and Network Performance

A MTS dispatcher requires fewer physical network connections. Connection pooling allows the administrator to take full advantage of this. This resource utilization feature is achieved by sharing a dispatcher's set of connections among multiple client processes.

Connection pooling reuses physical connections. Older connections are made available for incoming clients while a logical session with the previous idle connection is maintained. Connections that have been idle for a specified period of time are temporarily released by a timeout mechanism. The idle connection can be used by another process until the previous client resumes work. At that time another physical connection is established with the dispatcher.

Connection pooling is disabled on both incoming and outgoing network connections by default. To enable connection pooling, add the POOL argument to the `mts_dispatchers` parameter in the `init.ora` file.

```
MTS_DISPATCHERS = "(PROTOCOL=TCP)(DISPATCHERS=3)(POOL=3)"
```

Connection pooling is enabled for both incoming and outgoing network connections whenever a number is specified. The number sets the timeout in ticks for both types of network connections.

To enable connection pooling for both incoming and outgoing networks while using the Oracle Net default timeout, set the POOL argument to ON, YES, TRUE, or BOTH.

```
MTS_DISPATCHERS = "(PROTOCOL=TCP)(DISPATCHERS=3)(POOL=ON)"
```

The POOL argument IN or OUT enables connection pooling for incoming or outgoing network connections respectively. The Oracle Net default timeout will be used.

```
MTS_DISPATCHERS = "(PROTOCOL=TCP)(DISPATCHERS=3)(POOL=IN)"
```

In practical administration, connection pooling is used rarely unless the database server is overwhelmed with incoming Oracle Net requests.

ODBC and Network Performance

Open Database Connectivity (ODBC) is a standardized application programming interface (API). It makes it possible for applications to connect to SQL databases. The ODBC features can be used to develop applications that are independent from the database. These features include function calls, error codes, and data types, which can be defined by the designer to fit the needs of the application. The API does not communicate with the database directly, but serves as a link between the application and the generic interface routine. The interface routine is then able to communicate with the database drivers through a service provider interface.

Databases that are subject to high traffic may have performance problems when ODBC is used. Many Oracle applications experience increased overhead because connecting via ODBC is less efficient than using a native API call to the database. It is therefore recommended that ODBC be replaced with a native communications tool such as the Oracle call interface (OCI). ODBC generally works fine for occasional database queries but is too slow to be a permanent fixture in most production applications.

Oracle Replication Design

A replica is essentially a copy of a database. The replication process creates and maintains replicas of database objects, such as tables, in a distributed database system.

Replication can improve performance by increasing the availability of applications. This is done by providing alternate options for data retrieval. If a user is able to access a database on a local replica rather than on a remote server, network traffic is reduced. Replication provides the additional benefit of database access even when the distributed database is partially down. An application may still be able to function if part of the desired database is still available.

Oracle supports two forms of replication — basic and advanced. The CREATE SNAPSHOT or CREATE MATERIALIZED VIEW statements initialize basic replication. Basic replication only copies data (not procedures, indexes, etc.), the replication is always in one direction only, and only snapshot copies are read.

Advanced replication allows database objects (indexes, procedures, etc.) as well as data to be replicated. The advanced feature supports updateable-snapshot, multimaster, and update-anywhere replication in many different configurations. It is more difficult to configure than basic replication.

Yr.	Mo	Dy	Hr	EVENT	WAITS	AVG_WAIT_SECS
2002-11-07			11	SQL*Net message from client	541,157	1
2002-11-07			11	SQL*Net message to client	541,169	0
2002-11-07			11	SQL*Net more data from client	7,696	0
2002-11-07			11	SQL*Net more data to client	17,091	0
2002-11-07			11	latch free	2,198	0
2002-11-07			12	SQL*Net message from client	584,160	1
2002-11-07			12	SQL*Net message to client	584,153	0
2002-11-07			12	SQL*Net more data from client	7,475	0
2002-11-07			12	SQL*Net more data to client	20,393	0
2002-11-07			12	latch free	2,986	0
2002-11-07			13	SQL*Net message from client	342,213	1
2002-11-07			13	SQL*Net message to client	342,219	0

```
2002-11-07 13 SQL*Net more data from client    4,911        0
2002-11-07 13 latch free                       1,058        0
2002-11-07 14 SQL*Net message from client    563,049        1
2002-11-07 14 SQL*Net message to client      563,049        0
2002-11-07 14 SQL*Net more data from client    8,199        0
2002-11-07 14 latch free                       2,027        0
2002-11-07 15 LGWR wait for redo copy          3,724        0
2002-11-07 15 SQL*Net message from client    711,914        1
2002-11-07 15 SQL*Net message to client      711,912        0
2002-11-07 15 SQL*Net more data from client    8,868        0
2002-11-07 15 SQL*Net more data to client     16,408        0
```

ORACLE DISK DESIGN

Once you have your database design arsenal in place, you can begin the work of building correct physical designs from scratch and managing the physical design lifecycle once a system goes into production. But, how do you quickly spot physical design flaws in an up-and-running database?

It definitely takes a trained eye to uncover the root cause of identified performance problems, but Table 3.2 will help get you started. It lists just a few of the most common database performance problems and the possible physical design gremlins that could be the culprit in an Oracle database.

Using a quality performance monitor, you can be quickly led to the performance headaches in your database and then, using either your intelligent data-modeling tool or the combination of your database administration/change control product, you can remedy the situation.

Fixing foundational flaws in a database is never easy, but perhaps one day the DBA community will be treated to software that gets things right, before the situation turns ugly.

CONCLUSION

We have analyzed the tools and techniques that the designer must use to build a successful database environment. The designer must balance the requirements imposed by the hardware with a particular configuration of the database to adequately fulfill the purpose of the application, ensure the most efficient operation, and maximize the level of performance. Careful attention to the tuning methods described will reward the database designer with an efficient design that meets the needs of the client, while ensuring the optimum utilization of the resources available to him.

Next, let's look at Oracle design for the instance. The running instance is governed by the SGA and proper SGA design is a critical aspect of Oracle design.

Table 3.2   Performance Problems and Possible Causes

Performance Category	Performance Problem	Possible Design Cause
Memory	Poor data buffer cache hit ratio	Too many long table scans — invalid indexing scheme
		Not enough RAM devoted to buffer cache memory area
		Invalid object placement using Oracle's KEEP and RECYCLE buffer caches
		Not keeping small lookup tables in cache using CACHE table parameter
	Poor memory/disk sort ratio	Not presorting data when possible
Contention	Redo log waits	Incorrect sizing of Oracle redo logs
		Insufficient memory allocated to log buffer area
	Free list waits	Not enough free lists assigned to tables
		Not using Oracle9*i*'s auto segment management
	Rollback waits	Insufficient number of rollback segments
		Not using Oracle9*i*'s auto-UNDO management
I/O	Identified disk contention	Not separating tables and accompanying indexes into different tablespaces on different physical drives
	Slow access to system information	Not placing SYSTEM tablespace on little accessed physical drive
	Slow disk sorts	Placing tablespace used for disk sort activity on RAID5 drive or heavily accessed physical volume
	Abnormally high physical I/O	Too many long table scans — invalid indexing scheme
		Not enough RAM devoted to buffer cache memory area
		Invalid object placement using Oracle8's KEEP and RECYCLE buffer caches
		Not keeping small lookup tables in cache using CACHE table parameter

Table 3.2 Performance Problems and Possible Causes (Continued)

Performance Category	Performance Problem	Possible Design Cause
Space	Out of space conditions (storage structures)	Poorly forecasted data volumes in physical design
	Tablespace fragmentation	Invalid settings for either object space sizes or tablespace object settings (e.g., PCTINCREASE) Not using LMTs in Oracle8 and above
SQL	Large JOIN queries	Overnormalized database design
Object activity	Chaining in tables	Incorrect amount of PCTFREE, PCTUSED settings for objects Too small database block size
	Rollback extension	Incorrect sizing of rollback segments for given application transaction Not using Oracle9*i*'s auto-UNDO management
	Many large table scans	Incorrect indexing scheme
	Object fragmentation	Incorrect initial sizing Not using LMTs

4

ORACLE INSTANCE DESIGN

INTRODUCTION

The design of the Oracle instance can have a profound impact of the performance of the database. Starting in Oracle9*i,* you have the option of dynamically changing the SGA regions, but you still must design the instance configuration to handle your system's most common processing loads.

Because of the huge changes between Oracle releases, we will explore the design issues for Oracle8*i,* Oracle9*i,* and then explore the new Oracle Database 10*g* features for automatic SGA memory management.

If you are using Oracle9*i,* there are three ways to self-tune Oracle9*i*:

- Normal scheduled reconfiguration — a bimodal instance that performs OLTP and DSS during regular hours will benefit from a scheduled task to reconfigure the SGA and PGA.
- Trend-based dynamic reconfiguration — you can use Statspack to predict those times when the processing characteristics change and use the dbms_job package to fire *ad hoc* SGA and PGA changes.
- Reactive reconfiguration — just as Oracle9*i* dynamically redistributes RAM memory for tasks within the pga_aggregate_target region, the Oracle DBA can write scripts that steal RAM from an underutilized area and reallocate these RAM pages to another RAM area.

To illustrate, here is a script that can be used to change the SGA configuration when your processing requirements change:

```
#!/bin/ksh

# First, we must set the environment . . . .
ORACLE_SID=$1
export ORACLE_SID
ORACLE_HOME=`cat /etc/oratab|grep ^$ORACLE_SID:|cut
-f2 -d':'`
#ORACLE_HOME=`cat /var/opt/oracle/oratab|grep
^$ORACLE_SID:|cut -f2 -d':'`
export ORACLE_HOME
PATH=$ORACLE_HOME/bin:$PATH
export PATH

$ORACLE_HOME/bin/sqlplus -s /nologin<<!
connect system/manager as sysdba;
alter system set db_cache_size=1500m;
alter system set shared_pool_size=500m;
alter system set pga_aggregate_target=4000m;
exit
!
```

Let's review some guidelines for sizing the SGA and PGA regions.

Reserving RAM for Database Connections

Oracle allocates an OS area of RAM for every connected user if the system uses external PGA regions (i.e., if the pga_aggregate_target parameter is not used and you are not using the MTS). To determine the optimal RAM allocation for any Oracle server, the DBA may use a formula. We will assume in this example that the server is a dedicated Windows Oracle server and that Oracle is the only program running on the server. For dedicated Oracle servers, the maximum total RAM is computed as follows:

- OS reserved RAM — this is the amount of RAM required to run the OS kernel and system functions:
  – 20 percent of total RAM for Windows
  – 10 percent of total RAM for UNIX
- Oracle database connections RAM — each Oracle connection requires OS RAM regions for sorting and hash joins. (This does not apply when using the Oracle MTS or pga_aggregate_target.) The maximum amount of RAM required for a session is as follows:

- 2 megabytes (MB) RAM session overhead
- plus `sort_area_size`
- plus `hash_area_size`
■ Oracle SGA RAM — this is determined by the Oracle parameter settings. The total is easily found by either the `show sga` command or the value of the `sga_memory_max` parameter.

We should subtract 20 percent from the total available RAM to allow for Windows overhead. Windows uses RAM resources even when idle, and the 20 percent deduction is necessary to get the real free RAM on an idle server. Once the amount of RAM on the server is known, we will be in a position to size the Oracle database for RAM usage.

First, we need to know the high water mark (HWM) of Oracle connections. As noted previously, each session connected to the Windows server requires a memory region for the PGA, unless Oracle's MTS architecture or `pga_aggregate_target` is utilized.

The HWM of connected Oracle sessions can be determined in several ways. One popular method uses Oracle login and logoff system-level triggers to record sessions in a statistics table. Another method uses Oracle Statspack to display the values from the `stats$sysstat` table or the `v$resource_limit` view (only after release 8.1.7, because of a bug).

RAM Used by Oracle Connections

We have seen that an isolated memory region called the PGA is allocated in UNIX RAM memory whenever a dedicated connection is made to Oracle. The PGA consists of the following areas:

■ Sort area — this is the largest and most important area of the PGA.
■ Session information — this small area allows the user connection to communicate with the Oracle database by storing the internal connection addresses.
■ Cursor state — this area stores all reentrant values for the executing connection.
■ Stack space — this area contains miscellaneous control structures.

Oracle has the ability to dynamically change the largest component of a PGA — the sort area size — at either the system level or the session level. For example, here are some Oracle9i commands to dynamically change the sort area:

```
alter session set sort_area_size=10m deferred;
alter system  set sort_area_size=10m;
```

The `alter session` command instructs UNIX to expand the PGA sort area as the sort requires. If external PGA RAM is used, Oracle issues the `malloc()` command, creating a RAM sort area. The RAM sort area is not allocated until the retrieval from the databases has been completed and the memory only exists for the duration of the sort. In this way, the RAM is only allocated when Oracle needs it and the memory demands on the server are reduced.

Determining the Optimal PGA Size

Our sample Windows server has 1250 MB of RAM. Subtracting 20 percent for overhead, we have 1000 MB available for Oracle.

Each PGA RAM region size is determined as follows:

- OS overhead — we reserve 2 MB for Windows and 1 MB for UNIX.
- `Sort_area_size` parameter value — this RAM is used for data row sorting inside the PGA.
- `Hash_area_size` parameter value — This RAM defaults to 1.5 times `sort_area_size` and is used for performing hash joins of Oracle tables.

The values for `sort_area_size` and `hash_area_size` are quickly shown with the Oracle `show parameters` command:

```
SQL> show parameters area_size

NAME                                        TYPE          VALUE
------------------------------------------- ------------- ---------
bitmap_merge_area_size                      integer       1048576
create_bitmap_area_size                     integer       8388608
hash_area_size                              integer       1048576
sort_area_size                              integer       524288
workarea_size_policy                        string        MANUAL
```

A quick dictionary query (`pga_size_each.sql`) against the `v$parameter` view will yield the correct value for each PGA RAM region size.

```
set pages 999;

column pga_size format 999,999,999

select
    2048576+a.value+b.value    pga_size
```

```
from
   v$parameter a,
   v$parameter b
where
   a.name = 'sort_area_size'
and
   b.name = 'hash_area_size'
;
```

The data dictionary query output shows that the Oracle PGA will use 3.6 MB of RAM memory for each connected Oracle session.

```
PGA_SIZE
------------
3,621,440
```

If we now multiply the number of connected users by the PGA demands for each user, we will know exactly how much RAM should be reserved for connected sessions. Alternatively, we could issue an SQL statement to obtain the same result. The script for such a statement is shown below.

A Script for Computing Total PGA RAM

This script reads both the sort_area_size and hash_area_size to compute the total PGA region. The script will display a prompt for the HWM of connected users and then computes the total PGA RAM to reserve for dedicated Oracle connections. The Windows PGA session incurs a 2 MB overhead in this example.

```
-- ***********************************************************
-- Compute PGA sizes
--
-- Copyright (c) 2003 By Donald K. Burleson -
 All Rights reserved.
-- ***********************************************************

set pages 999;

column pga_size format 999,999,999

accept hwm number prompt 'Enter the high-water mark of connected
users: '
```

```
select
    &hwm*(2048576+a.value+b.value) pga_size
from
   v$parameter a,
   v$parameter b
where
   a.name = 'sort_area_size'
and
   b.name = 'hash_area_size'
;
```

Running the script, we see that we are prompted for the HWM. We will assume that the HWM of connected sessions to the Oracle database server is 100. Oracle will do the math and display the amount of RAM to reserve for Oracle connections.

```
SQL> @pga_size

Enter the high-water mark of connected users: 100

old   2:     &hwm*(2048576+a.value+b.value) pga_size
new   2:        100*(2048576+a.value+b.value) pga_size


PGA_SIZE
------------
 362,144,000
```

Returning to our example Windows server, we are ready to calculate the optimum SGA size. Multiplying 100 by the amount needed for each PGA region (3.62 MB) and adding the 2 MB PGA overhead, gives us the total PGA size of 364 MB. The maximum size for the SGA is determined by subtracting the total PGA and the OS overhead from the total RAM on the server. Here is a summary:

Total RAM on Windows server	1250 MB
Less:	
Total PGA regions for 100 users:	364 MB
RAM reserved for Windows (20 percent)	250 MB
Maximum SGA size	636 MB

This leaves 636 MB of free memory for the SGA. Therefore, the RAM allocated to the data buffers should be adjusted to make the SGA size less than 636 MB. If the SGA size is greater than 636 MB, the server will begin to page RAM, impairing the performance of the entire server. We also see that the total Oracle RAM is 1000 MB, equivalent to the total PGA plus the total SGA.

Next, let's review the SGA instance parameters and see how the proper design is used to optimize performance.

SGA PARAMETER COMPONENTS

With many hundreds of Oracle initialization parameters, it's important for the DBA to focus on those parameters that have the most impact on the performance of the Oracle database. Oracle has a huge number of parameters in the Oracle initialization files (init.ora) that control the overall configuration of the Oracle instance. While there are dozens of init.ora parameters that affect performance, the following are some of the most important.

In Oracle8i, we have these parameters:

- shared_pool_size — the memory region allocated for the library cache and internal control structures
- db_block_size — the size of each data block
- db_block_buffers — the number of data buffers to allocate for the instance
- sort_area_size — the amount of RAM reserved for each user to perform sorting operations
- optimizer_mode — the default mode in which all SQL statements will be optimized for an execution plan
- db_file_multiblock_read_count — the parameter that controls the number of blocks that are read asynchronously in FTS operations

By Oracle9i, we see new SGA parameters that control SGA region behavior:

- pga_aggregate_target — this parameter defines the RAM area reserved for systemwide sorting and hash joins.
- sga_max_size — this parameter defines the maximum size of the Oracle SGA and cannot be modified while the instance is running.

By Oracle Database 10g, we have the option of using automatic tuning parameters. The automated memory management (AMM) component manages the RAM inside the SGA, much the same way as the automatic PGA management feature in Oracle9i (pga_aggregate_target) automates the sort and hash areas with PGA RAM. The AMM uses real-time workload data from automatic workload repository (AWR) and changes the sizes of the shared pool and data buffers according to the current workload.

- `sga_target` — just like `pga_aggregate_target`, setting this parameter allows the Oracle SGA to dynamically change itself as processing needs change. The size of the `shared_pool_size` and `db_cache_size` will adjust based upon current and historical processing requirements.

As we see, the SGA design is highly dependent on the version of Oracle that you are running. Next let's examine the design of the shared pool region.

DESIGNING THE SHARED POOL

An important area of Oracle instance design is the Oracle shared pool. The Oracle shared pool contains Oracle's library cache, which is responsible for collecting, parsing, interpreting, and executing all of the SQL statements that go against the Oracle database. Hence, the shared pool is a key component, so it's necessary for the Oracle DBA to check for shared pool contention.

When the Oracle shared pool is stressed, Oracle reports can quickly tell you if shared pool thrashing is occurring. One of the most common causes of Oracle shared pool problems occurs when an application does not utilize reusable SQL.

Oracle's parsing algorithm ensures that identical SQL statements do not have to be parsed each time they're executed. However, many Oracle DBAs fail to insert host variables into SQL statements and instead ship the SQL statements with the liberal host values. The following example illustrates this point.

With literals in the SQL (not reusable):

```
Select
   customer_details
from
   customer
where
   customer_name = 'BURLESON';
```

With host variables in the SQL (reusable):

```
Select
    customer_details
from
    customer
where
    customer_name = :var1;
```

As we can see, the addition of the host variable makes the SQL statement reusable and reduces the time spent in the library cache. This improves the overall throughput and performance of the SQL statement. In severe cases of nonreusable SQL, many Oracle DBAs will issue the `Alter Database Flush Shared Pool` command periodically to remove all of the nonreusable SQL and improve the performance of SQL statements within the library cache.

Library Cache Usage Measurement

The library cache consists of the shared SQL areas and the PL/SQL areas, which are, in turn, a subcomponent of the shared pool. The library cache miss ratio tells the DBA whether or not to add space to the shared pool and it represents the ratio of the sum of library cache reloads to the sum of pins. In general, if the library cache ratio is over 1, you should consider adding to the `shared_pool_size`. Library cache misses occur during the compilation of SQL statements.

The compilation of a SQL statement consists of two phases:

1. The parse phase — when the time comes to parse a SQL statement, Oracle first checks to see if the parsed representation of the statement already exists in the library cache. If not, Oracle will allocate a shared SQL area within the library cache and then parse the SQL statement.
2. The execution phase — at execution time, Oracle checks to see if a parsed representation of the SQL statement already exists in the library cache. If not, Oracle will reparse and execute the statement. During the execution phase, the query plan is run and the data is retrieved from Oracle.

Within the library cache, hit ratios can be determined for all dictionary objects that are loaded. These include table/procedures, triggers, indexes, package bodies, and clusters.

If any of the hit ratios fall below 75 percent, you should add to the `shared_pool_size`. The table V$LIBRARYCACHE is the internal Oracle psuedotable that keeps information about library cache activity. The table has three relevant columns — namespace, pins, and reloads. The namespace column indicates whether the measurement is for the SQL area, a table or procedure, a package body, or a trigger. The pins column counts the number of times an item in the library cache is executed. The reloads column counts the number of times the parsed representation did not exist in the library cache, forcing Oracle to allocate the private SQL areas in order to parse and execute the statement.

Listing 4.1 is an example of a SQL*Plus query to interrogate the V$LIBRARYCACHE table and retrieve the necessary performance information.

When we run this script, we see all of the salient areas within the library cache, as shown below.

```
                          Low data dictionary object hit ratio
                                     Rollup by hour

                                                    Data
                                            Data Dictionary        Data Object
                                       Dictionary   Cache Dictionary     Hit
    Yr.   Mo Dy Hr.  PARAMETER              Gets   Misses      Usage   Ratio
    -------------  ------------------  --------  ---------- ---------- ------
    2003-08-23 12  dc_histogram_defs      2,994        980        600      67
    2003-08-23 23  dc_histogram_defs      2,567        956        432      63
```

Again, we must always check to see if any component of the shared pool needs to be increased. Next, let's take a look at how instancewide sort operations affect the performance of the Oracle database.

ORACLE EVENT WAITS

An improperly sized shared pool will also lead to excessive internal wait events and you can use the Oracle Statspack utility to monitor a too-small shared pool (Listing 4.2).

Listing 4.3 shows a sample listing. As we see, this measures all excessive wait events.

In addition to monitoring for shared pool wait events, you can also use the v$shared_pool_advice utility to help you get the optimal size for the shared pool.

THE SHARED POOL ADVISORY UTILITY

This shared pool advisory functionality has been extended in Oracle9*i*, release 2 to include a new advice called v$shared_pool_advice. There is talk to expanding the advice facility to all SGA RAM areas in future releases of Oracle.

Listing 4.1   Example of a SQL*Plus Query to Interrogate the V$LIBRARYCACHE Table

```
-- prompt
-- prompt
-- prompt  ************************************************************
-- prompt  Excessive library cache miss ratio
-- prompt  ************************************************************
-- prompt
-- prompt

ttitle 'High Library cache miss ratio|Increase shared_pool_size'

column c1 heading "execs"       format 9,999,999
column c2 heading "Cache Misses|While Executing"    format 9,999,999
column c3 heading "Library Cache|Miss Ratio"      format 999.99999

break on mydate skip 2;

select
   to_char(snap_time,'yyyy-mm-dd HH24')   mydate,
   sum(new.pins-old.pins)                 c1,
   sum(new.reloads-old.reloads)           c2,
   sum(new.reloads-old.reloads)/
   sum(new.pins-old.pins)                 library_cache_miss_ratio
from
   stats$librarycache old,
   stats$librarycache new,
   stats$snapshot       sn
where
   snap_time > sysdate-&1
and
   new.snap_id = sn.snap_id
and
   old.snap_id = new.snap_id-1
and
   old.namespace = new.namespace
having
   sum(new.reloads-old.reloads)/
   sum(new.pins-old.pins) > .05
group by
   to_char(snap_time,'yyyy-mm-dd HH24')
;
```

**Listing 4.2   Using the Oracle Statspack Utility to Monitor
a Too-Small Shared Pool**

```
-- prompt
-- prompt  **********************************************************
-- prompt  Excessive event waits indicate shared pool contention
-- prompt  **********************************************************
-- prompt
-- prompt

ttitle 'High event waits|Check for shared pool contention'

set pages 999;
set lines 80;

column mydate heading 'Yr.  Mo Dy Hr'      format a13;
column event                               format a30;
column waits                               format 99,999,999;
column secs_waited                         format 999,999,999;
column avg_wait_secs                       format 999,999;

break on to_char(snap_time,'yyyy-mm-dd') skip 1;

select
   to_char(snap_time,'yyyy-mm-dd HH24')            mydate,
   e.event,
   e.total_waits - nvl(b.total_waits,0)            waits,
   ((e.time_waited_micro - nvl(b.time_waited_micro,0))/100) /
   nvl((e.total_waits - nvl(b.total_waits,0)),0)  avg_wait_secs
from
   stats$system_event b,
   stats$system_event e,
   stats$snapshot       sn
where
   snap_time > sysdate-&1
and
   e.snap_id = sn.snap_id
and
   b.snap_id = e.snap_id-1
and
   b.event = e.event
and
  (
   e.event like 'SQL*Net%'
   or
   e.event in (
```

Listing 4.2 Using the Oracle Statspack Utility to Monitor a Too-Small Shared Pool (Continued)

```
      'latch free',
      'enqueue',
      'LGWR wait for redo copy',
      'buffer busy waits'
     )
  )
and
   e.total_waits - b.total_waits  > 100
and
   e.time_waited_micro - b.time_waited_micro > 100
;
```

Listing 4.3 High Event Waits

```
                      High event waits
               Check for shared pool contention


Yr.  Mo Dy Hr EVENT                                WAITS AVG_WAIT_SECS
------------ ------------------------------ ----------- -------------
2003-08-26 03 SQL*Net message to client        653,541             0
2003-08-26 03 SQL*Net message from client      653,532         1,377
2003-08-26 03 SQL*Net more data from client      4,155             1
2003-08-26 03 SQL*Net break/reset to client     62,166             7
2003-08-26 04 latch free                        43,341             8
2003-08-26 04 enqueue                            3,222        25,534
2003-08-26 04 buffer busy waits                  3,034            33
2003-08-26 04 LGWR wait for redo copy             250             2
2003-08-26 04 SQL*Net message to client        775,522             0
2003-08-26 04 SQL*Net more data to client       12,180             1
2003-08-26 04 SQL*Net message from client      775,505         1,717
2003-08-26 04 SQL*Net more data from client      4,900             1
2003-08-26 04 SQL*Net break/reset to client     74,054             7
2003-08-26 05 latch free                        32,033             8
2003-08-26 05 enqueue                            4,214        27,203
2003-08-26 05 LGWR wait for redo copy             235             2
2003-08-26 05 SQL*Net message to client        566,420             0
2003-08-26 05 SQL*Net more data to client        8,910             1
2003-08-26 05 SQL*Net message from client      566,395         1,555
```

Listing 4.3 High Event Waits (Continued)

```
2003-08-26 05 SQL*Net more data from client    3,588          1
2003-08-26 05 SQL*Net break/reset to client   53,578          7
2003-08-26 06 latch free                      41,587          8
2003-08-26 06 enqueue                          3,522     25,746
2003-08-26 06 buffer busy waits                  676         47
2003-08-26 03 SQL*Net more data to client     10,386          1
2003-08-25 12 SQL*Net message to client    1,266,653          0
2003-08-25 12 SQL*Net more data to client     21,475          1
2003-08-25 12 SQL*Net message from client  1,266,690      1,178
2003-08-25 12 SQL*Net more data from client    6,558          1
2003-08-25 12 SQL*Net break/reset to client   85,546          7
2003-08-25 13 latch free                      14,431          6
2003-08-25 13 enqueue                          4,485     27,703
2003-08-25 13 LGWR wait for redo copy            225          1
2003-08-25 13 SQL*Net message to client      833,371          0
2003-08-25 13 SQL*Net more data to client     11,453          1
2003-08-25 13 SQL*Net message from client    833,355      1,332
2003-08-25 13 SQL*Net more data from client    4,008          1
2003-08-25 13 SQL*Net break/reset to client   59,288          7
2003-08-25 14 latch free                      16,850          7
2003-08-25 14 enqueue                          4,312     27,418
2003-08-25 14 buffer busy waits                1,550         33
2003-08-25 14 LGWR wait for redo copy            209          2
2003-08-25 14 SQL*Net message to client      675,660          0
2003-08-25 14 SQL*Net more data to client     21,057          1
2003-08-25 14 SQL*Net message from client    675,642      2,402
2003-08-25 14 SQL*Net more data from client    4,214          1
2003-08-25 14 SQL*Net break/reset to client   62,844          8
2003-08-25 15 latch free                      14,644          7
2003-08-25 15 enqueue                          5,011     28,436
2003-08-25 15 buffer busy waits                3,339         32
2003-08-25 15 LGWR wait for redo copy            283          2
2003-08-25 09 SQL*Net message to client      510,794          0
2003-08-25 09 SQL*Net more data to client     21,264          1
2003-08-25 09 SQL*Net message from client    510,776      2,127
2003-08-25 09 SQL*Net more data from client    3,183          1
2003-08-25 09 SQL*Net break/reset to client   47,880          8
2003-08-25 11 latch free                      61,649          9
```

In Oracle9*i*, release 2, the v$shared_pool_advice shows the marginal differences in SQL parses as the shared pool changes in size from 10 percent of the current value to 200 percent of the current value.

The Oracle documentation contains a complete description for the set up and use of shared pool advice, which is simple to configure. Once it is installed, you can run a simple script to query the v$shared_pool_advice view and see the marginal changes in SQL parses for different shared_pool sizes (Listing 4.4).

Here we see the statistics for the shared pool in a range from 50 percent of the current size to 200 percent of the current size. These statistics can give you a great idea about the proper size for the shared_pool_size. If you are automating the SGA region sizes with automated alter system commands, creating this output and writing a program to interpret the results is a great way to ensure that the shared pool and library cache always have enough RAM.

Next let's examine the most important SGA component — the internal data buffers.

DESIGNING THE DATA BUFFERS

The design of the Oracle data buffers is an important aspect of Oracle tuning because the data buffer has a direct impact on disk I/O. Oracle provides an in-memory cache for data blocks that have been retrieved by earlier SQL requests. When a request is made to Oracle to retrieve data, Oracle will first check the internal memory structures to see if the data is already in the buffer. If the block is in memory, Oracle reads the data from the RAM buffer and avoids doing unnecessary disk I/O.

Before you can fully complete the design, you must implement the system on a best-guess basis and develop a mechanism to monitor the data buffer hit ratio (DBHR) for all pools you have defined. You can monitor all seven data buffers with this script:

```
--  ***********************************************************
-- Display avg. BHR since database startup time
--
-- Copyright (c)2003 By Donald K. Burleson - All Rights reserved.
--  ***********************************************************
select
   name,
   block_size,
   (1-(physical_reads/ decode(db_block_gets+consistent_gets, 0,
.001, db_block_gets+consistent_gets)))*100   cache_hit_ratio
from
   v$buffer_pool_statistics;
```

Here, we see the output from this script. Note that the names of the sized block buffers remain DEFAULT and you must select the

Listing 4.4 Display Shared Pool Advice

```
-- **************************************************
-- Display shared pool advice
-- **************************************************

set lines  100
set pages  999

column       c1     heading 'Pool |Size(M)'
column       c2     heading 'Size|Factor'
column       c3     heading 'Est|LC(M)   '
column       c4     heading 'Est LC|Mem. Obj.'
column       c5     heading 'Est|Time|Saved|(sec)'
column       c6     heading 'Est|Parse|Saved|Factor'
column c7     heading 'Est|Object Hits'   format 999,999,999

SELECT
   shared_pool_size_for_estimate c1,
   shared_pool_size_factor       c2,
   estd_lc_size                  c3,
   estd_lc_memory_objects        c4,
   estd_lc_time_saved                 c5,
   estd_lc_time_saved_factor          c6,
   estd_lc_memory_object_hits         c7
FROM
   v$shared_pool_advice;
```

				Est	Est	
				Time	Parse	
Pool	Size	Est	Est LC	Saved	Saved	Est
Size(M)	Factor	LC(M)	Mem. Obj.	(sec)	Factor	Object Hits
48	.5	48	20839	1459645	1	135,756,032
64	.6667	63	28140	1459645	1	135,756,101
80	.8333	78	35447	1459645	1	135,756,149
96	1	93	43028	1459645	1	135,756,253
112	1.1667	100	46755	1459646	1	135,756,842
128	1.3333	100	46755	1459646	1	135,756,842
144	1.5	100	46755	1459646	1	135,756,842
160	1.6667	100	46755	1459646	1	135,756,842
176	1.8333	100	46755	1459646	1	135,756,842
192	2	100	46755	1459646	1	135,756,842

block_size column to differentiate between the buffers. Here we see all seven data buffers.

NAME	BLOCK_SIZE	CACHE_HIT_RATIO
DEFAULT	32,767	.97
RECYCLE	16,384	.61
KEEP	16,384	1.00
DEFAULT	16,384	.92
DEFAULT	4,096	.99
DEFAULT	8,192	.98
DEFAULT	2,048	.86

This report is not very useful because the v$sysstat view only shows averages since the instance was started. To perform self-tuning of the data buffers, we can use Oracle's Statspack utility to measure the DBHRs every hour.

It would be ideal if you could create one buffer for each database page, ensuring that Oracle would read each block only once. With Oracle8i and the very large memory features, it's now possible to specify a data buffer that's large enough to hold an entire multigigabyte database, but most large databases do not have enough RAM to allow for the full caching of data pages.

In Oracle8i, we have three buffer pools for holding data blocks:

1. DEFAULT pool — used for all data blocks that are not marked for the KEEP or RECYCLE pools
2. KEEP pool — reserved for tables and indexes that are used frequently
3. RECYCLE pool — reserved for data blocks that are read when performing large FTSs

Because most Oracle databases do not have enough RAM to cache the whole database, the data buffers manage the data blocks to reduce disk I/O. Oracle utilizes a LRU algorithm to determine which database pages are to be flushed from memory.

As I mentioned earlier, the measure of the effectiveness of the data buffer is called the DBHR. This ratio computes the likelihood that a data block is present in the data buffer when the block is requested. The more data blocks that are found in the buffer, the higher the DBHR. Oracle recommends that all databases exhibit a DBHR of at least 90 percent.

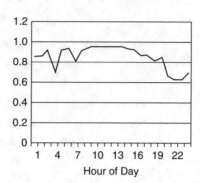

Figure 4.1   A Sample Listing from a Statspack DBHR Report

It's important to note that the DBHR is an elapsed-time measurement. If you use the Oracle Statspack utility to compute the DBHR over short intervals (every five minutes), you will see that the buffer hit ratio varies from 50 to 100 percent, depending upon the type of SQL requests that are being processed.

Many Oracle shops will keep their buffer hit ratio information in the Statspack tables and plot it to show trends in the effectiveness of the data buffer to reduce I/O. Figure 4.1 shows an example of a plot of Statspack data for the DBHR.

The predictive models for Oracle RAM areas began with the v$db_cache_advice utility in Oracle9*i*. The new v$db_cache_advice view is similar to an Oracle7 utility that also predicted the benefit of adding data buffers. The Oracle7 utility used the x$kcbrbh view to track buffer hits and the x$kcbcbh view to track buffer misses.

Oracle9*i*, release 2 now has three predictive utilities:

1. PGA advice — Oracle9*i* has introduced a new advisory utility dubbed v$pga_target_advice. This utility will show the marginal changes in optimal, one-pass, and multipass PGA execution for different sizes of pga_aggregate_target, ranging from 10 to 200 percent of the current value.
2. Shared pool advice — this advisory functionality has been extended in Oracle9*i*, release 2 to include a new advice called v$shared_pool_advice. There is talk to expanding the advice facility to all SGA RAM areas in future releases of Oracle.

3. Data cache advice — the v$db_cache_advice utility shows the marginal changes in physical data block reads for different sizes of db_cache_size. Bear in mind that the data from Statspack can provide similar data as v$db_cache_advice. Most Oracle tuning professionals use Statspack and v$db_cache_advice to monitor the effectiveness of their data buffers.

These advisory utilities are extremely important for the Oracle DBA who must adjust the sizes of the RAM areas to meet current processing demands.

Using v$db_cache_advice

The following query can be used to perform the cache advice function, once the db_cache_advice has been enabled and the database has run long enough to give representative results.

```
-- ***********************************************************
-- Display cache advice
-- ***********************************************************

column c1    heading 'Cache Size (meg)'      format 999,999,999,999
column c2    heading 'Buffers'               format 999,999,999
column c3    heading 'Estd Phys|Read Factor' format 999.90
column c4    heading 'Estd Phys| Reads'      format 999,999,999

select
    size_for_estimate          c1,
    buffers_for_estimate       c2,
    estd_physical_read_factor  c3,
    estd_physical_reads        c4
from
    v$db_cache_advice
where
    name = 'DEFAULT'
and
    block_size   = (SELECT value FROM V$PARAMETER
                    WHERE name = 'db_block_size')
and
    advice_status = 'ON';
```

The output from the script is shown below. Note that the values range from 10 percent of the current size to double the current size of the db_cache_size.

Cache Size (meg)	Buffers	Estd Phys Read Factor	Estd Phys Reads	
30	3,802	18.70	192,317,943	<== 10% size
60	7,604	12.83	131,949,536	
91	11,406	7.38	75,865,861	
121	15,208	4.97	51,111,658	
152	19,010	3.64	37,460,786	
182	22,812	2.50	25,668,196	
212	26,614	1.74	17,850,847	
243	30,416	1.33	13,720,149	
273	34,218	1.13	11,583,180	
304	38,020	1.00	10,282,475	Current Size
334	41,822	.93	9,515,878	
364	45,624	.87	8,909,026	
395	49,426	.83	8,495,039	
424	53,228	.79	8,116,496	
456	57,030	.76	7,824,764	
486	60,832	.74	7,563,180	
517	64,634	.71	7,311,729	
547	68,436	.69	7,104,280	
577	72,238	.67	6,895,122	
608	76,040	.66	6,739,731	<== 2x size

From this listing, we see that increasing the db_cache_size from 304 MB to 334 MB would result in approximately 700,000 less physical reads.

These advisory utilities are important for Oracle9i DBAs who must adjust their SGA regions to meet current processing demands. Remember, SGA tuning is an iterative process and busy shops continually monitor and adjust the size of their data cache, PGA, and shared pool.

DESIGN WITH THE DBHR

The goal of the DBA is to keep as many of the frequently used Oracle blocks in buffer memory as possible. The DBHR measures how often requested data blocks are found in the buffer pool. In sum, the DBHR is the ratio of logical reads to physical disk reads. As the hit ratio approaches 100 percent, more data blocks are found in memory, resulting in fewer disk I/Os and faster overall database performance.

On the other hand, if the DBHR falls below 90 percent, fewer data blocks are resident in memory, therefore Oracle must perform a disk I/O to move them into the data buffer. The formula for calculating the DBHR in Oracle8 was:

$$\frac{1 - (\text{Physical Reads} - \text{Physical Reads Direct})}{(\text{session logical reads})}$$

It should be noted that the formula for calculating the hit ratio in Oracle7 and Oracle8 does not include direct block reads. Direct block reads become a separate statistic in Oracle8*i*.

It is important to realize that the DBHR is only one small part of Oracle tuning. You should also use Statspack, interrogate system wait events, and tune your SQL for optimal execution plans.

The hit ratio for Oracle8*i* can be gathered from the v$ views, as shown below. However, the value is not very useful because it shows the total buffer hit ratio since the beginning of the instance.

```
select
    1 - ((a.value -
    (b.value))/d.value) "Cache Hit Ratio"
from
    v$sysstat a,
    v$sysstat b,
    v$sysstat d
where
    a.name='physical reads'
and
    b.name='physical reads direct'
and
    d.name='session logical reads';
```

Many novice DBAs make the mistake of using the DBHR from the v$ views. The v$buffer_pool_statistics view does contain the accumulated values for data buffer pool usage, but computing the DBHR from the v$ tables only provides the average since the database was started.

For the DBA to determine how well the buffer pools are performing, it is necessary to measure the hit ratio at more frequent intervals. Calculating the DBHR for Oracle8 and beyond is more complicated than earlier versions, but the results enable the DBA to achieve a higher level of tuning than was previously possible.

In the next section, we will look at the wealth of information that Statspack can provide for tracking buffer pool utilization and computing the DBHR.

Using Statspack for the DBHR

Statspack uses the `stats$buffer_pool_statistics` table for monitoring buffer pool statistics. This table contains the following useful columns:

- `name` — this column shows the name of the data buffer (KEEP, RECYCLE, or DEFAULT).
- `free_buffer_wait` — this is a count of the number of waits on free buffers.
- `buffer_busy_wait` — this is the number of times a requested block was in the data buffer but unavailable because of a conflict.
- `db_block_gets` — this is the number of database block gets, which are either logical or physical.
- `consistent_gets` — this is the number of logical reads.
- `physical_reads` — this is the number of disk block fetch requests issued by Oracle. (Remember, this is not always a real read because of disk array caching.)
- `physical_writes` — this is the number of physical disk write requests from Oracle. If you have a disk array, the actual writes are performed asynchronously.

These Statspack columns provide information that can be used to measure several important metrics, including the most important, the DBHR.

Data Buffer Monitoring with Statspack

There are two ways to use Statspack to compute the DBHR. In Oracle8*i* and beyond, we may use the `stats$buffer_pool_statistics` table. For Oracle 8.0, the `stats$sesstat` table should be used.

> **NOTE**: There is an important difference between `stats$ buffer_pool_statistics` in Oracle 8.0 and Oracle8*i*. If Statspack was back-ported into Oracle 8.0, the `stats$buffer_pool_statistics` view does not give accurate DBHRs for the DEFAULT, KEEP, and RECYCLE pools. Instead, there is only one pool defined as FAKE VIEW. This uses the `stats$sysstat` table and should be used for Oracle 8.0 (see Listing 4.5).

Listing 4.6 is used for Oracle 8.1 and beyond.

Listing 4.5   Display DBHR for Oracle8

```
--  ****************************************************************
-- Display BHR for Oracle8
--
-- Copyright (c) 2003 By Donald K. Burleson - All Rights reserved.
--  ****************************************************************

set pages 9999;

column logical_reads  format 999,999,999
column phys_reads     format 999,999,999
column phys_writes    format 999,999,999
column "BUFFER HIT RATIO" format 999

select
   to_char(snap_time,'yyyy-mm-dd HH24'),
   a.value + b.value  "logical_reads",
   c.value            "phys_reads",
   d.value            "phys_writes",
   round(100 * (((a.value-e.value)+(b.value-f.value))-(c.value-
g.value)) /
(a.value-e.value)+(b.value-f.v
value)))
        "BUFFER HIT RATIO"
from
   perfstat.stats$sysstat a,
   perfstat.stats$sysstat b,
   perfstat.stats$sysstat c,
   perfstat.stats$sysstat d,
   perfstat.stats$sysstat e,
   perfstat.stats$sysstat f,
   perfstat.stats$sysstat g,
   perfstat.stats$snapshot    sn
where
   a.snap_id = sn.snap_id
and
   b.snap_id = sn.snap_id
and
   c.snap_id = sn.snap_id
and
   d.snap_id = sn.snap_id
and
   e.snap_id = sn.snap_id-1
and
   f.snap_id = sn.snap_id-1
```

Listing 4.5   Display DBHR for Oracle8 (Continued)

```
and
   g.snap_id = sn.snap_id-1
and
   a.statistic# = 39
and
   e.statistic# = 39
and
   b.statistic# = 38
and
   f.statistic# = 38
and
   c.statistic# = 40
and
   g.statistic# = 40
and
   d.statistic# = 41
;
```

A sample output from this script is shown below:

```
yr.    mo dy Hr  BUFFER_POOL_NAME        BHR
-------------    --------------------    -----
2001-12-12 15  DEFAULT                  .92
2001-12-12 15  KEEP                     .99
2001-12-12 15  RECYCLE                  .75
2001-12-12 16  DEFAULT                  .94
2001-12-12 16  KEEP                     .99
2001-12-12 16  RECYCLE                  .65
```

This script provides us with the DBHR for each of the buffer pools at one-hour intervals. It is important that the KEEP pool always has a 99 to 100 percent DBHR. If this is not the case, data blocks should be added to the KEEP pool to make it the same size as the sum of all object data blocks that are assigned to the KEEP pool.

To summarize, the DBA can control the DBHR by adding blocks within the Oracle parameters. Oracle recommends that the DBHR not fall below 90 percent.

Listing 4.6   Display DBHR for Oracle8*i* and beyond

```
--   *************************************************************
--   Display BHR for Oracle8i & beyond
--
--   Copyright (c) 2003 By Donald K. Burleson - All Rights reserved.
--   *************************************************************

column bhr format 9.99
column mydate heading 'yr.  mo dy Hr.'

select
    to_char(snap_time,'yyyy-mm-dd HH24')        mydate,
    new.name                                    buffer_pool_name,
    (((new.consistent_gets-old.consistent_gets)+
    (new.db_block_gets-old.db_block_gets))-
    (new.physical_reads-old.physical_reads))
    /
    ((new.consistent_gets-old.consistent_gets)+
    (new.db_block_gets-old.db_block_gets))      bhr
from
    perfstat.stats$buffer_pool_statistics old,
    perfstat.stats$buffer_pool_statistics new,
    perfstat.stats$snapshot                sn
where
    (((new.consistent_gets-old.consistent_gets)+
    (new.db_block_gets-old.db_block_gets))-
    (new.physical_reads-old.physical_reads))
    /
    ((new.consistent_gets-old.consistent_gets)+
    (new.db_block_gets-old.db_block_gets)) < .90
and
    new.name = old.name
and
    new.snap_id = sn.snap_id
and
    old.snap_id = sn.snap_id-1
;
```

PINNING PACKAGES IN THE SGA

To prevent paging, packages can be marked as nonswappable. Marking a package as nonswappable tells a database that after the package is initially loaded, the package must always remain in memory. This is called pinning or memory fencing. Oracle provides a procedure called dbms_shared_pool.keep to pin a package. Packages can be unpinned with dbms_shared_pool.unkeep.

> **Note:** Only packages can be pinned. Stored procedures cannot be pinned unless they are placed into a package.

The choice of whether to pin a package in memory is a function of the size of the object and the frequency of its use. Large packages that are called frequently might benefit from pinning, but any difference might go unnoticed because the frequent calls to the procedure have kept it loaded into memory anyway. Therefore, because the object never pages out in the first place, pinning has no effect. Also, the way procedures are grouped into packages can have some influence. Some Oracle DBAs identify high-impact procedures and group them into a single package, which is pinned in the library cache.

In an ideal world, the `shared_pool` parameter of the `init.ora` should be large enough to accept every package, stored procedure, and trigger that can be used by the applications. However, reality dictates that the shared pool cannot grow indefinitely and wise choices must be made in terms of which packages are pinned.

Because of their frequent usage, Oracle recommends that the `standard`, `dbms_standard`, `dbms_utility`, `dbms_describe`, and `dbms_output` packages always be pinned in the shared pool. The following snippet demonstrates how a stored procedure called `sys.standard` can be pinned:

```
Connect system/manager as sysdba;
@/usr/oracle/rdbms/admin/dbmspool.sql
EXECUTE dbms_shared_pool.keep('sys.standard');
```

A standard procedure can be written to pin all of the recommended Oracle packages into the shared pool. Here is the script:

```
EXECUTE dbms_shared_pool.keep('DBMS_ALERT');
EXECUTE dbms_shared_pool.keep('DBMS_DDL');
EXECUTE dbms_shared_pool.keep('DBMS_DESCRIBE');
EXECUTE dbms_shared_pool.keep('DBMS_LOCK');
EXECUTE dbms_shared_pool.keep('DBMS_OUTPUT');
EXECUTE dbms_shared_pool.keep('DBMS_PIPE');
EXECUTE dbms_shared_pool.keep('DBMS_SESSION');
EXECUTE dbms_shared_pool.keep('DBMS_SHARED_POOL');
EXECUTE dbms_shared_pool.keep('DBMS_STANDARD');
EXECUTE dbms_shared_pool.keep('DBMS_UTILITY');
EXECUTE dbms_shared_pool.keep('STANDARD');
```

Automatic Repinning of Packages

UNIX users might want to add code to the /etc/rc file to ensure that the packages are repinned after each database startup, guaranteeing that all packages are repinned with each bounce of the box. A script might look like this:

```
[root]: more pin
ORACLE_SID=mydata
export ORACLE_SID
su oracle -c "/usr/oracle/bin/svrmgrl /<<!
connect internal;
select * from db;
    @/usr/local/dba/sql/pin.sql
exit;
!"
```

The DBA also needs to remember to run the pin.sql script whenever restarting a database. This is done by reissuing the PIN command from startup trigger immediately after the database has been restarted.

Listing 4.7 shows a handy script to look at pinned packages in the SGA. The output from this listing should show those packages that are frequently used by your application.

This is an easy way to tell the number of times a nonpinned stored procedure is swapped out of memory and required a reload. To effectively measure memory, two methods are recommended.

The first method is to regularly run the estat-bstat utility (usually located in ~/rdbms/admin/utlbstat.sql and utlestat.sql) for measuring SGA consumption over a range of time. The second method is to write a snapdump utility to interrogate the SGA and note any exceptional information relating to the library cache. This would include the following measurements:

- Data dictionary hit ratio
- Library cache miss ratio
- Individual hit ratios for all namespaces

Also, be aware that the relevant parameter — shared_pool_size — is used for other objects besides stored procedures. This means that one parameter fits all. Oracle offers no method for isolating the amount of storage allocated to any subset of the shared pool.

Listing 4.7   Pinned Packages in the SGA

```
SET PAGESIZE 60;

COLUMN EXECUTIONS FORMAT 999,999,999;
COLUMN Mem_used   FORMAT 999,999,999;

SELECT SUBSTR(owner,1,10) Owner,
       SUBSTR(type,1,12)  Type,
       SUBSTR(name,1,20)  Name,
       executions,
       sharable_mem       Mem_used,
       SUBSTR(kept||' ',1,4)   "Kept?"
  FROM v$db_object_cache
  WHERE TYPE IN ('TRIGGER','PROCEDURE','PACKAGE BODY','PACKAGE')
  ORDER BY EXECUTIONS DESC;

SQL> @memory
```

OWNER	TYPE	NAME	EXECUTIONS	MEM_USED	KEPT
SYS	PACKAGE	STANDARD	867,600	151,963	YES
SYS	PACKAGE BODY	STANDARD	867,275	30,739	YES
SYS	PACKAGE	DBMS_ALERT	502,126	3,637	NO
SYS	PACKAGE BODY	DBMS_ALERT	433,607	20,389	NO
SYS	PACKAGE	DBMS_LOCK	432,137	3,140	YES
SYS	PACKAGE BODY	DBMS_LOCK	432,137	10,780	YES
SYS	PACKAGE	DBMS_PIPE	397,466	3,412	NO
SYS	PACKAGE BODY	DBMS_PIPE	397,466	5,292	NO
HRIS	PACKAGE	S125_PACKAGE	285,700	3,776	NO
SYS	PACKAGE	DBMS_UTILITY	284,694	3,311	NO
SYS	PACKAGE BODY	DBMS_UTILITY	284,694	6,159	NO
HRIS	PACKAGE	HRS_COMMON_PACKAGE	258,657	3,382	NO
HRIS	PACKAGE BODY	S125_PACKAGE	248,857	30,928	NO
HRIS	PACKAGE BODY	HRS_COMMON_PACKAGE	242,155	8,638	NO
HRIS	PACKAGE	GTS_SNAPSHOT_UTILITY	168,978	11,056	NO
HRIS	PACKAGE BODY	GTS_SNAPSHOT_UTILITY	89,623	3,232	NO
SYS	PACKAGE	DBMS_STANDARD	18,953	14,696	NO
SYS	PACKAGE BODY	DBMS_STANDARD	18,872	3,432	NO
KIS	PROCEDURE	RKA_INSERT	7,067	4,949	NO
HRIS	PACKAGE	HRS_PACKAGE	5,175	3,831	NO
HRIS	PACKAGE BODY	HRS_PACKAGE	5,157	36,455	NO
SYS	PACKAGE	DBMS_DESCRIBE	718	12,800	NO
HRIS	PROCEDURE	CHECK_APP_ALERT	683	3,763	NO
SYS	PACKAGE BODY	DBMS_DESCRIBE	350	9,880	NO
SYS	PACKAGE	DBMS_SESSION	234	3,351	NO
SYS	PACKAGE BODY	DBMS_SESSION	65	4,543	NO
GIANT	PROCEDURE	CREATE_SESSION_RECOR	62	7,147	NO
HRIS	PROCEDURE	INIT_APP_ALERT	6	10,802	NO

DESIGNING LOGON TRIGGERS TO TRACK USER ACTIVITY

Starting with Oracle8*i*, Oracle introduced special triggers that are not associated with DML events (e.g., INSERT, UPDATE, and DELETE). These system-level triggers included database startup triggers, Data Definition Language (DDL) triggers, and end-user logon/logoff triggers.

While Oracle provided the functionality for these new triggers, it was not clear how they could be used to track systemwide usage. This chapter describes our work in creating end-user logon/logoff procedures to facilitate tracing end-user activity. Please be advised that the initial implementation of system-level triggers for end-user tracking is quite new and as such is still a bit lacking in robust functionality.

While the user logon/logoff triggers will accurately tell you the time of the user logon and user logoff, unfortunately the code does not capture any information regarding the specific tasks that were performed during the user's session.

Also note that these user logon and logoff triggers are best used for those types of applications that utilize time stamped users. By time stamped users, we mean those users who are given a unique Oracle user ID when they access the application. Applications that do not utilize the time stamped Oracle user IDs (e.g., products from SAP® and PeopleSoft®) may not benefit greatly by using these logon and logoff triggers.

Now that we understand the basics, let's look at how we can design the user audit table to track user activity.

Designing a User Audit Table

The first step is to create an Oracle table that can store the information gathered by the end-user logon/logoff triggers. To properly design these triggers, we begin by taking a look at the information that is available to us inside the system-level triggers. First, we gather the information available at logon:

- User ID — this is the user ID that was used to perform the sign-on operation.
- Session ID — this is the Oracle control session ID for the user.
- Host — this is the host name of the computer.
- Logon date — this is an Oracle date data type corresponding to the user logon time, accurate to 1/1000 of a second.

Now we gather the information available just prior to user logoff. At user logoff time, the Oracle system-level trigger provides us with some information about the current session that the user was performing:

- Last program — this provides the name of last program that the user was executing at the time of system logoff.
- Last action — this provides the last action performed by the user during the session.
- Last module — this provides the name of the last module accessed by the user prior to logoff time.
- Logoff date — this is an Oracle date data type corresponding to the actual user logoff time, accurate to 1/1000 of a second.

Now we know the information available to us at logon and logoff, but how do we collect this information and make it accessible to management? Let's take a look at the available options.

User Table Normalization

Since the user logon and user logoff triggers are separate entities, we have several choices in the design of a table to support this information. We could design two separate tables — a user logon table and a user logoff table. However, then we would have the difficulty of joining these two tables together and correlating which logon corresponds to which logoff and so on. This can be a tricky process, which presents several opportunities for error. How did user 24 logoff before they logged on ... and so on ... and so on?

In Listing 4.8, we take a look at the better option. To get around this table issue, a database design was created whereby a single table is used to record both logon and logoff events. This eliminates the need for table joins and the correlation of the data. In addition, we added a field to compute the elapsed minutes for each user's specific session. This pre-computation done by the trigger saves time and makes for a more informative report, as we shall see later.

Designing a Logon Trigger

Once the table is designed, the next issue is to create a system-level logon trigger that will fill in as much information as possible at the time of the logon event. Listing 4.9 illustrates the logon audit trigger that we created. As you can see, we populate this table with four values that are available at logon time:

1. User — this is the Oracle user ID of the person establishing the Oracle session.
2. Session ID — this uses Oracle's SYS context function to capture the Oracle session ID directly from the v$session table.

Listing 4.8   The Table Definition that We Used

```
create table
   stats$user_log
(
   user_id           varchar2(30),
   session_id          number(8),
   host              varchar2(30),
   last_program      varchar2(48),
   last_action       varchar2(32),
   last_module       varchar2(32),
   logon_day                  date,
   logon_time        varchar2(10),
   logoff_day                 date,
   logoff_time       varchar2(10),
   elapsed_minutes     number(8)
)
;
```

Listing 4.9   The Logon Trigger Definition that We Used

```
create or replace trigger
   logon_audit_trigger
AFTER LOGON ON DATABASE
BEGIN
insert into stats$user_log values(
   user,
   sys_context('USERENV','SESSIONID'),
   sys_context('USERENV','HOST'),
   null,
   null,
   null,
   sysdate,
   to_char(sysdate, 'hh24:mi:ss'),
   null,
   null,
   null
);
COMMIT;
END;
/
```

3. Host — this uses Oracle's SYS context function to capture the name of the host from which the Oracle session originated. Please note that capturing the host name is vital for systems using Oracle parallel server or real application clusters (RACs), because we can have many sessions connecting from many different instance hosts.
4. Logon date — this captures the date of the actual work logon, accurate to 1/1000 of a second. Notice how we partitioned logon date into two separate fields. Having a separate field for logon day and logon time produces a reader friendly report.

Now that the logon trigger is in place, we have the challenge of creating a logoff trigger to capture all of the information required to complete the elapsed time for the user session.

Designing the Logoff Trigger

To make a single table function for both logon and logoff events, it is first necessary to locate the logon row that is associated with the individual user session. As you might imagine, this is tricky, because you may have many users who are signed on with identical user names. To get around this limitation, the Oracle session ID was used. As we know, Oracle assigns a unique session ID into the v$session table for each individual user logged on to Oracle. We can use this session ID as a primary key to update our user audit table with logoff information.

Now let's take a look at the information that becomes available as a result of using our logoff trigger. We begin by updating the user log table to include the last action performed by the user. As shown in Listing 4.10, updating the last action is accomplished by using the SYS context function to grab the action column from the v$session table.

Next, update the audit table to show the last program that was accessed during the session. Again, invoke the SYS context function to select the program column from the v$session table.

Update the last module that was accessed by the user session. This is accomplished by selecting the module column from the v$session table and then placing it into the user audit table.

The final and most important step of this procedure is to insert the logoff time and compute the elapsed time for the user session. As the code in Listing 4.10 shows, this is achieved by updating the user logon table with logoff date data type and then computing the elapsed time.

As we noted before, precomputing the elapsed time for each user session makes each individual record in the stats$user_log audit table very useful because it shows the entire duration of the session.

Listing 4.10 The Logoff Trigger Definition that We Used

```
create or replace trigger
   logoff_audit_trigger
BEFORE LOGOFF ON DATABASE
BEGIN
-- ***************************************************
-- Update the last action accessed
-- ***************************************************
update
stats$user_log
set
last_action = (select action from v$session where
sys_context('USERENV','SESSIONID') = audsid)
where
sys_context('USERENV','SESSIONID') = session_id;
--***************************************************
-- Update the last program accessed
-- ***************************************************
update
stats$user_log
set
last_program = (select program from v$session where
sys_context('USERENV','SESSIONID') = audsid)
where
sys_context('USERENV','SESSIONID') = session_id;
-- ***************************************************
-- Update the last module accessed
-- ***************************************************
update
stats$user_log
set
last_module = (select module from v$session where
sys_context('USERENV','SESSIONID') = audsid)
where
sys_context('USERENV','SESSIONID') = session_id;
-- ***************************************************
-- Update the logoff day
-- ***************************************************
update
   stats$user_log
set
   logoff_day = sysdate
```

Listing 4.10 The Logoff Trigger Definition that We Used (Continued)

```
where
   sys_context('USERENV','SESSIONID') = session_id;
-- ***************************************************
-- Update the logoff time
-- ***************************************************
update
   stats$user_log
set
   logoff_time = to_char(sysdate, 'hh24:mi:ss')
where
   sys_context('USERENV','SESSIONID') = session_id;
-- ***************************************************
-- Compute the elapsed minutes
-- ***************************************************
update
stats$user_log
set
elapsed_minutes =
round((logoff_day - logon_day)*1440)
where
sys_context('USERENV','SESSIONID') = session_id;
COMMIT;
END;
/
```

We'll take a look at a few sample reports that can be produced by the system. These reports can be enhanced to fit specific needs. It is now obvious why the precomputing of elapsed minutes is such a valuable feature. It produces a more useful report.

User Activity Reports

Using our user audit table to generate reports can provide a wealth of information that may prove to be critical to you as an Oracle administrator. Our first report is a summary of total session time shown below.

We can start by creating a simple query against our user audit table that will show the day and date, the individual user ID, and the total number of minutes that the user spent on the system. While primitive, this can give us an indication of the total amount of time that was spent on our system by each individual user.

This information is especially useful where there are different user IDs going to different functional areas of the system. For example, if the Oracle

Listing 4.11 A Sample User Activity Report

```
                           Total
Day           User         Minutes
----------    ----------   -------
02-03-06      APPLSYSPUB         0
              APPS            466
              OPS$ORACLE        7
              PERFSTAT         11

02-03-07      APPLSYSPUB        5
              APPS          1,913
              CUSJAN            1
              JANEDI            5
              OPS$ORACLE        6
              PERFSTAT        134
              SYS              58

02-03-08      APPLSYSPUB        1
              APPS          5,866
              OPS$ORACLE       15
              PERFSTAT         44
              SYS               6

02-03-09      APPS              0
              OPS$ORACLE        0
              PERFSTAT         29
```

user IDs can be correlated directly to screen functions, then the Oracle administrator can get a good idea of the amount of usage within each functional area of the Oracle applications (Listing 4.11).

Now let's examine yet another type of report.

User Logon Detail Reports

We can also use the same table to show the number of users that are on our system at any given hour of the day. This information is especially useful for Oracle administrators who are in charge of tracking user activity.

By examining the user audit table for user logon times, we can get an accurate count of generated sessions at any given hour of the day. This information can be represented as shown in Listing 4.12.

At this point, the information can then be put into an Excel spreadsheet and expanded into impressive charts. Figure 4.2 shows a nice example.

Listing 4.12 Number of Users per Hour

```
Day        HO NUMBER_OF_LOGINS
---------- -- ----------------
02-03-06   01                2
           02                3
           03                1
           04                3
           05                6
           06                9
           07               14
           08               19
           09               21
           10               22
           11               26
           12               28
           13               45
           14               38
           15               26
           16               26
           17               25
           18               26
           19               26
           20               26
           21               49
           22               26
           23               24
```

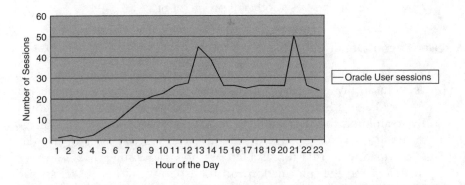

Figure 4.2 Example of Hourly Sessions over Time

As we can see, this produces a clear graph showing user activity by the hour of the day. Once you get a large amount of user activity in your system, you can also summarize this information by the day of the week or the hour of the day. This provides a tremendous amount of information regarding the user signature for the system. By signature, we mean trend lines or spikes in user activity. For example, we might see high user activity every Wednesday afternoon at 1:00 PM. Using this user audit table, we can quickly identify these user signatures and adjust Oracle to accommodate these changes and end-user usage.

Related DDL, system errors, and user activity can easily be captured using the system-level triggers. However, it is clear that system-level triggers are not as sophisticated as they might be, and Oracle indicates that efforts are underway to enhance system-level trigger functionality with the introduction of Oracle10*i*.

However, the judicious use of the system logon and system logoff triggers can provide an easy and reliable tracking mechanism for Oracle user activity. For the Oracle administrator who is committed to tracking user activity over long-term periods, the user audit table can provide a wealth of interesting user information, including user usage signatures, aggregated both by the hour of the day and the day of the week.

DESIGNING ORACLE FAILOVER OPTIONS

There are four levels of failover technology within the Oracle software (Figure 4.3). Each failover option has its own costs, advantages, and disadvantages:

1. Oracle9*i* RAC — this is the most powerful and complex of the failover solutions and offers continuous availability using TAF.
2. Oracle Streams — this is a high-speed replication solution that takes SQL directly from the `log_buffer` RAM area and replicates transactions to a remote database. During a server crash, transactions can be quickly redirected to the replicated system.
3. Oracle Data Guard — this is a free option with Oracle Enterprise Edition and provides for an automated standby database. Upon server failure, a series of database procedures synchronizes the standby database and opens it to accept connections.
4. Oracle Standby Database — this is not an Oracle product. It is a procedure used prior to Oracle Data Guard to create a standby database. Oracle7 introduced mechanisms that allowed a standby database to be constantly in recovery mode and to be refreshed from Oracle's archived redo logs. In case of failure, the last redo

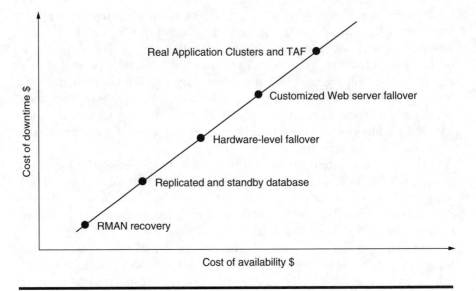

Figure 4.3   Oracle Failover Options

log could be added to the standby database and the database could be started in just a few minutes.

Note: Oracle standby servers need to be fully licensed if they are hot standby servers that can be used for queries. Cold standby servers used less than 10 days per year do not need to be licensed.

CONCLUSION

The point of this chapter is that the SGA must be properly designed and that the SGA can change dramatically as the system is implemented. Hence, you must constantly monitor and change the Oracle instance to optimize it according to your current demands.

Next, let's take a look at the proper design for tablespaces and review the various Oracle physical design options.

5

ORACLE TABLESPACE DESIGN

INTRODUCTION

Unlike the CODASYL databases of the 1980s, today's Oracle databases allow for tables to grow according to specified rules and procedures. In the Oracle model, one or more tables may reside in a tablespace. A tablespace is a predefined container for the tables that map to fixed files of a finite size. Tables that are assigned to the tablespace may grow according to the growth rules that are specified, but the size of the tablespace supersedes the expansion rules. In other words, a table may have more extents available according to the table definition, but there may not be room in the tablespace to allocate those extents.

Over the past few years, Oracle has gradually recognized the benefits of bitmap data structures. As Oracle has evolved, we've seen the following progressive introduction of bitmaps into the database engine:

- Oracle7 — bitmap indexes
- Oracle8 — LMTs
- Oracle8*i* — bitmap freelists ASSM
- Oracle Database 10*g* — ASM

It's important to note that these are optional structures. Bitmap ASSM in Oracle9*i* is optional and can only be implemented at the tablespace level. Existing systems can continue to use the traditional method of free list management. In Oracle Database 10*g*, LMTs have become the default.

This chapter will begin with a discussion of Oracle data blocks and then review the segment storage parameters. We'll then explore the Oracle tablespace option and understand how proper physical design can improve performance and manageability.

SIZING ORACLE DATA BLOCKS

It's ironic that the Oracle developer must choose a block size when the data warehouse is initially created — a time when knowledge of system performance is limited. While it is possible to use the Oracle import/export utility to change block sizes, too little attention is given to the proper sizing of database blocks. The physical block size is set with the DB_BLOCK_SIZE parameter in the init.ora file. While the default is to have 4 K block sizes, many Oracle developers choose at least 8 K block sizes for large, distributed data warehouses. Some DBAs believe that 16 K is the best block size, even for OLTP systems that seldom perform FTSs.

Depending upon the host platform and OS, Oracle block sizes may be set from 2 K up to 32 K. The Oracle OS documentation will provide the acceptable ranges for your OS, but the generally accepted wisdom is to create your database blocks as large as your OS will allow. Remember, minimizing disk I/O is one of the most important factors in data warehouse tuning.

Disk I/O is the single most expensive and time-consuming operation within an Oracle database. As such, the more data that can be read in a single I/O, the faster the performance of the Oracle database. This principle is especially true for databases that have many reports that read the entire contents of a table. For systems that read random single rows from the database, block size is not as important — especially with database clusters. An Oracle cluster is a mechanism whereby an owner row will reside on the same database block as its subordinate rows in other tables.

For example, if we cluster order rows on the same block as their customer owners, Oracle will only need to perform a single I/O to retrieve the customer and all of the order rows. Of course, in a distributed database where joins take place across different Oracle instances, clustering cannot be used. The additional I/O will be required to read the rows individually.

Bear in mind that increasing the block size of an Oracle database will also affect the number of blocks that can be cached in the buffer pool. For example, if we set the DB_BLOCK_BUFFERS init.ora parameter to 8 MB, Oracle will be able to cache 1000 4 K blocks, but only 500 8 K blocks.

Smaller block size means latches for block access (data and index) are held for shorter time, increasing concurrency. For other workloads (e.g., DSS), larger block sizes may better suit the usage profile of the data.

The same is true for UNDO, for which Oracle used 8 K blocks in the benchmark. What about a situation where your table has large rows (say 16 K each) with small index entries (say a numeric primary key)? Do you really want them both stored in blocks of the same size?

Now that we see the block sizing issues, let's examine the storage options within Oracle tablespaces.

THE EVOLUTION OF ORACLE FILE STRUCTURES

Starting with Oracle8i, Oracle has introduced three new tablespace parameters that automate tablespace and file storage management functions:

1. LMT — the LMT is implemented by adding the EXTENT MANAGE-MENT LOCAL clause to the tablespace definition. LMTs automate extent management and remove the ability to specify the NEXT storage parameter.
2. ASSM — the ASSM tablespace is new in Oracle9i and is implemented by adding the SEGMENT SPACE MANAGEMENT AUTO clause to the tablespace definition. ASSM tablespaces automate free list management and remove the ability to specify PCTFREE, PCTUSED, FREELISTS, and FREELIST GROUPS storage parameters.
3. ASM — the ASM features allow for the automatic stripe-and-mirror everywhere approach to be used to automatically load balance the disk I/O subsystem and remove the need for the DBA to specify physical file locations when allocating a tablespace.

Here is an example of a tablespace with these new parameters:

```
create tablespace
    asm_test
datafile
    'c:\oracle\oradata\diogenes\asm_test.dbf'
size
    5m
EXTENT MANAGEMENT LOCAL
SEGMENT SPACE MANAGEMENT AUTO
;
```

In Oracle9i, we expect an error if we try to specify PCTFREE or PCTUSED for a table defined inside a tablespace with ASM:

```
SQL> create table
  2                         test_table
  3                         (c1 number)
  4   tablespace
```

```
5                        asm_test
6  storage
7                           ( pctfree 20 pctused 30 )
8  ;

   ( pctfree 20 pctused 30 )
      *
ERROR at line 7:
ORA-02143: invalid STORAGE option
```

However, here we see an important point. While Oracle9*i* rejects the PCTFREE and PCTUSED parameter with LMTs with automatic space management, it does allow you to enter invalid settings for NEXT and FREELISTS settings:

```
SQL> create table
2                        test_table
3                        (c1 number)
4  tablespace
5                        asm_test
6  storage
7                        ( freelists 30 next 5m ) ;

Table created.
```

This could be a serious issue for the Oracle professional unless they remember that LMTs with automatic space management ignore any specified values for NEXT and FREELISTS.

Before we explore the details of designing with each of these options, it's important to understand the segment storage options and see how they relate to the tablespace options. Let's start with a review of the segment storage parameters.

DESIGN FOR ORACLE SEGMENT STORAGE

Since the earliest days of Oracle, we have the following individual segment parameters to manage the growth of each segment (table, index, IOT) within our Oracle database:

■ PCTFREE — this storage parameter determines when a block can be unlinked from the free list. You must reserve enough room on each data block for existing rows to expand without chaining onto other blocks. The purpose of PCTFREE is to tell Oracle when to remove a block from the object's free list. Since the Oracle default is PCTFREE=10, blocks remain on the free list while they are less than 90 percent full. Once an insert makes the block grow beyond 90 percent full, it is removed from the free list, leaving 10 percent of the block for row expansion. Furthermore, the data block will remain off the free list even after the space drops below 90 percent. Only after subsequent deletes cause the space to fall below the PCTUSED threshold of 40 percent will Oracle put the block back onto the free list.

■ PCTUSED — this storage parameter determines when a block can relink onto the table free list after DELETE operations. Setting a low value for PCTUSED will result in high performance. A higher value of PCTFREE will result in efficient space reuse but will slow performance. As rows are deleted from a table, the database blocks become eligible to accept new rows. This happens when the amount of space in a database block falls below PCTUSED and a free list relink operation is triggered. For example, with PCTUSED=60, all database blocks that have less than 60 percent will be on the free list, as well as other blocks that dropped below PCTUSED and have not yet grown to PCTFREE. Once a block deletes a row and becomes less than 60 percent full, the block goes back on the free list. As rows are deleted, data blocks become available when a block's free space drops below the value of PCTUSED for the table and Oracle relinks the data block onto the free list chain. As the table has rows inserted into it, it will grow until the space on the block exceeds the threshold PCTFREE, at which time the block is unlinked from the free list.

■ FREELISTS — Oracle allows tables and indexes to be defined with multiple free lists. All tables and index free lists should be set to the HWM of concurrent INSERT or UPDATE activity. Too low a value for free lists will cause poor Oracle performance.

There is a direct trade-off between the setting for PCTUSED and efficient use of storage within the Oracle database. For databases where space is tight and storage within the Oracle data files must be reused immediately, the Oracle DBA will commonly set PCTUSED to a high value. This ensures the blocks go on the free list before they are completely empty.

However, the downside to this approach is that every time the data block fills, Oracle must unlink the data block from the free list and incur another I/O to get another free data block to insert new rows. In sum, the DBA must strike a balance between efficient space usage and the amount of I/O in the Oracle database.

Let's begin our discussion by introducing the relationship between object storage parameters and performance. Poor object performance within Oracle occurs in several areas:

- Slow INSERTs — INSERT operations run slowly and have excessive I/O. This happens when blocks on the free list have room for only a few rows before Oracle is forced to grab another free block.
- Slow SELECTs — SELECT statements have excessive I/O because of chained rows. This occurs when rows chain and fragment onto several data blocks, causing additional I/O to fetch the blocks.
- Slow UPDATEs — UPDATE statements run slowly with double the amount of I/O. This happens when updates expand a VARCHAR or BLOB column and Oracle is forced to chain the row contents onto additional data blocks.
- Slow DELETEs — large DELETE statements run slowly and cause segment header contention. This happens when rows are deleted and the database must relink the data block onto the free list for the table.

As you can see, the storage parameters for Oracle tables and indexes can have an important effect on the performance of the database. Let's take a look at the common storage parameters that affect Oracle performance.

Setting PCTFREE and PCTUSED

As any experienced DBA understands, the settings for PCTUSED can have a dramatic impact on the performance of an Oracle database. But many new Oracle DBAs fail to realize that PCTUSED is only used to relink full data onto the table free list. A relink occurs only when a DELETE or UPDATE statement has reduced the free space in the data block. The setting for PCTUSED will determine the amount of row space in this newly relinked data block.

The default setting for all Oracle tables is PCTUSED=40. This setting means that a block must become less than 40 percent full before being relinked on the table free list.

Let's take a closer look at how the PCTUSED operator works and how it affects the operation of relinks onto the table free list. As I said, a data block becomes available for reuse when its free space drops below the value of PCTUSED for the table, which triggers a free list relink operation.

There is a trade-off between the setting for PCTUSED and database performance on INSERT operations. In general, the higher the setting for PCTUSED, the less free space will be on reused data blocks at INSERT time. Hence, INSERT tasks will need to do more frequent I/Os than they would if they were inserting into empty blocks. In short, the value for PCTUSED should be set above 40 only when the database is short on disk space and it must make efficient reuse of data block space.

It should now be clear that the average row length needs to be .considered when customizing the values for PCTFREE and PCTUSED. You want to set PCTFREE such that room is left on each block for row expansion. You want to set PCTUSED so that newly linked blocks have enough room to accept rows.

Herein lies the trade-off between effective space usage and performance. If you set PCTUSED to a high value, say 80, then a block will quickly become available to accept new rows, but it will not have room for a lot of rows before it becomes logically full again. In the most extreme case, a relinked free block may have only enough space for single rows before causing another I/O operation.

Remember that the lower the value for PCTUSED, the less I/O your system will have at INSERT time and the faster your system will run. The downside, of course, is that a block will be nearly empty before it becomes eligible to accept new rows.

Because row length is a major factor in intelligently setting PCTUSED, a script can be written that allows the DBA to specifically control how many rows will fit onto a reused data block before it unlinks from the free list.

Note that this script provides only general guidelines; you will want to leave the default PCTUSED=40 unless your system is low on disk space or unless the average row length is large. Now let's take a close look at free lists and see how a free list shortage can cause performance slowdowns.

Free List Management for Oracle Objects

In systems where multiple tasks are concurrently inserting or deleting records from an Oracle database, it is not uncommon to see buffer busy waits within the database engine. A buffer busy wait is a condition where Oracle is waiting to access the segment header block for the table. As you may know, Oracle reserves the first block in a table (the segment header) to keep control information, including the header link for a list of free blocks for the table. When multiple tasks are attempting to simultaneously insert information into an Oracle table, tasks will have to wait their turn to get access to the segment header.

In sum, any time buffer busy waits occur, the Oracle DBA must try to find those tables or indexes that are experiencing the segment header contention and increase the free lists or `freelist_groups` parameters. The `freelist_groups` parameter allows an Oracle table to have several segment headers, so that multiple tasks can insert into the table. The setting for the `FREELISTS` parameter should be set equal to the HWM of the number of concurrent inserts for the target table.

Design to Control Oracle Row Chaining and Row Migration

Improper settings for `PCTFREE` and `PCTUSED` can also cause database fragmentation. Whenever a row in an Oracle database expands because of an update, there must be sufficient room on the data block to hold the expanded row. If a row spans several data blocks, the database must perform additional disk I/O to fetch the block into the SGA. This excessive disk I/O can cripple the performance of the database.

The space reserved for row expansion is controlled by the `PCTFREE` parameter. Row chaining is especially problematic in cases where a row with many `VARCHAR` data types is stored with `NULL` values and subsequent update operations populate the `VARCHAR` columns with large values.

Fortunately, row chaining is relatively easy to detect in the `chain_cnt` column of the `dba_tables` view. Note that you must analyze all of the tables in the Oracle database with the `analyze table xxx estimate statistics` command before you can see this value.

Once you have identified those tables with chained rows, you must increase `PCTFREE` for the table and then export and reload the table to remove the chains. While there are several third-party products for reorganizing tables, table reorganization is most commonly done by running Oracle export/import utilities.

For efficient space reuse, you want to set a high value for `PCTUSED`. A high value for `PCTUSED` will effectively reuse space on data blocks, but at the expense of additional I/O. A high `PCTUSED` means that relatively full blocks are placed on the free list. Hence, these blocks will be able to accept only a few rows before becoming full again, leading to more I/O.

For better performance, you want to set a low value for `PCTUSED`. A low value for `PCTUSED` means that Oracle will not place a data block onto the free list until it is nearly empty. The block will be able to accept many rows until it becomes full, thereby reducing I/O at insert time. Remember that it is always faster for Oracle to extend into new blocks than to reuse existing blocks. For superfast space acquisition on SQL

INSERTs, you can turn off free list link/unlinks. It takes fewer resources for Oracle to extend a table than to manage free lists.

In effect, free lists can be turned off by setting PCTUSED to 1. This will cause the free lists to be populated exclusively from new extents. This approach requires lots of extra disk space and the table must be reorganized periodically to reclaim space within the table.

Let's review the general guidelines for setting object storage parameters:

- Always set PCTUSED to allow enough room to accept a new row. We never want to have free blocks that do not have enough room to accept a row. If we do, this will cause a slowdown since Oracle will attempt to read five dead free blocks before extending the table to get an empty block.
- The presence of chained rows in a table means that PCTFREE is too low or that DB_BLOCK_SIZE is too small. In most cases within Oracle, RAW and LONG RAW columns make huge rows that exceed the maximum blocksize for Oracle, making chained rows unavoidable.
- If a table has simultaneous INSERT SQL processes, it needs to have simultaneous DELETE processes. Running a single purge job will place all of the free blocks on only one free list and none of the other free lists will contain any free blocks from the purge.
- The FREELISTS parameter should be set to the HWM of updates to a table. For example, if the customer table has up to 20 end users performing INSERTs at any time, then the customer table should have FREELISTS=20.
- FREELIST GROUPS should be set to the number of Oracle Parallel Server instances that access the table. For partitioned objects and cases of segment header contention, freelist_groups may be set for non-RAC systems.

The PCTFREE parameter is used to reserve space on each data block for the future expansion of row values (via the SQL UPDATE command). Table columns may be defined as allowing null values that do not consume any space within the row or with VARCHAR data types. A VARCHAR data type specifies the maximum allowable length for the column instance, but the acceptable range of values may be anywhere from 4 B (the size of the length holder) to the size of the field plus 4 B. Hence, a VAR-CHAR(2000) may range in size from 4 B to 2004 B.

If an application initially stores rows with empty values and later fills in the values, the PCTFREE parameter can dramatically reduce I/O contention. If a block of storage is filled by the addition of a row, subsequent updates to that row to fill in column values will cause the row to fragment — usually onto the next available contiguous block.

Next, let's cover the main tablespace types within Oracle and show you how an up-front tablespace design decision can make a huge difference after your system is implemented.

The Issue of PCTFREE

The PCTFREE parameter is used to specify the amount of free space on a data block to reserve for future row expansion. If PCTFREE is set improperly, SQL update statements can cause a huge amount of row fragmentation and chaining.

The setting for PCTFREE is especially important when a row is initially stored small and expanded at a later time. In such systems, it's not uncommon to set PCTFREE equal to 95, telling Oracle to reserve 95 percent of the data block space for subsequent row expansion.

Sadly, Oracle9*i* doesn't allow you to specify the value for PCTFREE if you're using automatic space management. This is a serious limitation because Oracle9*i* can't know in advance about the amount of VARCHAR expansion in a table row, leading to excessive row chaining and poor access performance.

To see this problem, let's start by creating a 2 K tablespace using automatic space management:

```
create tablespace
   asm_test
datafile
   'c:\oracle\oradata\diogenes\asm_test.dbf'
size
   30m
blocksize
   2k
EXTENT MANAGEMENT LOCAL
SEGMENT SPACE MANAGEMENT AUTO
;
```

We can create a table in this tablespace with an unexpanded VARCHAR2(2000) data type by entering the following commands. Later, we'll expand the rows and see if there is fragmentation.

```
create table
   test_frag
```

```
(
    tab_key      number,
    big_column varchar2(2000)
)
tablespace
    asm_test
;
```

We now have a table named `test_frag` in a 2 K tablespace. The next step is to populate 4000 rows, with only a single specification in the VARCHAR2 column:

```
declare
myint integer := 1;
begin
loop

    insert into test_frag
    values
    (
        test_frag_seq.nextval,
        ' '
    );

    myint := myint+1;

    if myint > 4000 then exit; end if;

end loop;
end;
/
```

Now that we have the rows inserted, let's take a look at how many rows are stored on the data block in DBA_TABLES:

Table	% Free	NUM_ROWS	AVG_ROW_LEN	CHAIN_CNT
TEST_FRAG	10	4000	9	0

In DBA_SEGMENTS, we see that the table is in a single extent. We also see that we used 32 data block at 2 K per block to store 4000 rows. This works out to 500 data rows per block.

Table name	Tablespace Name	Buffer Pool	Bytes	Blocks	Extents
TEST_FRAG	ASM_TEST	DEFAULT	65,536	32	1

Now let's make a mess and expand a large VARCHAR2 column from 1 B to 2000 B. After the update, we see in DBA_SEGMENTS that the table is much larger:

Table name	Tablespace Name	Buffer Pool	Bytes	Blocks	Extents
TEST_FRAG	ASM_TEST	DEFAULT	9,437,184	4,608	24

Now our table is on 4608 blocks and the table has taken 24 extents. When we examine DBA_TABLES, we see that the table now has an average row length of 1378 and every single row has chained.

Table	% Free	NUM_ROWS	AVG_ROW_LEN	CHAIN_CNT
TEST_FRAG	10	4000	1378	4000

Row chaining is a serious problem for the DBA and it appears that automatic space management is not appropriate for tables where you need to reserve space for large row expansions with PCTFREE.

The Issue of PCTUSED

Let's take a closer look at another automatic space management feature — bitmap free lists. As you probably know, improper settings for PCTUSED can cause huge degradations in the performance of SQL INSERTs. If a data block isn't largely empty, excessive I/O will happen during SQL inserts because the reused Oracle data blocks will fill quickly. Taken to the extreme, improper settings for PCTUSED can create a situation in which the free space on the data block is smaller than the average row length for the table. In such cases, Oracle will try five times to fetch a block from the free list chain. After five attempts, it will raise the HWM for the table and grab five fresh data blocks for the insertion.

In Oracle9*i* with automatic segment management, the PCTUSED parameter no longer governs the relink threshold for a table data block and the DBA must rely on the judgment of Oracle to determine when a block is empty enough to be placed onto the free list.

Unlike PCTFREE, where Oracle can't tell in advance how much row expansion will occur, Oracle9*i* does have information about the right time to relink a data block. Because Oracle knows the average row length for the table rows (`dba_tables.avg_row_len`), it should be able to adjust `PCTUSED` to ensure that the relinked data block will have room for new rows.

One benefit of automatic segment management is that the bitmap free lists are guaranteed to reduce buffer busy waits. Let's take a close look at this feature.

Prior to Oracle9*i*, buffer busy waits were a major issue. A buffer busy wait occurs when a data block is inside the data buffer cache, but it's unavailable because another SQL `INSERT` statement needed to get a block on which to place its row. Without multiple free lists, every Oracle table and index had a single data block at the head of the table to manage free blocks for the object. Whenever any SQL `INSERT` ran, it had to go to this block and get a data block on which to place its row.

Obviously, single free lists cause a backup. When multiple tasks want to insert into the same table, they are forced to wait while Oracle assigns free blocks, one at a time.

Oracle's ASSM feature claims to improve the performance of concurrent DML operations significantly, because different parts of the bitmap can be used simultaneously, eliminating serialization for free space lookups.

The Sparse Table Problem

Sparse tables generally occur when a highly active table is defined with multiple free lists and the table has heavy `INSERT` and `DELETE` activity. In a sparse table, the table will appear to have thousands of free blocks, yet the table will continue to extend and it will behave as if Oracle doesn't have any free data blocks.

A sparse table in a data warehouse can use a huge amount of unnecessary storage, consuming many gigabytes of new storage while the table appears to have lots of free space. Remember, with multiple free lists, the free lists are independent and Oracle can't share free list blocks. An `INSERT` task will only attach to one free list and it's only able to use free blocks that are attached to that free list.

The cause of a sparse table is a lack of balance between `INSERT` and `DELETE` activity. In our example, there are three free lists defined for the table, yet a purge job (SQL `DELETES`) ran as a single task. Prior to Oracle9*i*, the DBA had to parallelize all purge jobs to the value of `FREELISTS` to ensure that all free lists were evenly populated with empty data blocks.

Prior to Oracle9*i*, the DBA would have had to reorganize the table using export/import or `alter table move` to balance the free blocks on each free list chain. Oracle9*i* makes this much easier with the `dbms_repair.rebuild_freelists` procedure. The purpose of the `rebuild_freelists` procedure is to coalesce bitmap free list blocks onto the master free list and zero out all other free lists for the segment. For tables and indexes accessed by RAC (using multiple free list groups), Oracle9*i* will evenly distribute all free blocks among the existing free list groups.

This is an important feature for table and indexes with multiple free lists because the DBA no longer has to reorganize a table to rebalance the bitmap free lists. Here's an example of using this procedure to rebuild the free lists for the BOOK table:

```
dbms_repair.rebuild_freelists('PUBS','BOOK');
```

Now that we understand the segment parameters we are ready to explore ASSM.

AUTOMATIC SEGMENT SPACE MANAGEMENT

Before we describe the differences between ASSM (also known as bitmap free lists) with traditional Oracle space management, let's examine how bitmap free lists are implemented. We'll begin by creating a tablespace with the SEGMENT SPACE MANAGEMENT AUTO parameter:

```
create tablespace
    asm_test
datafile
    'c:\oracle\oradata\diogenes\asm_test.dbf'
size
    5m
EXTENT MANAGEMENT LOCAL
SEGMENT SPACE MANAGEMENT AUTO
;
```

Once a table or index is allocated in this tablespace, the values for PCTUSED will be ignored and Oracle9*i* will automatically manage the free lists for the tables and indexes inside the tablespace. For objects created in this tablespace, the NEXT extent clause is now obsolete because of the LMT. The INITIAL parameter is still required because Oracle can't know in advance the size of the initial table load. When using automatic space management, the minimum value for INITIAL is three blocks.

There's some debate about whether a one-size-fits-all approach is best for Oracle. In large databases, individual object settings can make a huge difference in performance and storage. ASSM is a simpler and more efficient way of managing space within a segment. It completely eliminates any need to specify and tune the PCTUSED, FREELISTS, and FREELIST GROUPS storage parameters for schema objects created in the tablespace. If any of these attributes are specified, they are ignored.

When you create a LMT using the CREATE TABLESPACE statement, the SEGMENT SPACE MANAGEMENT clause lets you specify how free and used space within a segment is to be managed.

For example, the following statement creates tablespace mytbs1 with ASSM:

```
CREATE TABLESPACE mytbs1
DATAFILE '/u01/oracle/data/mytbs01.dbf' SIZE 500M
EXTENT MANAGEMENT LOCAL
SEGMENT SPACE MANAGEMENT AUTO;
```

When an object such as a table or index is created using the LMT, with ASSM enabled, there is no need to specify the PCTFREE or FREELISTS.

The in-segment free/used space is tracked using bitmaps as opposed to the free lists. When you cannot use the LMT and therefore the automatic management space feature, you have to depend on the traditional method of managing free lists and free list groups. ASSM offers the following benefits:

- It provides administrative ease of use by avoiding the specification of storage parameters.
- It is a good method for handling objects with varying row sizes.
- It provides better runtime adjustment for variations in concurrent access and avoids tedious tuning methods.
- It provides better multi-instance behavior in terms of performance and space utilization.

However, note that ASSM is available only with LMTs and their objects. A new column called SEGMENT_SPACE_MANAGEMENT has been added to the dba_tablespaces view to indicate the segment space management mode used by a tablespace.

Use the Oracle procedure dbms_space.space_usage to provide the space usage ratio within each block in the bitmap managed block (BMB) segments. It provides information regarding the number of blocks in a segment with the following ranges of free space:

- 0 to 25 percent free space within a block
- 25 to 50 percent free space within a block

- 50 to 75 percent free space within a block
- 75 to 100 percent free space within a block

One huge benefit of automatic segment management is the bitmap FREELISTS that are guaranteed to reduce buffer busy waits. Let's take a close look at this feature.

Prior to Oracle9*i*, buffer busy waits were a major issue. As a review, a buffer busy wait occurs when a data block is inside the data buffer cache, but it is unavailable because it is locked by another DML transaction. A block was unavailable because another SQL INSERT statement needed to get a block on which to place its row. Without multiple FREELISTS, every Oracle table and index had a single data block at the head of the table to manage the free block for the object. Whenever any SQL INSERT ran, it had to go to this block and get a data block on which to place its row.

Oracle's ASSM feature claims to improve the performance of concurrent DML operations significantly since different parts of the bitmap can be used, simultaneously eliminating serialization for free space lookups.

According to Oracle benchmarks, using bitmap FREELISTS removes all segment header contention and allows for super-fast concurrent INSERT operations (Figure 5.1).

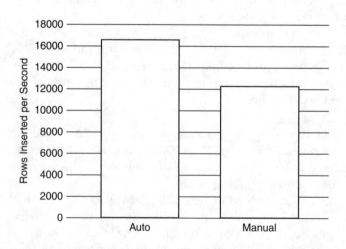

Figure 5.1 Oracle Corporation Benchmark on SQL INSERT Speed with Bitmap FREELISTS

Along with the automatic segment management features, we get some new tools for the DBA. Let's take a look at how the Oracle9*i* DBA will use these tools.

Internal Freelist Management with ASSM

With ASSM, Oracle controls the number of bitmap FREELISTS, up to 23 per segment. Internally within Oracle, a shortage of FREELISTS is manifested by a buffer busy wait. This is because the segment header is available in the data cache, but the block cannot be accessed because another task has locked the block to INSERT, DELETE, or UPDATE a row. Oracle9*i* may have a mechanism to allocate a new segment header block (with another bitmap FREELIST) whenever buffer busy waits are detected for the segment. As you may know, Oracle introduced dynamic FREELIST addition in Oracle8*i*.

- Free list unlinks — while it is possible for Oracle9*i* to detect the average row length for segments in a bitmap managed tablespace, Oracle9*i* has no way of predicting how much space to reserve of each data block for row expansion. This is because Oracle9*i* has no knowledge of VARCHAR data types that may later be expanded with SQL UPDATE statements. Logic dictates that Oracle9*i* must examine the updated row length for every UPDATE and relocate the row if it would chain onto another data block if left on its target block. Row relocation can have a high overhead, especially for batch-oriented SQL updates.
- Free list relinks — for Oracle to optimize the threshold for relinking a data block, it needs *a priori* knowledge of the volume of subsequent INSERT statements. If the threshold is set too high, only a small amount of space is reserved on the relinked data block and only a few rows can be INSERTED before Oracle is forced to perform an I/O to grab another data block. Oracle9*i* could detect high-volume INSERTS and use the APPEND option to bypass the FREELISTS and use empty table blocks for subsequent inserts.

Bitmap space management uses four bits inside each data block header to indicate the amount of available space in the data block. Unlike traditional space management with a fixed relink and unlink threshold, bitmap space managements allow Oracle to compare the actual row space for an INSERT with the actual available space on the data block. This enables better reuse of the available free space, especially for objects with

Table 5.1 Bitmap Value Meanings

Value	Meaning
0000	Unformatted block
0001	Block is logically full
0010	Less than 25 percent free space
0011	Greater than 25 percent but less than 50 percent free space
0100	Greater than 50 percent but less than 75 percent free space
0101	Greater than 75 percent free space

rows of highly varying size. Table 5.1 lists the values inside the four-bit space.

The value of this bitmap indicates how much free space exists in a given data block. In traditional space management, each data block must be read from the FREELIST to see if it has enough space to accept a new row. In Oracle9i, the bitmap is constantly kept up-to-date with changes to the block, which reduces wasted space because blocks can be kept fuller because the overhead of FREELIST processing has been reduced.

Another enhancement of Oracle9i space management is that concurrent DML operations improve significantly. This is because different parts of the bitmap can be used simultaneously, thereby eliminating the need to serialize free space lookups.

Please note that Oracle9i segment control structures are much larger than traditional FREELIST management. Because each data block entry contains the four-byte data block address and the four-bit free space indicator, each data block entry in the space management bitmap will consume approximately six bytes of storage.

It is also important to note that space management blocks are not required to be the first blocks in the segment. In Oracle8, the segment headers were required to be the first blocks in the segment. In Oracle8i, this restriction was lifted and the DBA could allocate additional FREELISTS with the ALTER TABLE command. In Oracle9i, Oracle automatically allocates new space management blocks when a new extent is created and maintains internal pointers to the bitmap blocks (refer to Figure 5.2).

Just like traditional FREELISTS, the BMB is stored in a separate data block within the table or index. Because Oracle does not publish the internals of space management, we must infer the structure from block dumps. Hence, this information may not be completely accurate, but it will give us a general idea about the internal mechanisms of Oracle9i automatic space management.

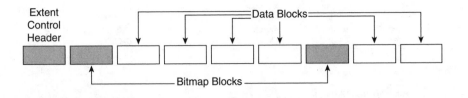

Figure 5.2   Noncontiguous Bitmap Blocks within a Segment

Unlike a linear-linked list in traditional FREELISTS, bitmap blocks are stored in a B-tree structure, much like a B-tree index structure. This new structure has important ramifications for concurrent DML. In traditional FREELISTS, free blocks must be accessed one at a time and this causes segment header contention in applications with high-volume INSERT operations. Because Oracle9i can use the FREELISTS blocks much like a B-tree index, multiple transactions can simultaneously access free blocks without locking or concurrency problems.

As we have noted, the purpose of bitmap blocks is to track the free blocks in the segment. Since the free blocks are organized in a B-tree, we see the information inside the segment control block. Three data blocks comprise the segment header.

The extent control header block contains the following components:

- The extent map of the segment
- The last block at each level of the B-tree
- The low HWM (LHWM)
- The high HWM (HHWM)

The HWM in the segment header has also changed in Oracle9i bitmap blocks. Instead of having a single pointer to the highest free block in an object, the B-tree index structure allows for a range of HWM blocks. Hence, we see two pointers for the HWM:

1. LHWM — all blocks below this block have been formatted for the table.
2. HHWM — all blocks above this block have not been formatted. Internally, the HHWM is required to ensure that Oracle direct load operations can access contiguous unformatted blocks.

Let's look at each block in detail to understand how space is managed in bitmap segment control. The Extent Control Header Block contains the HHWM, the LHWM, the extent map, and the data block addresses for each of the three levels of bitmap blocks.

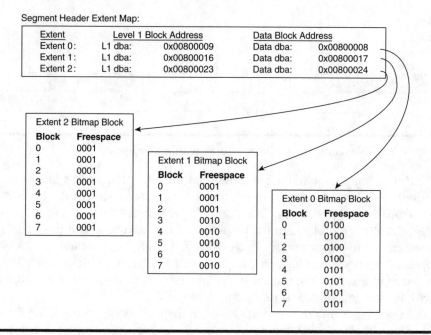

Figure 5.3   Segment Header Extent Map Points to All Extent Bitmaps in Segments

The extent map lists all of the data block addresses for each block within each extent within the segment and shows the four-bit free space of each block within the extent. Since the extent size is controlled by Oracle9i LMTs, each extent size within the tablespace is uniform, regardless of the NEXT extent size for each object in the tablespace.

Note that the first three blocks of the first extend list (blocks 0–2) are used for metadata and are not available for segment block addresses. For each extent in the segment, Oracle9i keeps an entry pointing to the bitmap for that segment (Figure 5.3).

Oracle9i also has pointers to the last bitmap block within each logical bitmap level (Figure 5.4).

This new pointer structure allows Oracle9i to quickly access multiple bitmaps to improve concurrency of high-volume INSERTs.

Potential Performance Issues with ASSM

The Oracle9i community has mixed feelings about using ASSM tablespaces. Among the top points about ASSM, we find both pros and cons:

■ Pros of ASSM:
– Varying row sizes — ASSM is better than a static PCTUSED. The bitmaps make ASSM tablespaces better at handling rows with wide variations in row length.

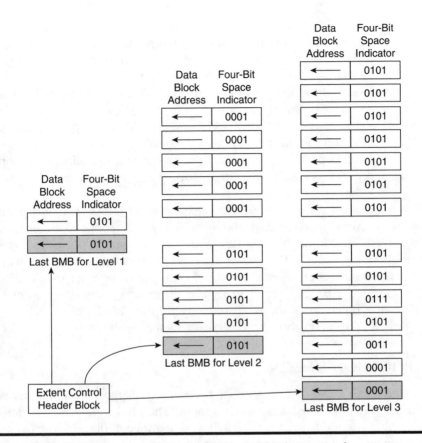

Figure 5.4 Pointers to Last Bitmap Block on Each Bitmap Level

  - Reducing buffer busy waits — ASSM will remove buffer busy waits better than using multiple FREELISTS. As we may know, when a table has multiple FREELISTS, all purges must be parallelized to reload the FREELISTS evenly. Whereas, ASSM has no such limitation.
  - Great for RAC — the bitmap FREELISTS remove the need to define multiple FREELISTS groups for RAC and provide overall improved FREELIST management over traditional FREELISTS.
■ Cons of ASSM:
  - Slow for FTSs — several studies have shown that large-table FTSs will run longer with ASSM than standard bitmaps. ASSM-FTS tablespaces are consistently slower than Freelist-FTS operations. This implies that ASSM may not be appropriate for DSSs and warehouse applications, unless partitioning is used with Oracle Parallel Query.

- Slower for high-volume concurrent INSERTS — numerous experts have conducted studies that show that tables with high volume bulk loads perform faster with traditional multiple FREELISTS.

■ ASSM will influence index clustering — for row-ordered tables, ASSM can adversely affect the clustering_factor for indexes. Bitmap FREELISTS are less likely to place adjacent rows on physically adjacent data blocks. This can lower the clustering_factor and the cost-based optimizer's propensity to favor an index range scan.

It remains to be seen how many experienced DBAs will start using automatic space management and how many will continue to use the older method. Although automatic space management promises faster throughput for multiple DML statements, Oracle professionals must always be on the watch for chained rows caused by a generic setting for PCTFREE. The seasoned DBA may want to bypass these new features in order to control the behavior of the table rows inside the data blocks.

Now let's examine how to design for Oracle replication.

REPLICATION DESIGN

Managing an Oracle data warehouse becomes challenging when we move into the distributed database environment. The challenge arises because so many components within the database software contribute to the overall performance. The number of concurrent users, the availability of space within the buffer and lock pools, and the balancing of access across processors all can affect database performance.

When a data warehouse accesses several remote databases in a single warehouse query, another dimension of complexity is added to the data warehouse. Not only must the DBA look at each individual database, but the DBA also must consider transactions that span several servers.

Although accessing several servers in a distributed warehouse query may seem trivial, performance problems can be introduced by PC hardware, network bottlenecks, router overloads, and many other sources. Let's take a look at distributed data warehouses and examine how they differ from traditional data warehouse environments.

CONCLUSION

This chapter has been concerned with the physical design of the file and tablespace structures. The main points of this chapter include:

- LMTs are now the default in Oracle Database 10*g* and should be used whenever feasible.
- ASSM relieves the one-way chains and relieves buffer busy waits on high-update segments.
- You still have the option of manually setting PCTFREE, PCTUSED, and FREELISTS for individual segments.

Now we are ready to look at the physical design options for Oracle tables and indexes. The next chapter will explore all of the table options to illustrate the advantages of each and show how they interface with the logical database design.

6

ORACLE TABLE DESIGN

INTRODUCTION

The data storage structures within Oracle are plentiful and range from simple to complex. During your physical design, you have a choice between standard relational tables and one of the many table extensions offered within the Oracle software. This chapter will address the following table design issues:

- Design with replicated tables
- Design with external tables
- Design with materialized views
- Design with Oracle object tables
- Design with ADTs
- Design with Oracle OIDs
- Design with pointer-based tables
- Design with nested tables
- Design with Oracle member methods

Let's begin with a review of the Oracle replicated table structure and see how it can be incorporated into a physical design.

TABLE REPLICATION DESIGN

Determining which type of replication your situation requires is very important. Remember these two adages:

1. More is not always better.
2. Just because Oracle includes it in the database, you don't have to use it.

One of the biggest mistakes a company can make is to implement advanced replication when all they need are read-only materialized views. With replication, more is harder to implement, harder to maintain, harder to troubleshoot, and takes more of your time.

Here are some criteria that you can use to determine the level of replication that best fits your situation.

Is the Transfer of Data Time Sensitive?

Many DBAs believe that data is time sensitive when in fact it is not. If the data is being moved to a data warehouse to be used for data mining or report generation, the data probably is not time sensitive. A daily transfer (or even weekly) may meet the entire business requirement. Ask management; a daily report in the morning may be acceptable, instead of a report available on demand with the most recent data. Many DBAs are finding that even internal materialized views are taking so long to update that they have to update them at night or only on weekends.

Is the Number of Tables Manageable?

If you are using Oracle Applications, forget about replicating the entire database. Oracle Apps consists of tens of thousands of tables. This is not a candidate for replication. However, replicating parts of large databases are possible. Remember that each replicated object adds overhead to the databases and takes network bandwidth. There are practical limits to the number of objects you can replicate, depending on the capability of the database server and the network connections. Replicating 100 tables is easy, 1000 may not be possible, 10,000 — forget it.

Do All Your Replicated Tables Need to Be Updatable?

This is a big one. A shop will often set up full multimaster replication because the database is supporting an application that has to update certain tables. Tables that need to be updated at both locations must use advanced replication, however all remaining tables can use basic replication. This ability to mix replication types can significantly lower the replication overhead. Remember, less is best.

Does Your Database Change Constantly?

Does Quality Assurance roll in a new update every weekend? If so, replication may not be for you. Table changes may force you either to rebuild the replication or implement advanced replication. Maintaining replication in a changing database will entail a significant increase in the DBA's workload.

Is the Number of Transactions Manageable?

The number of transactions per minute is another one of those variables that must be considered. A replication based on a few tables will be better able to handle high numbers of transactions. A large replication may not be able to keep up on a high transaction system; this again depends on the server capabilities and the network bandwidth.

Are You Replicating between Different Versions of Oracle or Different OSs?

Many shops choose replication rather than a standby database precisely because replication can operate between either different versions of the Oracle database or between Oracle databases running on different OSs. Because replication is passed across database links, different versions of Oracle can be used. An Oracle database on Windows can be replicated in a database on a Sun server, thereby providing a failover solution if needed.

Do Both Sites Require the Ability to Update the Same Tables?

If both sides of the replication must update data (INSERT, UPDATE, DELETE), then you must implement advanced replication. Use advanced replication only on the tables that must be updated on both sides of the replication.

Does the Replicated Site Require the Ability to Replicate to Another Site?

A master site can replicate with other sites. If the remote site only replicates with one master site, use updatable materialized views. If the remote site must replicate the data further, then it too must be a master site and multimaster replication is required.

As you might have figured, replication is difficult to understand and time-consuming to set up. But its daunting reputation is much worse than reality. Once you get it set up and operating, you will find it really isn't very intimidating. Remember to replicate at the lowest level possible. Don't use advanced replication where basic replication will work. Don't try to replicate more objects than your server and network are able to support.

Now let's look at Oracle9*i* external tables and see how they can be incorporated into your logical data model.

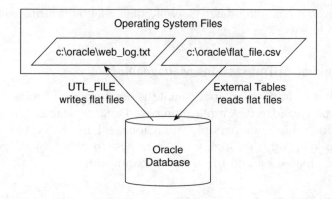

Figure 6.1   Oracle Read and Write Interfaces to OS Files

ORACLE EXTERNAL TABLES

One of the most exciting advances in Oracle9*i* is the ability to access non-Oracle files with Oracle SQL. This new functionality, called external tables, has important ramifications for systems where external files need to be available for nondatabase applications and appear to be a table within Oracle.

External tables allow you to define the structure of almost any flat file on your server and have it appear to Oracle as if it were a real table, as we've diagrammed (Figure 6.1).

As you can see, Oracle lets a database program write to flat files using the utl_file utility. Combined with external tables' read ability, this new topology removes the requirement that all Oracle data resides inside Oracle tables, opening new applications for Oracle. Let's take a closer look at how this feature works.

Defining an External Table

Let's say you want Oracle to refer to this comma-delimited flat file:

```
7369,SMITH,CLERK,7902,17-DEC-80,800,20
7499,ALLEN,SALESMAN,7698,20-FEB-81,1600,300,30
7521,WARD,SALESMAN,7698,22-FEB-81,1250,500,30
7566,JONES,MANAGER,7839,02-APR-81,2975,,20
7654,MARTIN,SALESMAN,7698,28-SEP-81,1250,1400,30
7698,BLAKE,MANAGER,7839,01-MAY-81,2850,,30
7782,CLARK,MANAGER,7839,09-JUN-81,2450,,10
7788,SCOTT,ANALYST,7566,19-APR-87,3000,,20
```

```
7839,KING,PRESIDENT,,17-NOV-81,5000,,10
7844,TURNER,SALESMAN,7698,08-SEP-81,1500,0,30
7876,ADAMS,CLERK,7788,23-MAY-87,1100,,20
```

The file contains the following employee information:

- Employee ID
- Last name
- Job description
- Manager's employee ID
- Hire date
- Salary
- Commission
- Department

So, how do we define this file to Oracle? First, we must create an Oracle directory entry in the data dictionary that points to the Windows directory where the flat file resides. In this example, we'll name the directory `testdir` and point it to `c:\docs\pubsdb\queries`:

```
SQL> create directory testdir as 'c:\docs\pubsdb\queries';
Directory Created.
```

Now that we have the directory, we can define the structure of the external file to Oracle. You'll see this code in Listing 6.1.

In this syntax, we define the column of the external table in much the same way as you would an internal Oracle table. The external definitions occur in the organization external clause, as shown in Table 6.1.

Now that we've defined the external table, we can run reports against the external table using SQL, just as if the table resided inside the database. In the query shown in Listing 6.2, note the use of the sophisticated ROLLUP parameter to summarize salaries by both department and job title. The results are available in Listing 6.3.

Because external tables are new, Oracle has not yet perfected their use. In Oracle9*i*, the feature has several limitations, including:

- No support for DML — external tables are read-only, but the base data can be edited in any text editor.
- Poor response for high-volume queries — external tables have a processing overhead and are not suitable for large tables.

Accessing flat files via Oracle has a number of uses. For example, you can define spreadsheets to Oracle. This technique has important

Listing 6.1   Defining the Structure of the External File

```
create table
   emp_ext
(
   empno     number(4),
   ename     varchar2(10),
   job       varchar2(9),
   mgr       number(4),
   hiredate date,
   sal       number(7,2),
   comm      number(7,2),
   deptno    number(2)
)
organization external
(
   type oracle_loader
   default directory testdir
   access parameters
   (
      records delimited by newline
      fields terminated by ','
   )
location ('emp_ext.csv')
)
reject limit 1000;
```

Table 6.1   External Definitions for the Comma-Delimited File

Syntax	Meaning
default directory `testdir`	The directory where the file resides
records delimited by `newline`	The new line character
fields terminated by `','`	The column termination character
location (`'emp_ext.csv'`)	The name of the external file

ramifications for shops where users can control systemwide parameters inside desktop spreadsheets and Oracle knows immediately about changes.

The advent of external tables in Oracle9*i* is exciting because it allows SQL queries to access any type of flat file, as if the data were stored inside an Oracle table. We'll examine some caveats to this new approach, specifically:

Listing 6.2   Sophisticated ROLLUP Parameter to Summarize Salaries

```
ttitle 'Employee Salary|Cubic Rollup'
col deptno    heading 'Department|Number'
col job       heading 'Job|Title'
col num_emps heading 'Number of|Employees' format 9,999
col sum_sal  heading 'Total|Salary'        format $99,999
SELECT
   deptno,
   job,
   count(*)  num_emps,
   sum(sal)  sum_sal
FROM
   emp_ext
GROUP BY
   ROLLUP
   (
      deptno,
      job
   );
```

Listing 6.3   Results of Listing 6.2

```
Wed Jun 12                                  page    1
                  Employee Salary
                   Cubic Rollup
Department Job       Number of    Total
   Number Title      Employees   Salary
---------- --------- --------- --------
       10  MANAGER          1   $2,450
       10  PRESIDENT        1   $5,000
       10                   2   $7,450
       20  ANALYST          1   $3,000
       20  CLERK            1   $1,100
       20  MANAGER          1   $2,975
       20                   3   $7,075
       30  MANAGER          1   $2,850
       30  SALESMAN         4   $5,600
       30                   5   $8,450
                           10  $22,975
```

- The external file must be comma-delimited and stored on the server as a file with a `.csv` extension.
- External spreadsheets are not good for large files because the entire file must be reread into Oracle whenever a change is saved to the spreadsheet.
- End users must never reformat the data columns inside the spreadsheet environment.

The next code listing shows the syntax used to make the file appear as an Oracle external table. Note the `csv` file name suffix.

```
create directory testdir as 'u01/oracle/oradata/testdb';

create table emp_ext (
EMPNO      NUMBER(4),
ENAME      VARCHAR2(10),
JOB        VARCHAR2(9),
MGR        NUMBER(4),
HIREDATE DATE,
SAL        NUMBER(7,2),
COMM       NUMBER(7,2),
DEPTNO     NUMBER(2))
Organization external
(type oracle_loader
default directory testdir
access parameters (records delimited by newline
fields terminated by ',')
location ('emp_ext.csv'))
reject limit 1000;
```

However, when defining the flat file as an external table, the file remains on the OS as a flat file, where it can be read and updated with a variety of tools, including spreadsheets. Using Excel spreadsheets, the external table data can be read just as if it were standard spreadsheet data (Figure 6.2).

End users can now manage critical tables inside easy-to-use spreadsheets. Oracle immediately notices whenever a change is made to the spreadsheet. However, there are important limitations to using spreadsheets as Oracle tables, the foremost being excessive disk I/O whenever the spreadsheet has changed. Let's take a closer look.

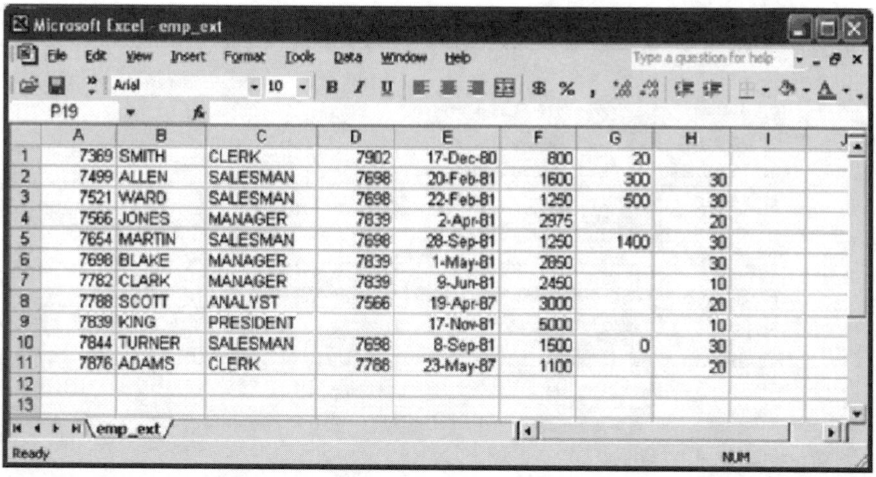

	A	B	C	D	E	F	G	H	I
1	7369	SMITH	CLERK	7902	17-Dec-80	800	20		
2	7499	ALLEN	SALESMAN	7698	20-Feb-81	1600	300	30	
3	7521	WARD	SALESMAN	7698	22-Feb-81	1250	500	30	
4	7566	JONES	MANAGER	7839	2-Apr-81	2975		20	
5	7654	MARTIN	SALESMAN	7698	28-Sep-81	1250	1400	30	
6	7698	BLAKE	MANAGER	7839	1-May-81	2850		30	
7	7782	CLARK	MANAGER	7839	9-Jun-81	2450		10	
8	7788	SCOTT	ANALYST	7566	19-Apr-87	3000		20	
9	7839	KING	PRESIDENT		17-Nov-81	5000		10	
10	7844	TURNER	SALESMAN	7698	8-Sep-81	1500	0	30	
11	7876	ADAMS	CLERK	7788	23-May-87	1100		20	
12									
13									

Figure 6.2 An External Table inside an Excel Spreadsheet

Internals of External Tables

It's important to recognize that Oracle data inside spreadsheets will not be accessible as quickly as internal row data. Oracle can't maintain row-level locking because the OS, not Oracle, is in command. When a spreadsheet is defined as an external table, Oracle has no way of knowing when individual row data changes. The OS will only tell Oracle that the entire spreadsheet has changed.

In addition, data blocks that are read from an external table are not placed inside the Oracle9*i* data buffers. The dictionary query shown in Listing 6.4 demonstrates that Oracle doesn't read the external table rows into the RAM data cache.

As we see in Listing 6.5, selections from our table don't reside in the data buffers following a SQL query.

Oracle doesn't make it clear whether a separate buffering mechanism is used for external tables. With this lack of buffering, Oracle9*i* must reread the entire spreadsheet for each SQL invocation that accesses the external table.

To maintain data integrity, Oracle must detect when the spreadsheet data has changed, but there is no way to discover when specific spreadsheet values have changed. When Oracle detects that the flat file has been updated, all data in the RAM data buffers becomes invalid and the entire spreadsheet must be reread. This is the primary reason external tables are not efficient for large volumes of data.

Listing 6.4 Dictionary Query

```
select
        bp.name             pool_name,
        ob.name             object,
        ob.subname      sub_name,
        sum(buf_count) buffer_blocks
from
        (select set_ds, obj, count(*) buf_count
        from x$bh group by set_ds, obj)     bh,
        obj$                                ob,
        x$kcbwds                            ws,
        v$buffer_pool                       bp
where
   ob.dataobj# = bh.obj
and
   ob.owner# > 0
and
   bh.set_ds = ws.addr
and
   ws.set_id between bp.lo_setid and bp.hi_setid
group by
        bp.name,
        ob.name,
        ob.subname
order by
        bp.name,
        ob.name,
        ob.subname
;
```

Because Oracle reads OS files in data blocks, we can compute the amount of disk I/O by determining the number of spreadsheet blocks with a simple shell script. In this script, we know the Oracle database has 8 KB block sizes:

```
bytes=`ls -al|grep emp_ext.csv|awk '{ print $5 }'`
num_bytes=`expr $bytes`
blocks=`expr $num_bytes / 8192`
echo $blocks
```

This script will tell us exactly how many disk reads are required to access the Oracle external table whenever a change is made.

Listing 6.5   Data Buffer Pool Contents

```
SQL> select ename from pubs.emp_ext;
SQL> @buf_data
POOL_NAME OBJECT                       SUB_NAME            BLOCKS
--------- ------------------------     ----------------    --------
DEFAULT   PUBLISHER                                           2
          REPCAT$_REPPROP                                     1
          SNS$BINDINGS$                                       2
          SNS$INODE$                                          2
          SNS$NODE_INDEX                                      1
          SNS$REFADDR$                                        3
          SNS$REFADDR_INDEX                                   3
          SYS_C001042                                         1
          SYS_C001414                                         1
```

Security for External Table Files

Any saved change to the spreadsheet causes the entire spreadsheet to be read again into Oracle from the disk. Spreadsheets can be password protected at the OS level and they can be marked read-only with the following DOS command:

```
c:\docs\pubsdb\queries> attrib +r emp_ext.csv
```

In UNIX, we can use this command to make the spreadsheet read-only for everyone except the owner of the spreadsheet:

```
chmod 744 emp_ext.csv
```

This ensures the file will not be updated, except by authorized users. It makes sure that Oracle caches the data in an efficient manner. Once defined to Oracle, the spreadsheet will be accessible both through Oracle and the Excel spreadsheet.

Limitations of Comma-Delimited Spreadsheet Files

For Oracle to successfully read comma-delimited (csv) files, it's important to avoid making spreadsheet-specific changes because Excel will change the internal storage of the column to accommodate the formatting. For example, let's assume that a manager reformats the SALARY column for comma display (Figure 6.3).

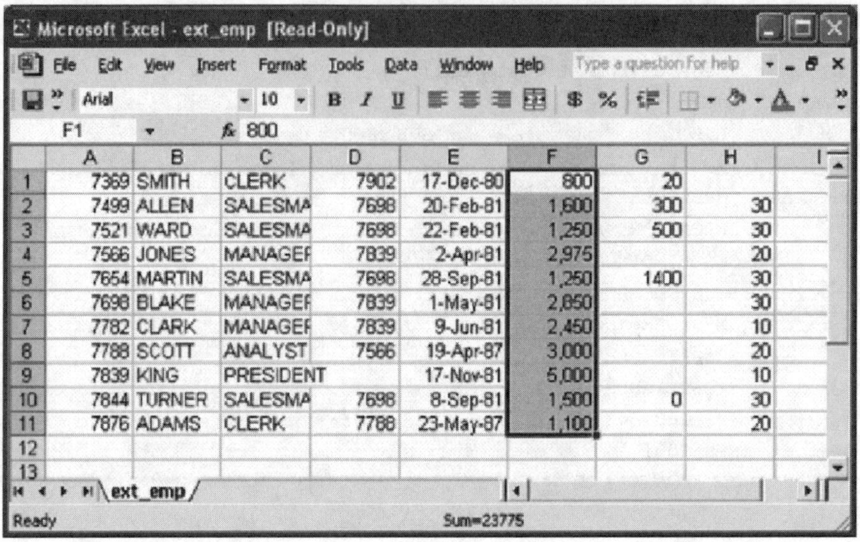

Figure 6.3 Reformatting a Comma-Delimited (csv) Spreadsheet

Once the file has been saved, Oracle can no longer read the SALARY column because the column has been stored in quotes. To Oracle, this defines the column as a character:

```
7369,SMITH,CLERK,7902,17-Dec-80,800,20,
7499,ALLEN,SALESMAN,7698,20-Feb-81,"1,600",300,30
7521,WARD,SALESMAN,7698,22-Feb-81,"1,250",500,30
7566,JONES,MANAGER,7839,2-Apr-81,"2,975",,20
7654,MARTIN,SALESMAN,7698,28-Sep-81,"1,250",1400,30
7698,BLAKE,MANAGER,7839,1-May-81,"2,850",,30
7782,CLARK,MANAGER,7839,9-Jun-81,"2,450",,10
7788,SCOTT,ANALYST,7566,19-Apr-87,"3,000",,20
7839,KING,PRESIDENT,,17-Nov-81,"5,000",,10
7844,TURNER,SALESMAN,7698,8-Sep-81,"1,500",0,30
7876,ADAMS,CLERK,7788,23-May-87,"1,100",,20
```

The accidental reformatting of the file makes it unreadable by Oracle. You must take special care to instruct end users to never change the formatting.

In summary, external tables are a great way to incorporate volatile data into the database without undergoing the task of physically loading the Oracle tables.

Next, let's examine how design with materialized views can allow multiple data structures (1NF and 3NF) to exist within the same Oracle database.

DESIGN WITH MATERIALIZED VIEWS

In the world of database architecture, the need to dynamically create complex objects conflicts with the demand for subsecond response time. Oracle's answer to this dilemma is the materialized view. Database designers can use materialized views to prejoin tables, presort solution sets, and presummarize complex data warehouse information. Because this work is completed in advance, it gives end users the illusion of instantaneous response time.

Materialized views are especially useful for Oracle data warehouses, where cross-tabulations often take hours to perform. This section explores the internals of materialized views and demonstrates how to precompute complex aggregates.

When accessing data against any relational database, the database developer is faced with a quandary of aggregation. As we know, extracting complex summaries and aggregations from a database can cause repeated large-table FTSs against the database. For very large systems, these kinds of large queries can run for many hours. So how can we provide subsecond response time when the queries may run for hours?

The answer is with Oracle materialized views. An Oracle materialized view allows us to presummarize information and store it inside Oracle tables. With Oracle's query rewrite facility enabled, Oracle will detect queries that can use the materialized views and automatically rewrite the SQL to reference the materialized view. The query optimizer can use materialized views by automatically recognizing when an existing materialized view can and should be used to satisfy a request. It then transparently rewrites the request to use the materialized view. Queries are then directed to the materialized view and not to the underlying detail tables, which should result in a significant performance gain.

This revolutionary technique can be used to take ordinary SQL queries down from hours to subsecond response time. This illusion of instantaneous response time is achieved by presummarizing the data.

However, there is a downside to using materialized views. Because materialized views are derived from subsets of the Oracle data, the information and the materialized views may become stale as soon as additional data is added into our database. Hence, the Oracle database provides a refresh mechanism for materialized views. The Oracle professional can specify that the materialized views be refreshed instantly, every ten minutes, every day, and so on, depending on the volatility of the data. Here is an example:

```
CREATE MATERIALIZED VIEW
     emp_sum
ENABLE QUERY REWRITE
REFRESH FAST
START WITH SYSDATE
NEXT  SYSDATE + 1/24
AS
        SELECT deptno, job, SUM(sal)
        FROM emp
        GROUP BY deptno, job
     ;
     Materialized View Created.
```

In the above example, the materialized view is recreated (refreshed) every 1/24 of a day (once per hour).

This refresh interval gives the database developer complete control over the refresh interval for the materialized views and allows them to take long-running expensive SQL queries and make them run super fast.

Materialized Views and Snapshots

Materialized views are an introduction of redundancy, along the same lines as Oracle snapshots. When an Oracle materialized view is created, Oracle treats the materialized view just as it would an Oracle snapshot. Oracle requires you to specify a schedule for periodic updates. Updates are accomplished by way of a refresh interval, which can range from instantaneous rebuilding of the materialized view to a hot refresh that occurs weekly.

Prerequisites for Using Materialized Views

The Oracle DBA must specify special initialization parameters in order to use materialized views. Special authorization must also be granted to all users of materialized views. We will first look at the initialization parameters and then explore the effective management and use of materialized views.

The initialization parameters are set within Oracle to enable the mechanisms for materialized views and query rewrite, as indicated below:

```
optimizer_mode = choose, first_rows, or all_rows
job_queue_interval = 3600
job_queue_processes = 1
query_rewrite_enabled = true
query_rewrite_integrity = enforced
compatible = 8.1.5.0.0 (or greater)
```

Several system privileges must be granted to anyone using materialized views. These grant statements can often be grouped into a single role and the role granted to the end user:

```
grant query rewrite to nelson;
grant create materialized view to nelson;
alter session set query_rewrite_enabled = true;
```

Invoking SQL Query Rewrite

After enabling materialized views, several methods are provided by Oracle for invoking query rewrite. In general, query rewrite is automatic, but it can be manually enabled by using alter session, alter system, or SQL hints:

```
ALTER {SESSION|SYSTEM} DISABLE QUERY REWRITE
Select /*+REWRITE(mv1)*/...
```

Refreshing Materialized Views

In Oracle9i, a materialized view log must be created for each single-table aggregate materialized view in order to use REFRESH FAST or the command will fail. The refresh can be set to occur manually (ON DEMAND) or automatically (ON COMMIT, DBMS_JOB) while creating a materialized view. The ON DEMAND mode must be specified to use the fast warehouse refresh facility. Call one of the procedures in DBMS_MVIEW to refresh the materialized view.

There are three types of refresh operations in the DBMS_MVIEW package:

1. DBMS_MVIEW.REFRESH — refreshes one or more materialized views
2. DBMS_MVIEW.REFRESH_ALL_MVIEWS — refreshes all materialized views
3. DBMS_MVIEW.REFRESH_DEPENDENT — refreshes all table-based materialized views

Manual Complete Refresh

When the materialized view is initially defined, a complete refresh occurs unless it references a prebuilt table. A complete refresh may be requested at any time after a materialized view is defined. This can be a time-consuming process since the results for the materialized view must be computed from the detail table. This is especially true if huge amounts of data need to be processed.

Manual Fast (Incremental) Refresh

When REFRESH FAST is specified, only changes performed by UPDATE, INSERT, or DELETE on the base tables will be refreshed. If any of the detail tables change, Oracle performs further verification of the query definition to ensure that fast refresh can be performed. These additional checks include:

- Each detail table must have a materialized view log.
- The SELECT list of the MVIEW query definition must have the ROWIDs of all the detail tables.
- Unique constraints must be placed on the join columns of the inner table if there are outer joins.

The DBMS_MVIEW package can manually invoke either a fast refresh or a complete refresh. F equals fast refresh and C equals complete refresh:

```
EXECUTE DBMS_MVIEW.REFRESH('emp_dept_sum','F');
```

Automatic Fast Refresh of Materialized Views

Oracle9*i* incorporates a new feature, the automatic fast refresh. A snapshot can be refreshed with DBMS_JOB in a short interval according to the snapshot log. It is possible to automatically refresh on the next COMMIT performed at the master table. ON COMMIT refreshing can be used with both materialized views on single-table aggregates and materialized views containing joins only. ON COMMIT MVIEW logs cannot be built as primary-key logs. They must be built as ROWID logs. It is suggested that indexes be created on the ROWIDs of the MVIEW to enhance performance. Note that the MVIEW underlying table can be prebuilt.

Here is an example of a materialized view with an ON COMMIT refresh:

```
CREATE MATERIALIZED VIEW
    empdep
```

```
ON PREBUILT TABLE
REFRESH FAST ON COMMIT
ENABLE QUERY REWRITE
    AS SELECT empno, ename, dname, loc,
             e.rowid emp_rowid,
             d.rowid dep_rowid
      FROM emp e, dept d
     WHERE e.deptno = d.deptno;
```

Creating a Materialized View

By taking it one step at a time, we can see the creation of a materialized view. The code for each step is shown in Listing 6.6.

It is important to note that some rewrites that were text-match based in release 8.1.5 may no longer be possible with release 8.1.6, if the CURSOR_SHARING parameter is set to FORCE. There are three acceptable values for query_rewrite_integrity:

1. enforced (default) — presents materialized view with fresh data
2. trusted — assumes that the materialized view is current
3. stale_tolerated — presents materialized view with both stale and fresh data

Tips for Using Materialized Views

When query rewrite is used, materialized views are created satisfying the largest number of SQL queries. For example, if there are 25 queries commonly applied to the detail or fact tables, they may be able to be satisfied with 6 or 7 well-written materialized views.

Oracle provides advisory functions in the DBMS_OLAP package if you are in doubt about which materialized views to create. These functions help in designing and evaluating materialized views for query rewrite.

A materialized view must be stored in the same database as its fact or detail tables in order to be used by query rewrite. A materialized view can be partitioned and it may be defined on a partitioned table and one or more indexes on the materialized view.

The performance of Oracle systems required to process complex SQL statements is significantly enhanced by the introduction of materialized views. It accomplishes this while delivering subsecond response time. We'll look at the internals of materialized views and SQL query rewrite in the next section and discuss how to implement this powerful performance feature.

Listing 6.6   Creating a Materialized View

1. Set the Oracle parameters

    ```
    optimizer_mode = choose, first_rows, or all_rows
    job_queue_interval = 3600
    job_queue_processes = 1
    query_rewrite_enabled = true
    query_rewrite_integrity = enforced
    compatible = 8.1.5.0.0 (or greater)
    ```

2. Create the materialized view

    ```
    CREATE MATERIALIZED VIEW
    emp_sum
    ENABLE QUERY REWRITE
    AS
    SELECT
        deptno,
        job,
        SUM(sal)
    FROM
        emp
    GROUP BY
        deptno,
        job
    PCTFREE 5
    PCTUSED 60
    NOLOGGING PARALLEL 5
    TABLESPACE users
        STORAGE (INITIAL 50K NEXT 50K)
        USING INDEX STORAGE (INITIAL 25K NEXT 25K)
    REFRESH FAST
    START WITH SYSDATE
    NEXT SYSDATE + 1/12;
    ```

3. Refresh the materialized view and get statistics

    ```
    execute dbms_utility.analyze_schema('NELSON','ESTIMATE');
    execute dbms_mview.refresh('emp_sum');
    ```

4. Verify the query rewrite

    ```
    set autotrace on explain;
    SELECT
        deptno,
        job,
        SUM(sal)
    ```

Listing 6.6   Creating a Materialized View (Continued)

```
FROM
    emp
GROUP BY
    deptno,
    job;
Execution Plan
------------------------------------
0 SELECT STATEMENT Optimizer=CHOOSE
1 0 TABLE ACCESS (FULL) OF 'EMP_SUM'
```

5. Create a materialized view log

```
CREATE MATERIALIZED VIEW LOG ON
    emp_sum
WITH ROWID;
CREATE MATERIALIZED VIEW LOG ON
    dept
WITH ROWID;
```

6. Test the refresh mechanism

```
EXECUTE DBMS_MVIEW.REFRESH('emp_sum');
```

DESIGN FOR PARTITIONED STRUCTURES

Partitioning is a divide-and-conquer approach to improving Oracle maintenance and SQL performance. Anyone with unpartitioned databases over 500 GB is courting disaster. Databases become unmanageable and serious problems occur:

- Files recovery takes days, not minutes
- Rebuilding indexes (important to reclaim space and improve performance) can take days
- Queries with FTSs take hours to complete
- Index range scans become inefficient

There are many compelling reasons to implement partitioning for larger databases and partitioning has become the *de facto* standard for systems over 500 GB. Oracle partitioning has many benefits to improve performance and manageability:

- Stable — partitioning is a stable technology and has been used in Oracle since Oracle8, back in 1997. Each new release of Oracle improves partitioning features.

- Robust — Oracle9*i* partitioning allows for multilevel keys, a combination of the range and list partitioning technique. The table is first range partitioned and then each individual range partition is further subpartitioned using a list partitioning technique. Unlike composite range-hash partitioning, the content of each subpartition represents a logical subset of the data, described by its appropriate range and list partition setup.
- Faster backups — a DBA can back up a single partition of a table, rather than backing up the entire table, thereby reducing backup time.
- Less overhead — because older partitioned tablespaces can be marked as read-only, Oracle has less stress on the redo logs, locks, and latches, thereby improving overall performance.
- Easier management — maintenance of partitioned tables is improved because maintenance can be focused on particular portions of tables. For maintenance operations across an entire database object, it is possible to perform these operations on a per-partition basis, thus dividing the maintenance process into more manageable chunks.
- Faster SQL — Oracle is partition-aware and some SQL may improve speed by several orders of magnitude (over 100 times faster).
- Index range scans — partitioning physically sequences rows in index order causing a dramatic improvement (over 10 times faster) in the speed of partition-key scans.
- FTSs — partition pruning only accesses those data blocks required by the query.
- Table joins — partitionwise joins take the specific subset of the query partitions, causing huge speed improvements on nested loop and hash joins.
- Updates — Oracle Parallel Query for partitions improves batch access speed by isolating the affected areas of the query.

In summary, partitioning has a fast payback time and the immediate improvements to performance and stress reduction on the Oracle server makes it a slam-dunk decision.

Next, let's examine the Oracle object-oriented table structures and see how they interface with physical design.

ORACLE OBJECT STRUCTURES

Oracle9*i* offers a variety of data structures to help create robust database systems. Oracle supports the full use of binary large objects, nested tables, non-1NF table structures (VARRAY tables), and object-oriented table structures. It even treats flat data files as if they were tables within the Oracle database.

OBJECTS **DATABASE ENTITIES**

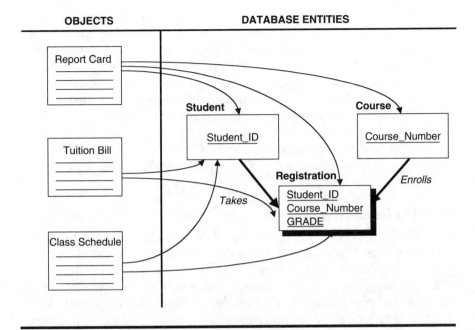

Figure 6.4   Oracle Models Complex Objects inside the Database

It is a challenge to many Oracle design professionals to know when to use these Oracle data model extensions. This section provides a brief review of advanced Oracle topics and how they are used to design high-performance Oracle databases.

Data Model Extension Capabilities

The new Oracle data model extensions provide the following capabilities:

- Modeling real-world objects — it is no longer required for the relational database designer to model complex objects in their smallest components and rebuild them at runtime. Using Oracle's object-oriented constructs, real-world objects can have a concrete existence just like C++ objects. Oracle can use arrays of pointers to represent these complex objects (Figure 6.4).
- Removing unnecessary table joins — this is achieved by deliberately introducing redundancy into the data model. Queries that required complex and time-consuming table joins can now be retrieved in a single disk I/O operation.
- Coupling of data and behavior — one of the important constructs of object orientation is the tight coupling of object behaviors with the objects themselves. In Oracle, a member method can be created

upon the Oracle object and all processes that manipulate the object are encapsulated inside Oracle's data dictionary. This functionality has huge benefits for the development of all Oracle systems. Prior to the introduction of member methods, each Oracle developer was essentially a custom craftsman writing custom SQL to access Oracle information. By using member methods, all interfaces to the Oracle database are performed using pretested methods with known interfaces. This way, the Oracle developer's role changes from custom craftsman to more of an assembly line coder. You simply choose from a list of prewritten member methods to access Oracle information.

Object Orientation and Oracle

Oracle9*i* offers numerous choices for the introduction of object-oriented data model constructs into relational database design. Oracle9*i* offers the ability to dereference table row pointers, ADTs, and limited polymorphism and inheritance support. In Oracle9*i*, data model constructs used in C++ or Smalltalk programming can be translated directly into an Oracle structure. In addition, Oracle supports abstract data typing whereby you create customized data types with the strong typing inherent in any of the standard Oracle data types like NUMBER, CHAR, VARCHAR, and DATE.

For example, here is an Oracle8 table created with ADTs and a nested table.

```
CREATE OR REPLACE TYPE
    employee
AS OBJECT
(
    last_name                varchar(40),
    full_address             full_mailing_address_type,
    prior_employers          prior_employer_name_arr
);
create table emp of employee;
```

Next, we use extensions to standard Oracle SQL to update these ADTs as shown below:

```
insert into emp
values (
    'Burleson',
    full_mailing_address_type('7474 Airplane Ave.','Rocky
Ford','NC','27445'),
```

```
prior_employer_name_arr(
    employer_name('IBM'),
    employer_name('ATT'),
    employer_name('CNN')
) );
```

Oracle Nested Tables

Using the Oracle nested table structure, subordinate data items can be directly linked to the base table by using Oracle's newest construct, the OID. One of the remarkable extensions of Oracle is the ability to reference Oracle objects directly by using pointers as opposed to joining relational tables together.

Oracle has moved toward allowing complex objects to have a concrete existence. To support the concrete existence of complex objects, Oracle introduced the ability to build arrays of pointers with row references directly to Oracle tables. Just as a C++ program can use the char** data structure to have a pointer to an array of pointers, Oracle allows similar constructs whereby the components of the complex objects reside in real tables with pointers to the subordinate objects. At runtime, Oracle simply needs to dereference the pointers and the complex object can be quickly rebuilt from its component pieces.

In this example, a nested table is used to represent a repeating group for previous addresses. Whereas a person is likely to have a small number of previous employers, most people have a larger number of previous addresses. First, we create a type using our full_mailing_address_ type:

```
create type prev_addrs as object (prior_address
full_mailing_address_type );
```

Next, we create the nested object:

```
create type nested_address as table of prev_addrs;
```

Now, we create the parent table with the nested table as we see below.

```
create table
   emp1 (
   last_name          char(40),
   current_address    full_mailing_address_type,
   prev_address       nested_address   )
```

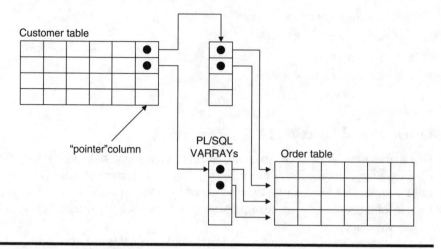

Figure 6.5 An Oracle Nested Table

```
nested table prev_address store as nested_prev_
address return as locator;
```

A nested table appears as a part of the master table. Internally, it is a separate table. The *store as* clause allows the DBA to give the nested table a specific name (Figure 6.5).

Note that the `nested_prev_address` subordinate table can be indexed just like any other Oracle table. Also, notice the use of the `return as locator` SQL syntax. In many cases, returning the entire nested table at query time can be time-consuming. The locator enables Oracle to use the pointer structures to dereference pointers to the location of the nested rows. A pointer dereference happens when you take a pointer to an object and ask the program to display the data the pointer is pointing to. In other words, if you have a pointer to a customer row, you can dereference the OID and see the data for that customer. The link to the nested tables uses an Oracle OID instead of a traditional foreign key value.

Performance of Oracle Object Extensions

To fully understand Oracle advanced design, we need to take a look at the SQL performance ramifications of using object extensions. Overall, the performance of ADT tables is the same as any other Oracle table, but we do see significant performance differences when implementing VARRAY tables and nested tables:

- ADT tables — creating user-defined data types simplifies Oracle database design. Doing ADTs also provides uniform data definitions for common data items. There is no downside for SQL performance. The only downside for SQL syntax is the requirement that all references to ADTs be fully qualified.
- Nested tables — nested tables have the advantage of being indexed and the repeating groups are separated into another table so as not to degrade the performance of FTSs. Nested tables allow for an infinite number of repeating groups. However, it sometimes takes longer to dereference the OID to access the nested table entries as opposed to ordinary SQL tables join operations. Most Oracle experts see no compelling benefit of using nested tables over traditional table joins.
- VARRAY tables — VARRAY tables have the benefit of avoiding costly SQL joins and they can maintain the order of the VARRAY items based upon the sequence when they were stored. However, the longer row length of VARRAY tables causes FTSs to run longer and the items inside the VARRAY cannot be indexed. More importantly, VARRAYs cannot be used when the number of repeating items is unknown or large.

There is much confusion concerning the implementation of the database object model by Oracle9*i*. The design of robust object systems using Oracle9*i* object features is explored in the following sections. Oracle designers are also shown how to plan ahead with these features in mind.

Design with ADTs

As mentioned earlier, Oracle9*i* allows the creation of ADTs. Oracle7 provided only a handful of built-in data types. While the data types in Oracle7 were sufficient for most relational database applications, developers are beginning to realize that the ability of Oracle9*i* to create ADTs can greatly simplify database design and improve system performance. These ADTs have been popular within languages such as C^{++} for some time; only recently have they been introduced into the mainstream world of database objects.

ADTs are implemented in Oracle9*i* by including a CREATE TYPE definition. CREATE TYPE defines the domains of the subtypes that exist in the ADT. An ADT is nothing more than a collection of smaller, basic data types. ADTs allow basic data types to be treated as a single entity. Even though this is a simple concept, the implications for Oracle database design are dramatic.

It is noteworthy that ADTs were commonly used within prerelational databases.

This ability was lost when the relational model was introduced. There were only a few allowable data types — such as numeric and character — in prerelational databases. However, these databases allowed for the component values to be grouped into larger units. These larger units could then be manipulated easily within the database. For example, if a full_address construct is copied into numerous record definitions, it can be handled as if it were a single unit.

Prerelational databases such as IMS and IDMS supported ADTs, but strong typing features were not introduced until about 1990, with the first commercial object-oriented databases. Actually, other DBMSs have offered many of Oracle9i's "new" features for years. For example, Dr. Wong Kim developed UniSQL, a relational/object-oriented database that supports the concept of nested tables. In UniSQL, a data field in a table can be a range of values or an entire table. In this way, the domain of values can be defined for a specific field in a relational database. Relationship data can be incorporated directly into a table structure using nested data tables.

Having considered the basic idea behind ADTs, we can investigate some of the compelling benefits to this approach. ADTs are useful within an Oracle9i design for several reasons:

■ Encapsulation — ADTs ensure uniformity and consistency because each type exists as a complete unit. Each type includes the data definitions, default values, and value constraints. Moreover, an ADT can interact with other ADTs. Regardless of where it appears in a database, the same logical data type always has the same definition, default values, and value constraints.
■ Reusability — common data structures can be reused within many definitions, ensuring uniformity and saving coding time.
■ Flexibility — the database object designer is able to model the real world by creating real-world representations of data.

If the data types are properly analyzed and incorporated into the database object model, abstract data typing is a powerful tool. Next, we'll consider implementing abstract data typing in Oracle9i.

The requirement to model all types at their lowest level was one of the shortcomings of Oracle7. For example, the address information of a customer could be accessed only by manipulating street_address, city_address, and zip_code as three separate statements. Oracle9i makes it possible to create an ADT called full_address and manipulate it as if it were a single data type. This is a huge improvement for Oracle, but as already mentioned, prerelational databases supported this construct.

A data type composed of subtypes has always been available to COBOL users. For example, a full address can be defined in COBOL as follows:

```
05  CUSTOMER-ADDRESS.
    07 STREET-ADDRESS       PIC X(80).
    07 CITY-ADDRESS         PIC X(80).
    07 ZIP-CODE             PIC X(5).
```

The CUSTOMER-ADDRESS can then be treated as if it were a single entity, like this:

```
MOVE CUSTOMER-ADDRESS TO PRINT-REC.
MOVE SPACES TO CUSTOMER-ADDRESS.
```

A customer_address data type can be defined in an object database as follows:

```
CREATE TYPE customer_address (
    street_address       CHAR(20),
    city_address         CHAR(20),
    state_name           CHAR(2)
      CONSTRAINT STATE_NAME IN ('CA','NY','IL','GA','FL')
,
    zip_code             NUMBER(9)) DEFAULT VALUE 0;
```

The data type definition contains much more than just the data and the data size. Default values can also be assigned to the data types and value constraints specified. When the object is created, default values are assigned and the constraint checks occur. In this way, the database designer is assured complete control over the data definition and the values inserted into the data type. Customer_address can then be manipulated as a valid data type and it can be used to create tables and select data as follows:

```
CREATE TABLE CUSTOMER (
    full_name            cust_name,
    full_address         customer_address,
    . . .
    );
```

Once an Oracle table is defined, you can reference full_address in your SQL, just as if it were a single data type:

```
SELECT DISTINCT full_address FROM CUSTOMER;

INSERT INTO CUSTOMER VALUES (
    full_name ('ANDREW','S.','BURLESON'),
    full_address('123 1st st.','Minot, ND','74635');

UPDATE CUSTOMER (full_address) VALUES ' ';
```

It is important to note that the Oracle SQL SELECT statements change when rows are accessed that contain ADTs. Here is the required Oracle SQL syntax to select a component within the full_address type:

```
SELECT full_address.zip_code
FROM CUSTOMER
WHERE
full_address.zip_code LIKE '144%';
```

By taking the concept of ADTs one step further, we can see how ADTs can be nested within other data types.

Nesting ADTs

ADTs were introduced primarily to give the database designer the ability to reuse components consistently across the entire database domain. DBAs need to be comfortable nesting ADTs within other ADTs, because data types are often created to include other data types. For example, a data type could be created that includes the data in an existing table. That data type could then be used to define a new table, as follows:

```
CREATE TYPE
    customer_stuff
AS OBJECT (
    full_name            customer_name,
    home_address         customer_address
    business_address     customer_address);
```

After the customer_stuff type is defined, the table definition becomes simple:

```
CREATE TABLE CUSTOMER (customer_data    customer_stuff);
```

Nesting ADTs in this way allows the duplication of the object-oriented concept of encapsulation. In other words, groups of related data types are placed into a container that is completely self-contained while retaining the full capability of the innate relational data types, such as INT and CHAR.

Nested ADTs are displayed in the same fashion as the sample queries seen earlier, except that the target data types require several dots to delimit the levels of nesting within the data structure. For example, the query below displays the street_address for a customer:

```
SELECT
    customer_stuff.customer_name.zip_code
FROM
    CUSTOMER
WHERE
    customer_stuff.customer_name.zip_code like '144%';
```

The above reference to zip_code must be preceded with customer_name since it is nested in this data type. In turn, the customer_name data type is nested within the customer_stuff data type. The proper SQL reference to zip_code is therefore expressed as follows:

```
customer_stuff.customer_name.zip_code.
```

With this general understanding of how ADTs function and operate within Oracle9*i*, we are ready to see how pointers are used within Oracle to establish relationships between table rows.

Design with Oracle OIDs

It is necessary to understand exactly what OIDs represent in Oracle9*i* and how they are implemented before we discuss navigating the database with pointers. Each record in a database has a unique database address in prerelational databases. The addresses correspond to a physical database block, similar to Oracle ROWIDs. The offset or displacement of the target record into the block is included in the address. For example, an address of 552:3 refers to the third record in block number 552 of the database. These addresses can be stored inside other records once defined. This method allows one record to point to another record. In prerelational databases, these pointers are the foundation of relationships between entities.

Modern object databases store objects in an object table with an assigned OID. An OID is guaranteed to be globally unique. Each OID consists of a 128 B hexadecimal value. An OID cannot be used to locate an object instance by itself. Only a REF (or reference, discussed later in this chapter) containing location data can be used to locate an object instance.

The concept of the ROWID, introduced in Oracle7, is also used in Oracle9*i* to uniquely identify each row in each table in a database. The ROWID in Oracle7 is a VARCHAR2 representation of a binary value shown in hexadecimal format. It is displayed as:

```
bbbbbbbb.ssss.ffff
```

where:

- bbbbbbbb is the block ID
- ssss is the sequence in the block
- ffff is the file ID

The ROWID can be used to detect and eliminate duplicate rows in instances where a primary key for a table allows duplicate values. ROWIDs for duplicate customers are displayed in the following SQL:

```
SELECT
  ROWID,
     cust_no
FROM
      CUSTOMER a
WHERE
a.cust_nbr >
    (SELECT
        MIN (b.ROWID)
        FROM
        CUSTOMER b
        WHERE
        a.cust_nbr = b.cust_nbr
    );
```

The concept of objects and OIDs is new in Oracle9*i*. Objects in Oracle9*i* have identifiers attached to ROWIDs, giving an EXTENDED ROWID format. This format is 10 B long instead of the 6 B format used in Oracle7. The

ROWID in Oracle9*i* is a VARCHAR2 representation of a base 64 number. The Oracle9*i* ROWID is displayed as:

```
oooooo.fff.bbbbbb.sss
```

where:

- oooooo is the data object number
- fff is the relative file number
- bbbbbb is the block number
- sss is the slot number

Oracle9*i* gives DBAs the ability to create a distinct OID that uniquely identifies each row within a table. These OIDs are 128 B in length, as noted. Oracle guarantees that OIDs will remain unique to the database software even after they have been deleted. OIDs are similar to traditional pointers in legacy databases because they can point to any row in a database once they have been embedded into the column. We have already mentioned that many prerelational databases used pointers and employed linked-list data structures. These data structures provided embedded pointers in the prefix of each database entity.

The pointers established one-to-many and many-to-many relationships among entities. The design of pointer-based databases was elegant since foreign keys were not needed to establish data relationships, but difficult implementation problems remained. The programmer had to remember the location, name, and type of each pointer in the database, making navigation a chore in network databases, such as CA-IDMS® database, and hierarchical databases, such as IMS. Considering these limitations, a declarative language such as SQL is a luxury.

Oracle database design is dramatically altered by the introduction of OIDs. SQL joins are no longer required to extract the values in an object since the OID can simply be dereferenced. Unfortunately, there is a price to pay: special utility programs are required to sweep every affected object in the database when a new OID is added. This is because the data relationships are hard linked with embedded pointers. Also, when an Oracle9*i* object containing an OID is deleted, the designer must still keep track of it. Otherwise, it is possible to have orphan OIDs that point to deleted objects. Oracle9*i* will alert you if an OID reference points to a deleted object by returning a True value with the SQL extension IF oid_column IS DANGLING.

Having clarified the concept of OIDs, we can investigate how to use pointers to navigate Oracle databases as an alternative to using JOIN operations to navigate between tables.

Navigating with Pointers (OIDs)

Prior to Oracle9i, relational databases required that rows be addressed by the contents of their data values (with the exception of the ROWID construct). Oracle9i gives database designers an alternative access method for rows — the OID. For example, consider the following Oracle query:

```
SELECT
        customer_stuff
FROM
        CUSTOMER
WHERE
        customer_ID = 38373;
```

Oracle9i also allows the use of SQL to address rows by their OIDs, permitting the following pointer-based navigation:

```
SELECT
        customer_stuff
FROM
        CUSTOMER
WHERE
    OID = :host_variable;
```

The concept of retrieval by OIDs supplies Oracle database designers with a powerful new navigational tool. It means that you can navigate your database one row at a time with PL/SQL, capturing an OID as you retrieve a row and using that OID to access another row, and so on. However, in Oracle SQL, the access path is usually determined at runtime by the SQL optimizer and therefore remains hidden. Now that we have a sophisticated understanding of OID-based navigation, we are ready to see how an Oracle database can be designed to contain repeating groups within a row definition. The introduction of repeating groups violates Codd's 1NF rule, so this feature is called non-1NF design.

DESIGN WITH VARRAY TABLES

The concept of repeating data items within an object has been repugnant to Oracle designers for many years. The tenets of data normalization dictated that the first step toward a clean data model was the removal of repeating data items. Even so, many of the earlier databases, such as IDMS, allowed repeating groups to be defined. The UniSQL database was the first to implement the introduction of lists of values into relational databases. Initially, non-1NF modeling raised the ire of the titans of relational modeling and was treated with suspicion. Repeating groups soon proved their utility, however, and became more respectable. C.J. Date introduced the set concept into the relational model to allow this construct to fit into the relational paradigm. Database designers now recognize that there are specific instances where the use of repeating groups improve an Oracle9*i* database design.

In an environment where 1NF is violated and repeating groups are introduced into tables, there is a need for a set of rules to specify when repeating groups are acceptable. The following guidelines address this need:

- The size of repeating data items should be small.
- Repeating data items should be stationary and rarely changed.
- Repeating data should never be queried as a set. In other words, you should never select all of the repeating values within a single SQL query.

This scenario illustrates the principle: suppose a university database needs to include the information that a student can take the ACT exam up to three times. There are only two choices without using repeating groups:

1. Unique columns can be created within the student table, assigning each repeating group a subscript, as follows:

```
CREATE TABLE STUDENT (
     student_ID       NUMBER(5),
     . . .
     act_score_one    NUMBER(3),
     act_score_two    NUMBER(3),
     act_score_three NUMBER(3))
```

2. The repeating groups can be normalized out and moved into another table, like this:

```
CREATE TABLE ACT_SCORE (
     student_ID       NUMBER(5),
     act_score        NUMBER(3));
```

Contrast the above with how the repeating group might be implemented:

```
CREATE TYPE act_type as VARRAY(3) OF act_score;
```

We have defined a data structure that can use an implied subscript to reference the data. For example, to insert the test scores for Don Burlington, we could enter:

```
INSERT INTO
    STUDENT
act_score(
    VALUES
        300
        566
        624)
WHERE
    student_name.last_name = 'Burlington'
AND
    student_name.first_name = 'Don';
```

We can query the `act_scores` by referring to the subscript of the data item in order to select the test score for Don Burlington, as follows:

```
SELECT
    act_score(1),
    act_score(2),
    act_score(3)
FROM
    STUDENT
WHERE
    student_name.last_name = 'Burlington'
AND
    student_name.first_name = 'Don';
```

This gives a basic understanding of the use of repeating values within a database object or relational table. We'll look at the advantages and disadvantages of this approach before determining when to use repeating groups.

Advantages of Repeating Groups

Improved performance is the main advantage of designing repeating groups. Repeating groups are available whenever a table row is fetched.

Previously, Oracle7 required the repeating group to be joined with another table. Moreover, as the above example illustrates, less disk space is consumed because another table need not be created to hold the ACT scores and the necessity of duplicating a foreign key into the new table is avoided. If another table is nevertheless created, the student_ID for each and every row of the ACT_SCORE table will have to be redundantly duplicated.

Disadvantages of Repeating Groups

The primary disadvantage of repeating groups is that Oracle SQL cannot easily query them as a separate set of values. For example, a query to see all students who have received an ACT score greater than 500 cannot be performed without writing a PL/SQL snippet such as the following:

```
DECLARE CURSOR c1 AS SELECT * FROM STUDENT;

     FOR score IN c1
     LOOP

        Fetch c1 into :score;

        FOR i = 1 to 3
        LOOP
           IF act_score(i) > 500
           THEN
                PRINT student_name
           END IF
        END LOOP
     END LOOP
```

Oracle9*i* SQL provides a rather clumsy alternative with the use of the SQL UNION operator. This involves creating a temporary table to hold the values in a single column, as shown:

```
create table temp as
(
select act_score(1) from student
union
select act_score(2) from student
union
select act_score(3) from student
```

```
)
select act_score from temp where act_score > 500;
)
```

Determining When to Use Repeating Groups

This leaves a simple central question: Do the advantages of enhanced performance and disk savings justify the use of repeating groups? Let's employ both techniques to the above example to answer this question. First, we remove the repeating group of act_score and place the scores in a table called ACT_SCORE. The table can easily be queried to get the list of students:

```
SELECT student_name
FROM STUDENT, ACT_SCORE
WHERE
    ACT_SCORE.student_ID = STUDENT.student_ID
    AND
    act_score > 500;
```

When we use repeating groups, we cannot know in advance how many cells contain data. Therefore, we must test to see how many values are present. To test whether the act_score column is NULL, we add the following special code to our example:

```
FOR i - 1 to 3
LOOP
    IF act_score(i) IS NOT NULL
    THEN
        . . .
    END LOOP
```

Repeating groups can be very useful within an Oracle9*i* design if the repeating groups are small and have the same number of repeating values. Repeating groups will greatly enhance performance in these cases, allowing us to avoid the additional work involved in joining several tables.

Next, we'll see how repeating values appear in the Oracle object/relational model and discuss how they interact with ADTs.

Repeating Groups and ADTs

Repeating groups are indicated in the Oracle9*i* engine by use of the varying-array language construct of PL/SQL (the VARRAY). Repeating groups are declared within table columns by using the VARRAY mechanism.

Oracle9*i* permits repeating groups to be introduced in two ways. We can either define repeating groups of data items or repeating groups of OIDs with rows in another table. We'll consider OIDs first and then examine repeating groups of data values using an equivalent structure.

Repeating Groups of OIDs

Repeating groups of OIDs are best understood through an example. The SQL seen below adds a repeating group called job_history to a customer table. To begin, a TYPE needs to be created called job_history with a maximum of three values:

```
CREATE TYPE customer_address (
        street_address      CHAR(20),
        city_address        CHAR(20),
        state_name          CHAR(2),
        zip_code            CHAR(5));

CREATE TYPE job_details AS OBJECT (
        job_dates               CHAR(80),
        job_employer_name       CHAR(80),
        job_title               CHAR(80),
        job_address             customer_address);

CREATE TYPE job_history (
        VARRAY(3) OF REF job_details);
```

After defining the data types, we can use them to create the Oracle9*i* object:

```
CREATE TABLE CUSTOMER (
        customer_name       full_name,
        cust_address        customer_address,
        prior_jobs          job_history);

CREATE TABLE JOB_HISTORY OF job_details;
```

We have created a repeating list of references. We can now store job_history objects, capture the OIDs for these objects, and store them as reference columns in the prior_jobs column. We are now ready to extract the data from the remote object using the following DEREF statement. As we know from basic programming, when a pointer type is placed inside the DEREF function, the data corresponding to the pointer location is returned:

```
SELECT DEREF(CUSTOMER.prior_jobs.job_title(3))
  FROM CUSTOMER
  WHERE
  CUSTOMER.customer_name.last_name LIKE 'JONES%';
```

Accessing remote job_history rows by OID is much faster than doing so with an SQL join, as you probably suspected. However, another Oracle9*i* method is even faster than dereferencing an OID. A repeating group can be stored directly inside a table with repeating groups of data values. Let's investigate how these repeating groups of data values can appear in Oracle9*i*.

Repeating Groups of Data Values

As we have seen, repeating groups can be indicated using the VARRAY construct. It should come as no surprise, then, that the job_history item can be declared with a VARRAY mechanism. For example:

```
CREATE TYPE customer_address (
      street_address      CHAR(20),
      city_address        CHAR(20),
      zip_code            CHAR(5));

CREATE TYPE job_details (
      job_dates           CHAR(80),
      job_employer_name   CHAR(80),
      job_title           CHAR(80)
      job_address         customer_address);

CREATE TYPE job_history (
      VARRAY(3) OF job_details);
```

Now the CUSTOMER table can be created using the data types already defined:

```
CREATE TABLE CUSTOMER (
      customer_name       full_name,
```

```
    cust_address        customer_address,
    prior_jobs          job_history);
```

A job_history table has been created with three details. We have seen that prior_jobs must be subscripted to inform the database which of the three items are wanted. This is done with the following code:

```
SELECT
    CUSTOMER.prior_jobs.job_title(3)
FROM
    CUSTOMER
WHERE
    CUSTOMER.customer_name.last_name LIKE 'CARSON%';
```

A repeating list has been created within our table definition (Figure 6.6). The street address of the first previous employer is selected by the following code:

```
SELECT
    CUSTOMER.prior_jobs.job_address.street_address(1)
FROM
    CUSTOMER
WHERE
    CUSTOMER.customer_name.last_name LIKE 'CARSON%';
```

It is important to note that repeating groups in Oracle9i can contain either data or pointers to rows within other tables. But what if nested data types themselves have repeating groups? It was easy to create a record that contained a finite repeating group in prerelational databases. For example, a record definition could contain three repeating groups of job history information in COBOL:

```
03 EMPLOYEE.
    05 EMPLOYEE-NAME                    PIC X(80).
    05 JOB-HISTORY OCCURS 3 TIMES.
        07 JOB-DATE                     PIC X(80).
        07 JOB-EMPLOYER-NAME  PIC X(80).
        07 JOB-TITLE                    PIC X(80).
        07 EMPLOYER-ADDRESS
            09 STREET-ADDRESS           PIC X(80).
            09 CITY-ADDRESS             PIC X(80).
            09 ZIP-CODE                 PIC X(80);
```

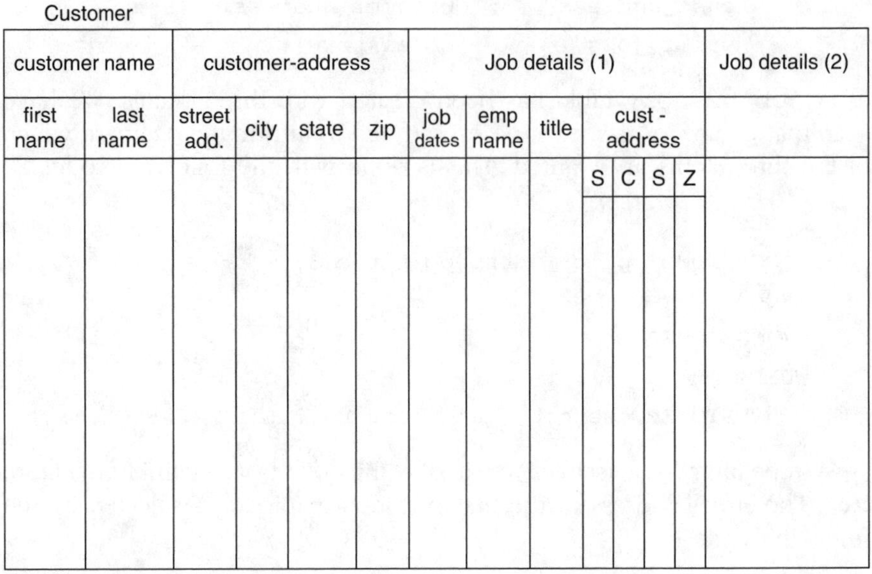

Customer

customer name		customer-address				Job details (1)							Job details (2)
first name	last name	street add.	city	state	zip	job dates	emp name	title	cust - address				
									S	C	S	Z	

Figure 6.6 A Repeating List within an Oracle Table Column

The JOB-HISTORY component is referenced by a subscript in COBOL, as the following examples clarify:

```
MOVE JOB-HISTORY(2) TO OUT-REC.
MOVE 'DATABASE ADMINISTRATOR' TO JOB-TITLE(3).
```

Database designers will notice that 1NF is directly violated by the use of Oracle9*i* VARRAYs.

If repeating values within a table cell are permissible, why not allow a reference to an entirely new table? Oracle9*i* provides this option with the nested table. We'll look at pointing to tables in the next section.

Pointing to Tables

Imagine a database that allows nesting of tables within tables. In such a database, a single cell of one table can point to another table. While this concept might initially seem foreign, it is easier to understand if you keep in mind that many real-world objects are composed of subparts.

Recall our discussion of OIDs. A pointer must be unique and permanent to establish data relationships between database entities. A relational ROWID is used to identify a row in relational databases. Because a ROWID is the number of a physical database block and row, a problem arises because it could be moved unintentionally to another block or, even worse, accidentally deleted. Oracle created OIDs for each row to solve this problem. With OIDs, each row is always identified uniquely, regardless of the physical placement of the row or its status. An OID associated with a row will never be reused by Oracle, even if the row is deleted.

To create a table with OIDs, a data type containing all the necessary row information must be created. Assume that the data type customer_stuff contains the required data structures for a customer table in the example below. The table could be created in a traditional relational database as shown:

```
CREATE TABLE CUSTOMER (customer_data   customer_stuff);
```

The table creation syntax is changed slightly when using OIDs. The following example creates exactly the same table as the preceding one, except that the table contains an OID for each row within the customer table:

```
CREATE TABLE CUSTOMER OF customer_stuff;
```

The utility of the relational model has always been seriously hampered by the inability to directly represent aggregate objects. Relational views were formerly required to assemble aggregate objects. Object technology professors used to ridicule the relational model's inability to represent aggregate objects. Finally, Oracle users have the ability to represent real-world objects without resorting to views by utilizing nested ADTs.

Let's see how Oracle represents this type of recursive data relationship. A TYPE definition is created for a list of orders in the following SQL. The pointers for the list of orders might become a column within an Oracle table, as indicated:

```
CREATE TYPE order_set
    AS TABLE OF order;

CREATE TYPE customer_stuff (
    customer_id                   integer,
    customer_full_name    full_name,
    customer_full_address customer_address,
    . . .
    order_list                    order_set);

CREATE TABLE CUSTOMER OF customer_stuff;
```

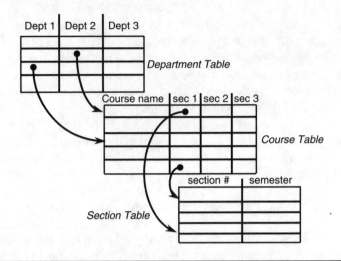

Figure 6.7 Oracle Pointers to Other Database Rows

We can see the new syntax style for table creation here. The following two table declarations are the same, except that the syntax establishes OIDs in the CREATE TABLE OF statement. This is done so that other tables can contain references to rows in the CUSTOMER table:

■ Without OIDs — CREATE TABLE CUSTOMER (cust_data customer_stuff);
■ With OIDs — CREATE TABLE CUSTOMER OF customer_stuff AS OBJECT;

Either way, we can now define a pointer column called order_list in the CUSTOMER table. This pointer refers to a list of pointers. Each cell of the list contains pointers to rows in the ORDER table (Figure 6.7).

Figure 6.7 shows how the pointer structure looks conceptually. However, to implement these repeating groups of pointers, object/relational databases must use internal arrays. Oracle9*i* uses variable-length arrays to represent this structure.

In a pointer table, each column contains a nested list of pointers. Each cell within a column also contains a list of pointers to rows in the ORDER table. The three orders for this customer can be prejoined with the ORDER table using object-oriented SQL extensions, as follows:

```
UPDATE CUSTOMER
    SET order_list (
        SELECT REF(order)      /* this returns the OIDs
    from all order rows */
```

```
FROM ORDER
WHERE
order_date = SYSDATE
AND
ORDER.customer_ID = (123)
)
```

We see that the use of the REF operator returns the reference, or OID, of the requested rows. This is similar to the retrieval of ROWIDs in a relational database, except that now the row information is stored inside a relational table.

We are now ready to see how navigation between tables can be done without having to join tables together. In our earlier discussion we mentioned that the object/relational model provides two ways to retrieve data from the database. We can gather the required information either by using SQL to specify the desired data, where the access path is chosen by the SQL optimizer, or by navigating the database one row at a time. The following code returns the content of the three rows contained in the order_list VARRAY:

```
SELECT
    DEREF(order_list)
FROM
    CUSTOMER
WHERE
    customer_id = 123;
```

The important concept in the above example is that navigation between tables can be accomplished without ever performing an SQL join. Take a moment to consider the possibilities. There is never a need to embed a foreign key in the order record for the CUSTOMER table because the pointers can be stored in each customer row. This prevents a relational join between the CUSTOMER and ORDER tables, but since the ability to navigate between customers and orders with pointers has been maintained it makes no difference.

Of course, the pointers from customers to orders work in only one direction. There is no method to get from the ORDER table to the CUSTOMER table unless a pointer has been embedded that points to the row containing the customer for each order. This can be done by creating an owner reference inside each order row containing the OID of the customer who placed the order.

Let's consider how Oracle9*i* represents this type of recursive data relationship:

```
CREATE TYPE order_set
    AS TABLE OF ORDER;

CREATE TABLE CUSTOMER (
     customer_id                integer,
     customer_full_name         full_name,
     customer_full_address      customer_address,
     . . .
     order_list                 order_set);
```

We see that the ORDER table is nested within the CUSTOMER table (more about nesting in the next section). Now we need to populate the new table structure, as below:

```
INSERT INTO CUSTOMER VALUES (
    full_name ('ANDREW','S.','BURLESON),
    customer_address('246 1st St.','Minot, ND','74635');
```

Three orders for this customer could be added as follows:

```
INSERT INTO ORDER values order_id, customer_id, order_date (
    9961
    123,
    SYSDATE);

INSERT INTO ORDER values order_id, customer_id, order_date (
    9962
    123,
    SYSDATE);

INSERT INTO ORDER values order_id, customer_id, order_date (
    9962
    123,
    SYSDATE);
```

We are now in a position to appreciate the performance gain. The CUSTOMER table can be prejoined with the ORDER table to add the three orders for this customer:

```
UPDATE CUSTOMER
    SET order_list (
        SELECT REF(order)       /* OID reference */
        FROM ORDER
        WHERE
        order_date = SYSDATE
        AND
        order.customer_ID = (123)
    )
```

The `order_list` entry in the CUSTOMER table now contains pointers to the three orders that have been placed by this customer. These pointers can be referenced without having to perform the task of a relational join:

```
SELECT
    DEREF(order_list)
FROM
    CUSTOMER
WHERE
    customer_id = 123;
    /* This will return 3 rows in the order table *
/
```

This query returns a pointer to the three rows in the ORDER table. It is now a trivial matter to dereference these pointers to retrieve the contents of the ORDER table. It might look something like this, depending on the vendor implementation of SQL:

```
SELECT
    DEREF(order_list)
FROM
    CUSTOMER
WHERE
    customer_ID = 123;
```

Now it's time to look deeper into the ability of Oracle9*i* to nest tables.

USING NESTED TABLES

We have seen that the new object/relational database contains an interesting pointer structure that permits a single cell in an entity to encapsulate a whole other entity. In this way, structures can be created where objects (or tables) can be nested within other objects (or tables). This means that values in a single column inside a table can contain an entire table in an object/relational database. In turn, these subtable tables can have single column values that point to other tables, and so on, ad infinitum.

This new data structure presents exciting possibilities for modeling complex aggregate objects, even though applications for it may not be obvious. Database designers can create a structure in C++ object-oriented databases, such as ONTOS and Objectivity, where an object contains a list of pointers. Each of these pointers refers to a separate list of pointers. These pointers, in turn, point to other objects in the database. This structure is known as **char in C language parlance, which is called a pointer to a pointer to a character.

This structure is implemented in Oracle9*i* with a store table. A store table is an internal table that is tightly linked to the parent table. The data storage characteristics of the parent table are inherited by the store table. These characteristics include the initial extent of the table as well as the size of any new extent.

A cell is defined as a pointer to a table in the highest level table. Each column value within the column pointing to a whole table must contain a pointer to a table with exactly the same definition. In other words, every pointer within the column is restricted to pointing to tables with an identical definition.

In practice, it may appear that each cell points to a whole table, but the object/relational databases actually implement this structure with the special store table.

A store table is essentially nothing more than an internal table with a fixed set of columns that is subordinate to the parent table. A simple example will illustrate the use of this data structure. Returning to the university database, the database has a many-to-many relationship between courses and student entities. A course has many students; a student can take many courses. This relationship between students and courses would be implemented in a traditional relational system by creating a junction table between the student and course entities. The primary keys from the student and course tables would then be copied into the junction table. This table is called GRADE in our example and the grade entity contains the student_ID and course_ID columns as foreign keys.

Let's see how this could be implemented using pointers to whole tables. In a traditional relational implementation, to generate a class schedule for a student we would need to select the student row, join with the GRADE table, and finally join with the CLASS table, as follows:

```
SELECT
        student_full_name,
        course_name,
        course_date,
        grade
FROM
        STUDENT, GRADE, COURSE
WHERE
        student_last_name = 'Burleson'
        AND
        STUDENT.student_ID = GRADE.student_ID
        AND
        GRADE.course_ID = COURSE.course_ID;
```

We can avoid the three-way SQL join of the tables by choosing to create a store table that is subordinate to the STUDENT table. This table would contain the course_name, course_date, and grade for each student:

```
CREATE TYPE
    student_list (
        student_full_name          full_name,
        student_full_address       full_address,
        grade                      CHAR(1));

CREATE TYPE student_list_type AS TABLE OF student_list;

CREATE TABLE
    COURSE (
        course_name                VARCHAR(20),
        dept_ID                    NUMBER(4),
        credit_hrs                 NUMBER(2),
        student_roster             student_list_type);
```

We see here that the student_roster column of the COURSE table contains a pointer to a table of TYPE student_list_type. Herein lies the illusion. While it appears that each distinct column value points to a whole table, the column actually points to a set of rows within the store table. The store table is common to all of the columns that contain

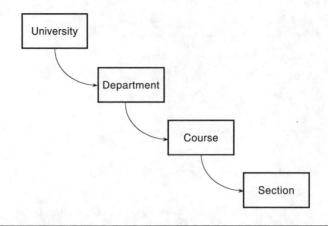

Figure 6.8   A Hierarchy of Data Relationships

this pointer structure. The store table also contains a special OID that points to the owner of the row in the parent table.

The concept of nesting tables within tables is an excellent method for modeling hierarchical structures, but there is still some question about the utility of this data structure with actual data applications. The main advantage of nested tables is that they simplify queries because a single SELECT statement returns the desired rows of a store table. There remains some question about whether it is better to use this structure or to simply create another table because the nested table is still just another table with the same column structure for each row.

With this basic understanding of OIDs and pointers, we are ready to look at one of the most sophisticated constructs in Oracle9*i* — the multidimensional array of OIDs.

Understanding Multidimensional Pointers and Oracle

We'll begin with a simple example of a natural hierarchy of data relationships (Figure 6.8) in order to understand multidimensional pointers. In this example, we see that each university has many departments, each department offers many courses, and each course offers many sections. This is a natural descending hierarchy of one-to-many relationships.

There are several options for modeling this type of descending one-to-many data relationship. Each entity would exist as a table in a traditional relational database, with the primary key of the owner table copied into the member table. The object/relational model offers an alternative to modeling this structure. We see in Listing 6.7 how Oracle9*i* might implement a hierarchical data structure.

Listing 6.7   Implementing a Hierarchical Data Structure

```
CREATE TYPE full_name (
        first_name    VARCHAR(20),
        MI            CHAR(1),
        last_name     VARCHAR(20));
CREATE TYPE section_type (
    section_number   NUMBER(5),
    instructor_name  full_name,
    semester         CHAR(3),
    building         VARCHAR(20),
    room             CHAR(4),
    days_met         CHAR(5),
    time_met         CHAR(20));
CREATE TABLE SECTION OF section_type;
CREATE TYPE section_array AS VARRAY(10) OF section_type;
CREATE TYPE course_type (
    course_ID        number(5),
    course_name      varchar(20),
    credit_hours     number(2),
    section_list     section_array);
CREATE TABLE COURSE OF course_type;
CREATE TYPE course_array AS VARRAY(20) OF course_type;
CREATE TYPE dept_type (
    dept_name            varchar(20),
    chairperson_name     full_name,
    course_list          course_array);
CREATE TABLE DEPARTMENT OF dept_type;
```

We see that pointers allow fast access from owner to member in the hierarchy. But, where are the owner pointers? A hierarchy must first be defined before we have the necessary definitions to include the pointers. Owner pointers can be added using the ALTER TYPE statement, as follows:

```
ALTER TYPE section_type
    ADD COLUMN course_owner_pointer      course_type;

ALTER TYPE course_type
    ADD COLUMN department_owner_pointer department_type;
```

We have now created a two-way pointer structure where all the owner rows within the hierarchy point to the member rows and all member rows point to their owners. We must remain aware, however, that these are merely data structures. The programmer must assign these pointers when the rows are created.

This Oracle9*i* data structure is similar to the C language `**char` data structure (as mentioned earlier). The department has an array of pointers to courses in our Oracle9*i* example, which, in turn, contain arrays of pointers to sections.

The question we now face is how to query these pointers with Oracle SQL? Most object/relational vendors are implementing the `CAST` and `MULTISET` extensions to SQL to accommodate the new object features. A query to populate the `STUDENT_LIST` internal table is implemented as shown below:

```
INSERT INTO
    COURSE (STUDENT_LIST)
    (CAST
        (MULTISET
            (SELECT
                    student_name,
                    student_address,
                    grade
            FROM
                    GRADE, STUDENT
            WHERE
                    GRADE.course_name = 'CS101'
                    AND
                    GRADE.student_name = STUDENT.student_name
            )
        )
);
```

Those accustomed to pure relational syntax may feel that the new SQL extensions are rather foreign.

With an understanding of how OIDs and VARRAYs operate within Oracle9*i*, we can consider the performance implications of these constructs to the Oracle database.

Reviewing the Implications of OIDs for Oracle Design

By now, it should be clear that the capabilities of ADTs provide database designers with a very powerful tool. It gives programmers the ability to:

- Store repeating groups inside a table cell
- Nest tables within tables
- Navigate using pointers to access relational data
- Represent aggregate objects

Consider the ramifications of pointer-based navigation for processing relational data. Imagine the possibilities of being free from SQL. Oracle9*i* allows us to navigate a data model without the cumbersome tasks of joining tables together. The new ability to represent complex objects is even more important. This means that we can precreate aggregate objects without having to construct them from their subobjects every time we need them. Methods can be attached to aggregate objects because they exist independently. Additionally, precreated complex database objects are instantly available and streamline database performance.

The ability to represent real-world objects in the database is one of Oracle9*i*'s most exciting features. Traditional relational databases were hampered by the requirement that all data be stored at the most primitive level (i.e., 3NF) and that aggregate objects be created by combining tables. This restriction has been removed by Oracle9*i*. Aggregate objects can now be prebuilt from their components and stored within the database. Let's see how this works.

Designing Aggregate Objects

We need to understand the nature of aggregation within Oracle9*i* to effectively design an aggregate object. Oracle9*i* features a new object called order_form that contains pointers to its various components. It is never necessary to rebuild an order_form object unless items are added or deleted from it. The order_form object automatically picks up the new value when the quantity_ordered column in the order_line table is changed.

This is how it works. We first define a pointer that references the row representing the customer who placed an order. We'll assume that we already have an object for the entire customer row. We define the CUSTOMER table as follows:

```
CREATE TABLE CUSTOMER (customer_data    customer_adt);
```

We can now create a customer_ref TYPE that points to the customer:

```
CREATE TYPE customer_ref AS TABLE OF customer_adt;
```

We can do the same thing for the ORDER table row since we will be retrieving one order row.

```
CREATE TYPE order_ref AS TABLE OF order_adt;
```

Therefore, the reference to the customer and order rows will be the first component of the ORDER_FORM object:

```
CREATE TABLE ORDER_FORM (
    customer        customer_ref,
    order           order_ref);
```

We now have the customer and order data. We still need to establish pointers to represent the many-to-many relationships between the ORDER and ITEM tables. We accomplish this by defining a repeating group of every order_line for each order:

```
CREATE TYPE item_list
    AS TABLE OF order_line;
```

This code defines item_list. We next define ORDER_FORM:

```
CREATE TABLE ORDER_FORM (
    customer        customer_ref,
    order           order_ref,
    lines           item_list);
```

The model lacks only pointers to every item referenced in the ORDER_LINE table. But, how can we create them? The item_ID numbers of the order are unknown until the order_line rows are retrieved. Therefore, owner pointers inside each order_line row must be established so that the item table can be dereferenced. Let's assume that the LINE_ITEM table has been defined to include a reference pointer to the item table, as follows:

```
/* example of an owner pointer */
CREATE TYPE item_ref
    AS TABLE OF item;

CREATE TABLE LINE_ITEM (
    order_ID            integer,
    item_ID             integer,
    item_pointer        item_ref,
    quantity_ordered integer);
```

The data for the ORDER_FORM object is now ready to be displayed:

```
CREATE TABLE ORDER_FORM (
    customer          customer_ref,
    order             order_ref,
    lines             item_list);

SELECT
    DEREF(CUSTOMER.customer_last_name),
    DEREF . . .
    DEREF(ORDER.order_date),
    DEREF(ITEM_LIST.item_name),  /* if item is a foreign key
in line item */
    DEREF(ORDER.quantity_ordered)
    DEREF(DEREF(ORDER_LINE.item_pointer))  /* this returns
item data */
```

Now that we understand how to create Oracle9i objects, we are ready to couple these objects using Oracle9i methods. Coupling data and methods requires careful design. The process typically begins by specifying prototypes for each of the Oracle9i methods.

Designing with Oracle Methods

Successfully coupling Oracle9i data and methods requires the use of method prototypes. The following example shows a hierarchy of methods. If we use the data type definitions in the data dictionary and the psuedocode from the minispec it will facilitate our discussion. The example references a set of DFDs. The fill_order process is described in level one, including all of the lower level DFDs in which each process is listed, including the submethods within the process:

```
1 - fill_order
    1.1 - check_customer_credit
    1.2 - check_inventory
        1.2.1 - check_stock_level
        1.2.2 - generate_backorder_notice
        1.2.3 - decrement_inventory
        1.2.4 - prepare_packing_slip
    1.3 - prepare_invoice
        1.3.1 - compute_order_cost
        1.3.2 - compute_shipping_charges
```

```
1.3.3 - add_handling_charge
1.3.4 - assemble_invoice
```

This hierarchy helps us visualize how methods are nested within other methods. After the hierarchy has been developed, we can translate these processes into the database classes.

The lowest level DFDs represent functional primitives, processes that cannot be decomposed into smaller processes. It is obvious that functional primitive processes become methods, but does this mean that they will never have subcomponents? With the exception of standalone methods, such as a compute_shipping_charges method, a method will never have subcomponents if the analyst has designed the process properly.

Using the primitive processes, we can design a method that accepts the same values as noted on the DFD and returns those values to the retrieving program. For example, we might have a process called compute_shipping_charges that accepts a valid_in_stock_order as input. The process gathers the weight and cost of the items, computes the charges, and returns the shipping charge and total weight.

A prototype is essentially a formal definition of a method that describes all of the input and output data flows. The accepted form for a prototype is:

```
return_data_type Method_name
        (input_data_name_1  input_data_type_1,
        input_data_name_2 input_data_type_2,
        . . .);
```

Let's review the data types that methods can use before going into further detail. These data types can return a data value or they can be an input parameter for a method:

- INT — integer value
- VARCHAR — variable length character string
- TYPE — pointer to a data structure (identical to an Oracle9*i* OID)

Object novices are often confused by TYPE because it refers to pointers. A pointer in an object database is nothing more than an OID pointing to an object that supplies method values. The various types of OIDs must be carefully differentiated because Oracle9*i* supports strong data typing in the SCOPE clause of the CREATE TABLE statement. For example, a pointer to an order (*order) is quite different from a pointer to a customer (*customer) object. It is more efficient to use pointers than the data itself because the OID pointer is more compact.

As mentioned, Oracle9*i* fully supports strong typing. Oracle9*i* uses the SCOPE verb in the CREATE TABLE statement to limit the type of a reference column to a particular OID table. For example, if a customer table is defined with a VARRAY of OIDs consisting of customer orders, the SCOPE clause can be used to ensure that only OIDs from the ORDER table are stored within these columns.

In object database parlance, a prototype is designed for each process in the DFD. This is illustrated by examining how the prototype is designed for the compute_shipping_charges method. According to the DFD, compute_shipping_charges accepts a valid_in_stock_order and outputs the shipping_charge for the order. Therefore, the proto-type could return an integer (the shipping charge, defined as INT) from compute_shipping_charges and accept a pointer to an order object:

```
INT compute_shipping_charge(valid_in_stock_order *order);
```

Here we see the prototype details:

- INT — this says that the returned value will be an integer.
- compute_shipping_charge — this is the name of the procedure.
- valid_in_stock_order — this is the first parameter pass to the procedure.
- *order — this is the second parameter passed and the * indicates that it is a pointer data type, pointing to an ORDER object.

We assume for the purpose of this example that the valid_in_stock_order contains the following four values, which the process requires to compute the shipping charges:

1. Weight in pounds
2. Desired class of shipping
3. Origination zip code
4. Destination zip code

How can the data items be retrieved when the order is represented by an OID? The method retrieves the data by dereferencing the OID and accessing the order object. In other words, the method captures the OID and dictates SQL to retrieve data items from the object. The SQL within the compute_shipping_charges method might look like this:

```
select
      item_weight,
      shipping_class,
```

```
        origination_zip_code,
        destination_zip_code
    from
        order
    where
        order.oid = :valid_in_stock_order;
```

The function above yields the shipping charge, expressed as an integer. If the method has no pointer to the order object, the prototype for compute_shipping_charges becomes far more complicated, as the following shows:

```
    INT compute_shipping_charge
            (weight                  int,
            class                    char(1),
            origination_zip_code number(9),
            destination_zip_code number(9));
```

Note that INT refers to the data type of the value returned by the method. If the method does not return a value, INT is replaced by VOID. For example, a method called give_raise would not return a value and could be prototyped as:

```
    VOID give_raise(emp_ID number(9), percentage int);
```

Armed with this basic understanding of prototyping, we are ready to prototype some methods. We need to know the names and data types of all input data, as well as the name and data types of the returned value. These are generally derived from the DFDs in the initial systems analysis.

```
*order          fill_order(cust_info *customer);
int             check_customer_credit(cust_info *customer);
int             check_inventory(item_number int);
*invoice        prepare_invoice(valid_in_stock_order *order_form);
int             check_stock_level(item_number int);
*backorder      generate_backorder_request(item_number   int);
void            decrement_inventory(item_number int);
*packing_slip   prepare_packing_slip(valid_in_stock_order
                                    *order_form);
int             compute_order_cost(valid_in_stock_order
                                    *order_form);
int             compute_shipping_charges(valid_in_stock_order
                                    *order_form);
int             add_handling_charge(total_weight int);
```

```
*invoice       assemble_invoice(item_total_cost   int,
                                shipping_charge int,
                                handling_charge int);
```

Let's describe these prototypes to become more comfortable with the definitions. We see that some methods return an integer, some return values, and others return object pointers. It is not uncommon to combine assignment statements with method calls in object-oriented databases. For example, the following process code computes the shipping charges for the order and assigns the result to a variable called my_shipping_charges:

```
my_shipping_charges =
compute_shipping_charges(:my_order_form_OID);
```

In the same way, a method call can also return an OID. This means that an OID can be embedded into another object. We assume in the code below that the data type for order_OID has been defined as a pointer to an order. Two things can now be done in a single statement. The fill_order method can be initialized while simultaneously returning the OID of the new order object into the order_OID variable, as follows:

```
order_OID = fill_order(:cust_info);
```

The name and data type of every input and output variable has been specified for each method. It is required that each method be tested independently. The internal variable might be unknown to the calling method. This is called information hiding. It is used whenever private variables are declared within a method. One of the goals of object-oriented databases is to make each method a reusable procedure that can always be counted on to function properly. This is the foundation of object method design.

Let's introduce the Oracle9*i* model into this system. It should be obvious by now that several components are used to describe an object/relational database design. First, the object/relational model must be delineated for the base objects. Figure 6.9 displays the base classes in the order processing system and describes the indexes, tablespaces, and subclasses for each class definition.

Now take a look at the aggregate class diagram shown in Figure 6.10. Here, we see two aggregate class definitions, their internal pointer structures, and the index and tablespace information for all classes that are composed of pointers to other objects.

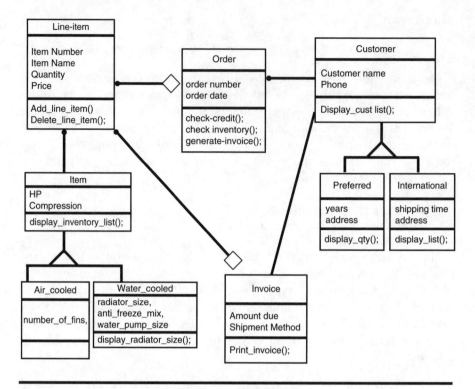

Figure 6.9 An Object/Relation Diagram for the Order Processing System

Note that the models show both base classes, as well as the aggregate classes. The problem now is mapping the method prototypes for these classes. Since all objects are represented as tables in the object/relational model, the aggregate object allows the owner table to be coupled with aggregate methods. The method informs the aggregate object in this way.

Automatic Method Generation

Most object-oriented and object/relational databases automatically create the basic methods for objects (e.g., new) when an object class is defined. These basic methods correspond to the INSERT, DELETE, and UPDATE SQL verbs and are used whenever objects are created. It is important to recognize that methods exist in several forms within a database engine:

- Standalone — these methods are not associated with a database class.
- Base class — these methods affect the lowest level objects in a database.
- Aggregate class — these methods operate on aggregate objects and reference data within component objects.

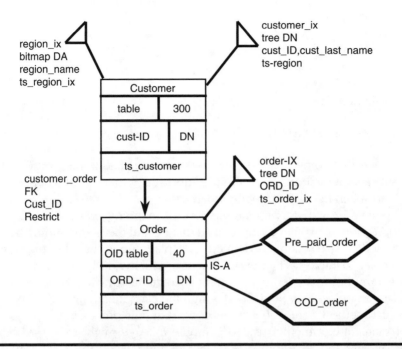

region_ix
bitmap DA
region_name
ts_region_ix

customer_ix
tree DN
cust_ID,cust_last_name
ts-region

Customer	
table	300
cust-ID	DN
ts_customer	

customer_order
FK
Cust_ID
Restrict

order-IX
tree DN
ORD_ID
ts_order_ix

Order	
OID table	40
ORD - ID	DN
ts_order	

IS-A

Pre_paid_order

COD_order

Figure 6.10   The Aggregate Class Diagram for the Order Processing System

However, more complex methods can be linked to their target objects. For example, an order_form object might contain a method called check_payment_history, which performs detailed checks into the prior payment history for a customer who is placing an order.

Let's analyze the methods that might be associated with these objects. If a method of the same name appears in multiple class definitions, the database first references the object and then searches for the method in the class hierarchy. The following example indicates some sample methods that might be associated with each type of student object.

```
Methods for student:

    Display_student();
    Compute_tuition();
    enroll_student();

Methods for graduate_student;

    assign_mentor();
    compute_tuition();
    update_thesis_status();
```

```
Methods for non_resident_students;

    Compute_tuition();
    record_transfer_statistics();

Methods for foreign_students;

    compute_tuition();
```

We see that some methods unique to the subclass appear only within the subclass definition. For example, `update_thesis_status` would have no meaning to an undergraduate student.

We have provided a general method for mapping processes with their database objects. We have emphasized that careful method planning occurs before a database schema is defined. This planning is critical in the design of an object database. The importance of careful method placement cannot be overemphasized. Method planning is crucial in Oracle9*i* because many types of an object may be defined within the class hierarchies, each having identical method names, but with vastly different processing.

To illustrate, a method called compute mileage might exist for both a sailboat class and an automobile class. The internals for the sailboat would use nautical miles while the automobile would use statute miles. Oracle9*i* allows a new method to be created that differentiates between the type of object used in either case. The new method will be known only to objects within that class of subclasses. Objects belonging to other classes will never know that the new method exists. This is called overloading. Overloading is extremely powerful because new code can be introduced into a system with absolute certainty that no unintended side effects will occur.

Now that we understand the performance implications of the Oracle9*i* object features for our database design, let's look at the design considerations within the base Oracle engine. Bear in mind that the most important factor in database performance is proper design. Proper design is crucial because no amount of tuning will correct a poorly designed database.

Stored Procedures and Oracle Tables

Objects such as stored procedures and triggers are becoming more popular, moving application code away from external programs and into the database engine. Oracle encouraged this trend in anticipation of the object-oriented features introduced in Oracle8. However, the Oracle DBA must be conscious of the increasing memory demands of stored procedures and plan carefully for the eventual storage of all database access code within the database.

Most Oracle databases today have only a small amount of code in stored procedures, but this is changing rapidly. Many compelling benefits accrue from placing all Oracle SQL inside stored procedures. These benefits include:

- Improved performance — stored procedures are loaded once into the SGA and remain there unless they become paged out. Subsequent runtimes of the stored procedures are far faster than external code.
- Coupling of data with behavior — relational tables can be coupled with the behaviors associated with them by using naming conventions. Oracle9*i* gives us the ability to store procedures that are directly associated with the database table through the use of methods. For example, if all behaviors associated with the EMPLOYEE table are prefixed with the table name (e.g., EMPLOYEE.hire, EMPLOYEE.give_raise), then the data dictionary can be queried to list all behaviors associated with a table (e.g., SELECT * FROM DBA_OBJECTS WHERE OWNER = 'EMPLOYEE') and code can be readily identified and reused.
- Isolation of code — all SQL is moved out of the external programs and into stored procedures. The application program becomes nothing more than a call to a stored procedure. This feature makes it a simple matter to interchange one database for another.

Stored procedures and triggers function faster than traditional code primarily because of Oracle's SGA. Once a procedure has been loaded into the SGA, it remains in the library cache until it is paged out of memory. Items are paged out of memory according to a LRU algorithm. The procedure will execute quickly once it has been loaded into the RAM memory of the shared pool. The trick is to prevent pool-thrashing during the period when many procedures are competing for a limited amount of library cache within the shared pool memory.

Two init.ora parameters emerge as more important than all other parameters combined for tuning Oracle. They are the db_block_buffers and the shared_pool_size parameters. These two parameters define the size of the in-memory region that Oracle consumes on startup and also determine the amount of storage available to cache data blocks, SQL, and stored procedures.

Oracle also provides the package construct. A package is essentially a collection of stored procedures and functions that can be organized in various ways. Stored procedures and functions for employees can be logically grouped together in an employee package as in the following example:

```
CREATE PACKAGE EMPLOYEE AS

    FUNCTION compute_raise_amount (percentage NUMBER);
    PROCEDURE hire_employee();
    PROCEDURE fire_employee();
    PROCEDURE list_employee_details();

END EMPLOYEE;
```

The code above creates a package to encapsulate all employee behaviors (Oracle functions and stored procedures) into a single package that will be added into Oracle's data dictionary. Stored procedures place the SQL directly into the database and out of the external application programs. The external programs are reduced to mere procedure calls.

The shared pool will become important as systems increasingly place process code within stored procedures. The shared pool consists of the following subpools:

- Dictionary cache
- Library cache
- Shared SQL areas
- Private SQL areas (these exist during `cursor open/cursor close`)
- Persistent area
- Runtime area

We mentioned that the shared pool utilizes a LRU algorithm to determine which objects are paged out of the shared pool. Fragments, or discontiguous chunks of memory, are created within the shared pool as this paging occurs.

This means that a large procedure that originally fit into memory may no longer fit into contiguous memory when it is reloaded after paging out. A problem can occur when the body of a package has been paged out of the SGA due to more recent (or more frequent) activity. The server might not find enough contiguous memory to reload the package body due to fragmentation. This would result in an ORA-4031 error. Paging can be avoided in Oracle by pinning packages in the SGA.

CONCLUSION

This chapter has dealt with the wealth of physical implementations of Oracle table storage structures with an eye toward using the appropriate physical structure to match the logical design model. We are now ready to conclude this book with a discussion of Oracle index design methods.

7

ORACLE INDEX DESIGN

INTRODUCTION

In Oracle, an index is used to speed up the time required to access table information. Internally, Oracle indexes are B-tree data structures in which each tree node can contain many sets of key values and ROWIDs.

In general, Oracle indexes exist for the purpose of preventing FTSs. FTSs create two problems. The main problem created by FTSs is the time lost in servicing a request, as each and every row of a table is read into Oracle's buffer pool. In addition to causing the task performance to suffer, a FTS also causes performance degradation at the system level.

When this happens, all other tasks on the system might have to incur additional I/O because the buffer block held by competing tasks will have been flushed by the FTS. As blocks are flushed from the buffer pool, other tasks are required to incur additional I/Os to reread information that would have remained in the buffer pool if the FTS had not been invoked.

Almost any Oracle table can benefit from the use of indexes. The only exception to this rule would be a small table that can be read in less than two-block I/Os. Two-block I/Os are used as this guideline because Oracle will need to perform at least one I/O to access the root node of the index tree and another I/O to retrieve the requested data.

For example, assume that a lookup table contains rows of 25 B each and you have configured Oracle to use 4 K block sizes. Because each data block would hold about 150 rows, using an index for up to 300 rows would not make processing any faster than a FTS.

Let's start with a review of Oracle index design basics and then move on to discuss design of indexes for high-speed data access within Oracle.

INDEX DESIGN BASICS

Oracle includes numerous data structures to improve the speed of Oracle SQL queries. Taking advantage of the low cost of disk storage, Oracle includes many new indexing algorithms that dramatically increase the speed with which Oracle queries are serviced. This section explores the internals of Oracle indexing; reviews the standard B-tree index, bitmap indexes, FBIs, and index-organized tables (IOTs); and demonstrates how these indexes may dramatically increase the speed of Oracle SQL queries.

Oracle uses indexes to avoid the need for large-table FTSs and disk sorts, which are required when the SQL optimizer cannot find an efficient way to service the SQL query. I begin our look at Oracle indexing with a review of standard Oracle B-tree index methodologies.

The Oracle B-Tree Index

The oldest and most popular type of Oracle indexing is a standard B-tree index, which excels at servicing simple queries. The B-tree index was introduced in the earliest releases of Oracle and remains widely used with Oracle (Figure 7.1). B-tree indexes are used to avoid large sorting operations. For example, a SQL query requiring 10,000 rows to be presented in sorted order will often use a B-tree index to avoid the very large sort required to deliver the data to the end user.

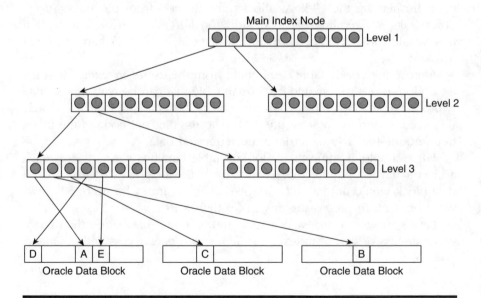

Figure 7.1   An Oracle B-Tree Index

Oracle offers several options when creating an index using the default B-tree structure. It allows you to index on multiple columns (concatenated indexes) to improve access speeds. Also, it allows for individual columns to be sorted in different orders. For example, we could create a B-tree index on a column called `last_name` in ascending order and have a second column within the index that displays the salary column in descending order.

```
create index
    name_salary_idx
on
    person
(
    last_name asc,
    salary desc);
```

While B-tree indexes are great for simple queries, they are not very good for the following situations:

- Low-cardinality columns — columns with less than 200 distinct values do not have the selectivity required to benefit from standard B-tree index structures.
- No support for SQL functions — B-tree indexes are not able to support SQL queries using Oracle's built-in functions. Oracle provides a variety of built-in functions that allow SQL statements to query on a piece of an indexed column or on any one of a number of transformations against the indexed column.

Prior to the introduction of Oracle FBIs, the Oracle cost-based SQL optimizer had to perform time-consuming long-table FTSs due to these shortcomings. Consequently, it was no surprise when Oracle introduced more robust types of indexing structures.

Bitmapped Indexes

Oracle bitmap indexes are very different from standard B-tree indexes. In bitmap structures, a two-dimensional array is created with one column for every row in the table being indexed. Each column represents a distinct value within the bitmapped index. This two-dimensional array represents each value within the index multiplied by the number of rows in the table. At row retrieval time, Oracle decompresses the bitmap into the RAM data buffers so it can be rapidly scanned for matching values. These matching values are delivered to Oracle in the form of a ROWID list. These ROWID values may directly access the required information.

The real benefit of bitmapped indexing occurs when one table includes multiple bitmapped indexes. Each individual column may have low cardinality. The creation of multiple bitmapped indexes provides a powerful method for rapidly answering difficult SQL queries.

For example, assume there is a motor vehicle database with numerous low-cardinality columns such as car_color, car_make, car_model, and car_year. Each column contains less than 100 distinct values by themselves and a B-tree index would be fairly useless in a database of 20 million vehicles. However, combining these indexes together in a query can provide blistering response times a lot faster than the traditional method of reading each one of the 20 million rows in the base table. For example, assume we wanted to find old blue Toyota Corollas manufactured in 1981.

```
select
    license_plat_nbr
from
    vehicle
where
    color = 'blue'
and
    make = 'toyota'
and
    year = 1981;
```

Oracle uses a specialized optimizer method called a bitmapped index merge to service this query. In a bitmapped index merge, each ROWID list is built independently by using the bitmaps and a special merge routine is used to compare the ROWID lists and find the intersecting values. Using this methodology, Oracle can provide subsecond response time when working against multiple low-cardinality columns (Figure 7.2).

Function-Based Indexes

One of the most important advances in Oracle indexing is the introduction of function-based indexing. FBIs allow the creation of indexes on expressions, internal functions, and user-written functions in PL/SQL and Java. FBIs ensure that the Oracle designer is able to use an index for its query. Prior to Oracle8, the use of a built-in function would not be able to match the performance of an index. Consequently, Oracle would perform the

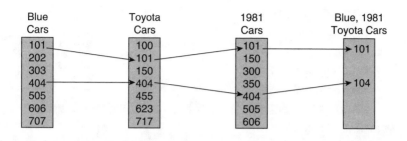

| Blue Cars | Toyota Cars | 1981 Cars | Blue, 1981 Toyota Cars |

Figure 7.2   Oracle Bitmap Merge Join

dreaded FTS. Examples of SQL with function-based queries might include the following:

```
Select * from customer where substr(cust_name,1,4) = 'BURL';
Select * from customer where to_char(order_date,'MM') = '01;
Select * from customer where upper(cust_name) = 'JONES';
Select * from customer where initcap(first_name) = 'Mike';
```

Remember, Oracle always interrogates the WHERE clause of the SQL statement to see if a matching index exists and then evaluates the cost to see if the index is the lowest-cost access method. By using FBIs, the Oracle designer can create a matching index that exactly matches the predicates within the SQL WHERE clause. This ensures that the query is retrieved with a minimal amount of disk I/O and the fastest possible speed.

Index-Organized Tables

Beginning with Oracle8, Oracle recognized that a table with an index on every column did not require table rows. In other words, Oracle recognized that by using a special table access method called an index fast full scan, the index could be queried without actually touching the data itself.

Oracle codified this idea with its use of IOT structure. When using an IOT, Oracle does not create the actual table but instead keeps all of the required information inside the Oracle index. At query time, the Oracle SQL optimizer recognizes that all of the values necessary to service the query exist within the index tree. Therefore, at that time, the Oracle cost-based optimizer has a choice of either reading through the index tree nodes to pull the information in sorted order or invoke an index fast full scan, which will read the table in the same fashion as a FTS, using sequential prefetch (as defined by the db_file_multiblock_read_count parameter). The multiblock read facility allows Oracle to quickly scan index blocks in linear order, quickly reading every block within the index tablespace. This listing includes an example of the syntax to create an IOT:

```
CREATE TABLE emp_iot (
    emp_id number,
    ename varchar2(20),
    sal number(9,2),
    deptno number,
    CONSTRAINT pk_emp_iot_index PRIMARY KEY (emp_id) )
ORGANIZATION index
TABLESPACE spc_demo_ts_01
PCTHRESHOLD 20 INCLUDING ename;
```

Oracle dominates the market for relational database technology, so Oracle designers must be aware of the specialized index structures and fully understand how they can be used to improve the performance of all Oracle SQL queries. Many of these techniques are discussed in my book *Oracle High-Performance SQL Tuning* (Oracle Press, 2001). This text details the process of creating all of Oracle's index tree structures and offers specialized tips and techniques for ensuring SQL queries are serviced using the fastest and most efficient indexing structure.

EVALUATING ORACLE INDEX ACCESS METHODS

Oracle9*i* offers a variety of indexing methods including B-tree, bitmapped, and FBIs. Regardless of the index structure, an Oracle index can be thought of as a pair bond of a symbolic key, paired with a ROWID. The goal of Oracle index access is to gather the ROWIDs required to quickly retrieve the desired rows from the table. Within Oracle, we see the following types of index access.

Index Range Scan

The index range scan is one of the most common access methods. During an index range scan, Oracle accesses adjacent index entries and then uses the ROWID values in the index to retrieve the table rows. An example of an index range scan would be the following query.

```
select
    employee_name
from
    employee
where
    home_city = 'Rocky Ford';
```

In practice, many Oracle SQL tuning professionals will resequence the table rows into the same physical order as the primary index. This technique can reduce disk I/O on index range scans by several orders of magnitude.

Fast Full-Index Scan

Index full scans are sometimes called fast full-index scans, which were introduced in Oracle7.3. There are some SQL queries that can be resolved by reading the index without touching the table data. For example, the following query does not need to access the table rows and the index alone can satisfy the query.

```
select distinct
    color,
    count(*)
from
    automobiles
group by
    color;
```

Oracle enhanced the fast full-index scan to make it behave similar to a FTS. Just as Oracle has implemented the db_file_multiblock_read_count parameter for FTSs, Oracle allows this parameter to take effect when retrieving rows for a fast full-index scan. Since the whole index is accessed, Oracle allows multiblock reads.

There is a huge benefit to not reading the table rows, but there are some requirements for Oracle to invoke the fast full-index scan.

- All of the columns required must be specified in the index. That is, all columns in the SELECT and WHERE clauses must exist in the index.
- The query returns more than 10 percent of the rows within the index. This 10 percent figure depends on the degree of multiblock reads and the degree of parallelism.
- You are counting the number of rows in a table that meet a specific criterion. The fast full-index scan is almost always used for count(*) operations.

You can also force a fast full-index scan by specifying the index_ffs hint, which is commonly combined with the parallel_index hint to improve performance. For example, the following query forces the use of a fast full-index scan with parallelism:

```
select distinct /*+ index_ffs(c,pk_auto)
parallel_index(automobile, pk_auto)
   color,
   count(*)
from
   automobiles
group by
   color;
```

It is not always intuitive whether a fast full-index scan is the fastest way to service a query, because of all of the variables involved. Hence, most expert SQL tuners will time any query that meets the fast full-index scan criteria and see if the response time improves.

If you plan to use the Oracle Parallel Query facility, all tables specified in the SQL query must be optimized for a FTS. If an index exists, the cost-based optimizer must be used with a hint to invalidate the index in order to use parallel query. For the rule-based optimizer, indexes can be turned off by using an Oracle function in the WHERE clause.

One important concept in indexing is the selectivity or the uniqueness of the values in a column. To be most effective, an index column must have many unique values. Columns having only a few values (e.g., sex = m/f, status = y/n) are not good candidates for traditional Oracle B-tree indexing, but they are ideal for bitmapped indexes. For a tree index, the sparse distribution of values would be less efficient than a FTS. To see the selectivity for a column, compare the total number of rows in the table with the number of distinct values for the column, as follows:

```
SELECT count(*) FROM CUSTOMER;

SELECT DISTINCT STATUS FROM CUSTOMER;
```

Another concept used in indexing is called distribution. Distribution refers to the frequency that each unique value is distributed within a table. For example, let's say you have a state_abbreviation column that contains 1 of 50 possible values. This is acceptable to use as an index column, provided that the state abbreviations are uniformly distributed across the rows. However, if 90 percent of the values are for New York, then the index will not be effective.

Oracle has addressed the index data distribution issue with the ANA-LYZE TABLE command. When using Oracle's cost-based SQL optimizer, ANALYZE TABLE looks at both the selectivity and distribution of the column values. If they are found to be out-of-bounds, Oracle can decide not to use the index. Oracle has provided a view called DBA_HISTOGRAMS that tells the cost-based optimizer about the distribution of values within a column. The purpose of a histogram is to provide a clear picture of the distribution of values within a low-cardinality index. Unfortunately, getting the histogram data requires each and every index column to be analyzed. Most Oracle designers favor bitmapped indexes over tree indexes for low-cardinality indexes.

Remember, indexes are a valuable shortcut for the Oracle optimizer and a careful design will help reduce unnecessary logical I/O at query runtime. Oracle recommends the following guidelines when considering whether to index a column:

- Columns frequently referenced in SQL WHERE clauses are good candidates for an index.
- Columns used to join tables (primary and foreign keys) should be indexed.
- Columns with poor selectivity should not be indexed using a B-tree. Any column with less than 10 percent of unique values should be indexed as a bitmap index.
- Frequently modified columns are not good candidates for indexing because excessive processing is necessary to maintain the structure of the index tree.
- Columns used in SQL WHERE clauses using Oracle functions or operators should not be indexed. For example, an index on last_name will not be effective if it is referred to in the SQL as upper (last_name).
- When using RI, always create an index on the foreign key.

Most programmers do not realize that database deadlocks occur frequently within the database indexes. It is important to note that a SELECT of a single row in a database can cause more than one lock entry to be placed in the storage pool because all affected index rows are also locked. In other words, the individual row receives a lock, but each index node that contains the value for that row will also have locks assigned.

If the last entry in a sorted index is retrieved, the database will lock all index nodes that reference the indexed value in case the user changes that value. Because many indexing schemes always carry the high-order key in multiple index nodes, an entire branch of the index tree can be locked — all the way up to the root node of the index.

While each database's indexing scheme is different, some relational database vendors recommend that tables with ascending keys be loaded in descending order, so the rows are loaded from Z to A on an alphabetical key field. Other databases, such as Oracle, recommend indexes be dropped and recreated after rows have been loaded into an empty table.

When an UPDATE or DELETE is issued against a row that participates in an index, the database will attempt an exclusive lock on the row. This attempt requires the database to check if any shared locks are held against the row as well as for any index nodes that will be affected. Many indexing algorithms allow for the index tree to dynamically change shape, spawning new levels as items are added and condensing levels as items are deleted.

However, for any table of consequential size, indexes are not recommended to improve performance. Indexes require additional disk space and a table with an index on each column will have indexes that consume more space than the table they support. Oracle will update indexes at runtime as columns are deleted, added, or modified. This index updating can cause considerable performance degradation. For example, adding a row to the end of a table will cause Oracle to adjust the high-key value for each node in the table.

Another guideline for determining when to use an index involves examination of the SQL issued against a table. In general, if the SQL can be collected and each value supplied in each SQL WHERE clause, then the SQL could be a candidate for inclusion in an index.

Another common approach for determining where to create indexes is to run an EXPLAIN PLAN for all SQL and carefully look for any FTSs. The Oracle cost-based optimizer operates in such a fashion that Oracle will sometimes perform a FTS, even if an index has been defined for the table. This occurs most commonly when issuing complex n-way joins. If you are using rule-based optimization in Oracle, the structure of an SQL statement can be adjusted to force the use of an existing index. For Oracle's cost-based optimizer, adding hints to the structure can ensure that all indexes are used. The cost-based optimizer sometimes chooses FTS when an index scan would be more efficient.

Indexes do much more than speed up an individual query. When FTSs are performed on a large Oracle table, the buffer pool begins to page out blocks from other queries. This causes additional I/O for the entire database and results in poor performance for all queries, not just the offending FTS.

Indexes are never a good idea for long descriptive columns. A column called customer_description would be a poor choice for an index because of its length and the inconsistency of the data within the column. Also, a field such as customer_description would usually be referenced in SQL by using Oracle extensions, such as SUBSTR, LIKE, and UPPER. Remember, these Oracle extensions invalidate the index. Suppose an index has been created on customer_last_name. The following query would use the index:

```
SELECT
    STATUS
FROM
    CUSTOMER
WHERE
    customer_last_name = 'BURLESON';
```

The following queries would bypass the index, causing a FTS:

```
SELECT
    STATUS
FROM
    CUSTOMER
WHERE
    customer_last_name = lower('burleson');

SELECT
    STATUS
FROM
    CUSTOMER
WHERE
    customer_last_name LIKE 'BURL%';
```

Unlike other relational databases, such as DB2®, Oracle cannot physically load a table in key order. Consequently, administrators can never guarantee that the rows in a table will be in any particular order.

The use of an index can help whenever the SQL ORDER BY clause is used. For example, even if there are no complex WHERE conditions, the presence of a WHERE clause will assist the performance of the query. Consider the following SQL:

```
SELECT
    customer_last_name,
    customer_first_name
FROM
    CUSTOMER
ORDER BY
    customer_last_name, customer_first_name;
```

Here, building a multivalued index on `customer_last_name` and `customer_first_name` will alleviate the need for an internal sort of the data, significantly improving the performance of the query:

```
CREATE INDEX
    cust_name
ON
    CUSTOMER
(
    customer_last_name,
    customer_first_name
)
ascending;
```

Now that we understand the basic index design principles, let's explore the use of indexes for high-speed systems. We will cover index parallelism, compression, and techniques to reduce index disk I/O.

DESIGNING HIGH-SPEED INDEX ACCESS

When using the `create index` syntax to build an Oracle index, there are many options that can dramatically improve the speed of the creation, the space used by the index, and the height of the resulting index. Let's review a few of these factors.

Speed Factors

Parallel Option

This option allows for parallel processes to scan the table. When an index is created, Oracle must first collect the symbolic key/ROWID pairs with a FTS. By making the FTS run in parallel, the index creation will run many times faster, depending on the number of CPUs, table partitioning, and disk configuration. I recommend a n-1 for the `degree` option, where *n* is the number of CPUs on your Oracle server. In this example, we create an index on a 36 CPU server and the index creates twenty times faster:

```
CREATE INDEX cust_dup_idx
    ON customer(sex, hair_color, customer_id)
PARALLEL 35;
```

But what if your goal is to minimize computing resources? If this SQL is inside a batch program, then it is not important to start returning rows

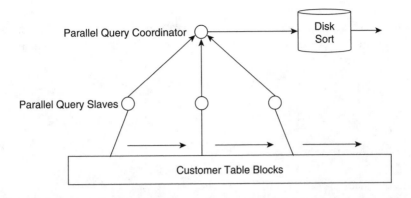

Figure 7.3 An Oracle Parallel Query

quickly and a different execution plan would take fewer resources. In this example, a parallel FTS followed by a back-end sort will require less machine resources and less I/O because blocks do not have to be reread to pull the data in sorted order (Figure 7.3). In this example, we expect the result to take longer to deliver (no rows until the sort is complete), but we will see far less I/O because blocks will not have to be reaccessed to deliver the rows in presorted order. Let's assume that this execution plan delivers the result in 10 seconds with 5000 `db_block_gets`.

Nologging Option

The `nologging` option bypasses the writing of the redo log, significantly improving performance. The only danger with using `nologging` is that you must rerun the CREATE INDEX syntax if you perform a roll-forward database recovery. Using `nologging` with CREATE INDEX can speed index creation by up to 30 percent:

```
CREATE INDEX cust_dup_idx
    ON customer(sex, hair_color, customer_id)
PARALLEL 35
NOLOGGING;
```

Space and Structure Factors

Compress Option

The `compress` option is used to repress duplication of keys in nonunique indexes. For concatenated indexes (indexes with multiple columns), the `compress` option can reduce the size of the index by more than half.

The `compress` option allows you to specify the prefix length for multiple column indexes. In this example, we have a nonunique index on several low cardinality columns (`sex` and `hair_color`) and a high cardinality column (`customer_id`):

```
CREATE INDEX
    cust_dup_idx
ON
    Customer
(
    sex,
    hair_color, customer_id
)
PARALLEL 35
NOLOGGING
COMPRESS 2;
```

Tablespace Block Size Option

The block size of the index tablespace will have a huge impact on the structure of the index. Here is an example of an index created in a 32 K tablespace:

```
create tablespace 32k_ts
datafile '/u01/app/oracle/prod/oradata/32k_file.dbf'
bocksize 32k;

CREATE INDEX
    cust_dup_idx
ON
    Customer
(
    sex,
    hair_color,
    customer_id
)
PARALLEL 35
NOLOGGING
COMPRESS 2
TABLESPACE 32k_ts;
```

In summary, there are many parameters that you can use to improve the performance of Oracle index creation, the size of the index tree, and the height of the tree structure. Now let's look at how you can adjust your block size when designing indexes to reduce disk I/O.

Designing Indexes to Reduce Disk I/O

You can use the large (16 K to 32 K) block size data caches to contain data from indexes or tables that are the object of repeated large scans. Does such a thing really help performance? A small but revealing test can answer that question.

For the test, the following query will be used against an Oracle9*i* database that has a database block size of 8 K, but also has the 16 K cache enabled along with a 16 K tablespace:

```
select
        count(*)
from
        eradmin.admission
where
        patient_id between 1 and 40000;
```

The ERADMIN.ADMISSION table has 150,000 rows in it and has an index build on the PATIENT_ID column. An EXPLAIN PLAN of the query reveals that it uses an index range scan to produce the desired end result:

```
Execution Plan
----------------------------------------------------------
0      SELECT STATEMENT Optimizer=CHOOSE
1        (Cost=41 Card=1 Bytes=4)
1    0    SORT (AGGREGATE)
2    1      INDEX (FAST FULL SCAN) OF 'ADMISSION_PATIENT_ID'
                (NON-UNIQUE) (Cost=41 Card=120002 Bytes=480008)
```

Executing the query (twice to eliminate parse activity and to cache any data) with the index residing in a standard 8 K tablespace produces these runtime statistics:

```
Statistics
----------------------------------------------------
          0   recursive calls
          0   db block gets
```

```
421  consistent gets
  0  physical reads
  0  redo size
371  bytes sent via SQL*Net to client
430  bytes received via SQL*Net from client
  2  SQL*Net roundtrips to/from client
  0  sorts (memory)
  0  sorts (disk)
  1  rows processed
```

To test the effectiveness of the new 16 K cache and 16 K tablespace, the index used by the query will be rebuilt into the 16 K tablespace that has the exact same characteristics as the original 8 K tablespace, except for the larger block size:

```
alter index
       eradmin.admission_patient_id
       rebuild nologging noreverse tablespace indx_
  16k;
```

Once the index is nestled firmly into the 16 K tablespace, the query is reexecuted (again twice) with the following runtime statistics being produced:

```
Statistics
----------------------------------------------------
  0  recursive calls
  0  db block gets
211  consistent gets
  0  physical reads
  0  redo size
371  bytes sent via SQL*Net to client
430  bytes received via SQL*Net from client
  2  SQL*Net roundtrips to/from client
  0  sorts (memory)
  0  sorts (disk)
  1  rows processed
```

As you can see, the amount of logical reads has been reduced in half simply by using the new 16 K tablespace and accompanying 16 K data cache. Clearly, the benefits of properly using the new data caches and multiblock tablespace feature of Oracle and above are worth your investigation and trials in your own database. Next, let's see how Oracle cost-based optimizer influences our index design decision.

ORACLE OPTIMIZER AND INDEX DESIGN

In some cases, the distribution of values within a column of a table will affect the optimizer's decision to use an index versus perform a FTS. This scenario occurs when the value with a where clause has a disproportional amount of values, making a FTS cheaper than index access.

A column histogram should only be created when we have data skew exists or is suspected. In the real world, that happens rarely and one of the most common mistakes with the optimizer is the unnecessary introduction of histograms into optimizer statistics. The histograms signals the optimizer that the column is not linearly distributed and the optimizer will peek into the literal value in the SQL WHERE clause and compare that value to the histogram buckets in the histogram statistics (Figure 7.4).

Many Oracle professionals misunderstand the purpose of histograms. While they are used to make a yes-or-no decision about the use of an index to access the table, histograms are most commonly used to predict the size of the intermediate result set from a multiway table join.

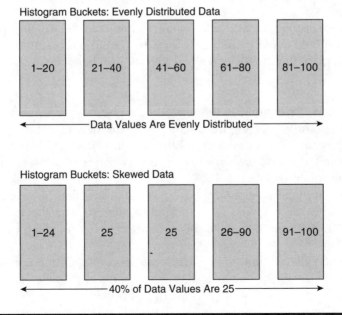

Figure 7.4   Oracle Histograms and Column Skew

For example, assume that we have a five-way table join where the result set will be only 10 rows. Oracle will want to join the tables together in such a way as to make the result set (cardinality) of the first join as small as possible. By carrying less baggage in the intermediate result sets, the query will run faster. To minimize intermediate results, the optimizer attempts to estimate the cardinality of each result set during the parse phase of SQL execution. Having histograms on skewed columns will greatly aid the optimizer in making a proper decision. (Remember, you can create a histogram even if the column does not have an index and does not participate as a join key.)

Because a complex schema might have tens of thousands of columns, it is impractical to evaluate each column for skew and thus Oracle provides an automated method for building histograms as part of the dbms_stats utility. By using the method_opt=>'for all columns size ske-wonly' option of dbms_stats, you can direct Oracle to automatically create histograms for those columns whose values are heavily skewed. We'll take a look at this option in more detail later.

As a general rule, histograms are used to predict the cardinality and the number of rows returned in the result set. For example, assume that we have a product_type index and 70 percent of the values are for the HARDWARE type. Whenever SQL with where product_type='HARDWARE' is specified, a FTS is the fastest execution plan, while a query with where product_type='SOFTWARE' would be fastest using index access.

Because histograms add additional overhead to the parsing phase of SQL, you should avoid them unless they are required for a faster optimizer execution plan. But, there are several conditions where creating histograms is advised:

- When the column is referenced in a query — remember, there is no point in creating histograms if the queries do not reference the column. This mistake is common: many DBAs will create histograms on a skewed column, even though it is not referenced by any queries.
- When there is a significant skew in the distribution of column values — this skew should be sufficiently significant that the value in the WHERE clause will make the optimizer choose a different execution plan.
- When the column values cause an incorrect assumption — if the optimizer makes an incorrect guess about the size of an intermediate result set, it may choose a suboptimal table join method. Adding a histogram to this column will often provide the information required for the optimizer to use the best join method.

Now that we understand histogram design, let's examine how the physical row order influences Oracle's choice of index usage.

PHYSICAL ROW-ORDERING AND INDEX DESIGN

Many Oracle developers are perplexed when the optimizer chooses a FTS when they are only retrieving a small number of rows, not realizing that the optimizer is considering the clustering of the column values within the table.

Oracle provides a column called clustering_factor in the dba_indexes view that tells the optimizer how synchronized the table rows are with the index. When the clustering factor is close to the number of data blocks, the table rows are synchronized with the index.

The selectivity of a column value, the db_block_size, the avg_row_len, and the cardinality all work together in helping the optimizer decide whether to use an index versus using a FTS. If a data column has high selectivity and a low clustering_factor, then an index scan is usually the fastest execution method (Figure 7.5).

In cases where most of the SQL references a column with a high clustering_factor, a large db_block_size, and a small avg_row_len, the DBA will sometimes periodically resequence the table rows or use a single-table cluster to maintain row order. This approach places all adjacent rows in the same data block, removing the FTS and making the query up to 30 times faster.

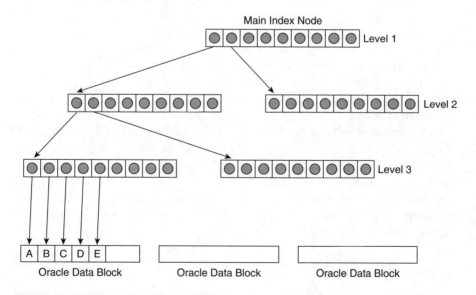

Figure 7.5   A Clustered Index

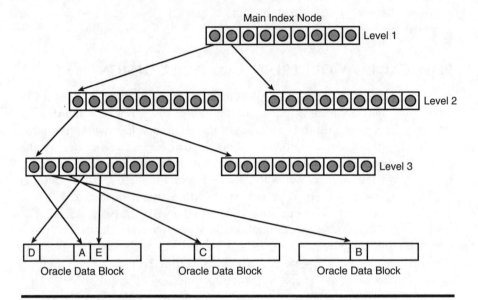

Figure 7.6 An Unclustered Index

Conversely, a high `clustering_factor`, where the value approaches the number of rows in the table (`num_rows`), indicates that the rows are not in the same sequence as the index and additional I/O will be required for index range scans. As the `clustering_factor` approaches the number of rows in the table, the rows are out of sync with the index.

However, even if a column has high selectivity, a high `clustering_factor` and small `avg_row_len` will indicate that the column values are randomly distributed across the table and additional I/O will be required to fetch the rows. In these cases, an index range scan would cause a huge amount of unnecessary I/O (Figure 7.6); a FTS would be far more efficient.

In summary, the `clustering_factor`, `db_block_size`, and `avg_row_len` all influence the optimizer's decision about performing a FTS versus an index range scan. It's important to understand how these statistics are used by the optimizer.

Now that we understand the basics of Oracle indexing and design for performance, let's move on to take a look at how indexes interact with RI and examine the performance implications of these features.

Constraints and Index Design

Constraints are used to enforce business rules and Oracle indexes are often used to support your constraints. In Oracle, some constraints create an index on your behalf. For example, creating a primary key constraint

Listing 7.1 Creating a Primary Key Constraint

```
CREATE TABLE
  CUSTOMER
(
  cust_nbr                    number
CONSTRAINT
  cust_ukey
PRIMARY KEY (CUST_NBR)
USING INDEX
PCTFREE   10
INITRANS 2
MAXTRANS 255
TABLESPACE TS1
STORAGE   (
  INITIAL    256000
  NEXT      102400
  MINEXTENTS  1
  MAXEXTENTS  121
  PCTINCREASE  1 ),
       dept_name            CHAR(10)
       CONSTRAINT dept_fk REFERENCES DEPT on delete cascade,


       organization_name    CHAR(20)
       CONSTRAINT org_fk REFERENCES ORG on delete restrict,


       region_name          CHAR(2)
       CONSTRAINT state_check
       CHECK region_name IN ('NORTH', SOUTH', 'EAST', 'WEST')
);
```

on the CUSTOMER table for the cust_id (Listing 7.1) will create an index on the field and it is not necessary to manually build an index.

Note that you should always specify the location clause when declaring constraints. In the previous example, had the cust_ukey constraint been defined without the STORAGE clause, then the index would have been placed in whatever tablespace was specified by the table owner's DEFAULT tablespace, with whatever default storage parameters were in effect for that tablespace.

In Listing 7.1, the first constraint is on the cust_nbr column, the primary key. When you use Oracle's RI to specify a primary key, Oracle automatically builds a unique index on the column to ensure that no duplicate values are entered.

The second constraint in the listing above is on the dept_name column of the DEPT table. This constraint tells Oracle that it cannot remove a department row if there are existing customer rows that reference that department. ON DELETE CASCADE tells Oracle that when the department row is deleted, all customer rows referencing that department will also be deleted.

The next RI constraint on organization_name ensures that no organization is deleted if customers are participating in that organization. ON DELETE RESTRICT tells Oracle not to delete an organization row if any customer row still references the organization. Only after each and every customer has been set to another organization can the row be deleted from the organization table.

The last RI constraint shown in the listing above is called a check constraint. Using a check constraint, Oracle will verify that the column is one of the valid values before inserting the row, but it will not create an index on the column.

In addition to basic indexes, Oracle8 allows for an index to contain multiple columns. This ability can greatly influence the speed at which certain types of queries function within Oracle.

USING MULTICOLUMN INDEXES

When an SQL request is issued using multiple columns, a concatenated or multicolumn index can be used to improve performance. Oracle supports the use of multivalued indexes, but there are some important limitations. Unlike other relational databases, Oracle requires that all columns in an index be sorted in the same order, either ascending or descending. For example, if you needed to index on customer_last_name ascending, followed immediately by gross_pay descending, you would not be able to use a multivalued index.

Sometimes two columns, each with poor selectivity (i.e., both columns have few unique values), can be combined into an index that has better selectivity. For example, you could combine a status field that has three values (good, neutral, bad) with another column such as state_name (only 50 unique values), thereby creating a multivalued index that has far better selectivity than each column would have if indexed separately.

Another reason for creating concatenated indexes is to speed the execution of queries that reference all the values in an index. For example, consider the following query:

```
SELECT     customer_last_name,
           customer_status,
           customer_zip_code
```

```
FROM CUSTOMER
ORDER BY customer_last_name;
```

Now, an index can be created, as follows:

```
CREATE INDEX last_status_zip
ON CUSTOMER
(customer_last_name, customer_status, customer_zip
_code) ascending;
```

If this query were issued against the CUSTOMER table, Oracle would never need to access any rows in the base table. Because all key values are contained in the index and the high-order key (customer_last_name) is in the ORDER BY clause, Oracle can scan the index and retrieve data without ever touching the base table.

With the assistance of this feature, the savvy Oracle developer can also add columns to the end of the concatenated index so that the base table is never touched. For example, if the preceding query also returned the value of the customer_address column, this column could be added to the concatenated index, dramatically improving performance. In summary, the following guidelines apply when creating a concatenated index:

- Use a composite index whenever two or more values are used in the SQL where the clause and the operators are ANDed together.
- Place the columns in a WHERE clause in the same order as in the index, with data items added at the end of the index.

Now that we understand the basic constructs of Oracle indexes, let's take a closer look at the SQL optimizer and examine how it chooses which indexes to use to service SQL requests.

HOW ORACLE CHOOSES INDEXES

It is interesting to note that the fastest execution for an individual task might not always be the best choice. For example, consider the following query against the CUSTOMER table:

```
SELECT
    customer_name
FROM
    CUSTOMER
WHERE
    credit_rating = 'POOR'
```

```
AND

    amount_due > 1000

AND

    state = 'IOWA'

AND

    job_description LIKE lower('%computer%');
```

Here, you can see a query where a FTS would be the most efficient processing method. Because of the complex conditions and the use of Oracle extensions in the SQL, it might be faster to perform a FTS. However, the fast execution of this task might be done at the expense of other tasks on the system as the buffer pool becomes flushed.

In general, the type of optimizer will determine how indexes are used. As you probably know, the Oracle optimizer can run as either rule-based or cost-based. As a general rule, Oracle is intelligent enough to use an index if it exists, but there are exceptions to this rule. The most notable exception is the n-way join with a complex WHERE clause. The cost-based optimizer, especially when the all_rows mode is used, will get confused and invoke a FTS on at least one of the tables, even if the appropriate foreign key indexes exist for the tables. The only remedy to this problem is to use the rule-based optimizer or use the first_rows mode of the cost-based optimizer.

Always remember, Oracle will only use an index when the index column is specified in its pure form. The use of the SUBSTR, UPPER, LOWER, and other functions will invalidate an index. However, there are a few tricks to help you get around this obstacle. Consider the following two equivalent SQL queries:

```
SELECT * FROM CUSTOMER
WHERE
total_purchases/10 > 5000;

SELECT * FROM CUSTOMER
WHERE
total_purchases > 5000*10;
```

The second query, by virtue of the fact that it does not alter the index column, would be able to use an index on the total_purchases column.

While index usage has an impact on database performance, the way that the Oracle8 tables are allocated can also influence the performance of systems, especially those that have a high amount of updating. Let's take a look at some of the most important considerations when allocating Oracle8 tables.

INDEX DESIGN FOR STAR SCHEMAS

In Oracle, bitmap indexes are required for all join columns on the fact table and Oracle will initially use these bitmap indexes as a path to the fact table. The SQL optimizer will then rewrite the original query, replacing the equi-join criteria with subqueries using the IN clause. These subqueries are used as sources of keys to drive the bitmap index accesses, using bitmap key iteration to access the dimension tables. Once the resulting bitmap-ROWID lists are retrieved, Oracle will use a hash join to merge the result sets.

To see how the Oracle SQL optimizer transforms a star query, consider the following query where we sum the sales by region for all southern regions during the months of March and April:

```
select
    store.region,
    time.month,
    sum(sales.sales_amount)
from
    sales,
    store,
    time,
    product
where
    sales.store_key = store.store_key
and
    sales.month = time.month
and
    store.region = `south'
  and
    time.month in (`01-03', `01-04')
group by
    store.region, time.month
;
```

The star optimizer replaces the WHERE clauses as follows. Note that the equi-join criteria is replaced by a subquery using the IN clause.

■ Region clause
  – Region clause before star transformation:

```
where
    store.region = `south'
and
    sales.store_key = store.store_key
```

  – Region clause after star transformation:

```
where
    sales.store_key in (select store_key from store
                            where region = `south')
```

We see a similar transformation in the join into the time table:

■ Month clause
  – Month clause before star transformation:

```
where
    sales.month = time.month
and
    time.month in (`01-03', `01-04')
```

  – Month clause after star transformation:

```
where
    sales.month in (select month from time
                        where month in (`01-03', `01-04'))
```

As we see, the query is significantly transformed, replacing all WHERE clause entries for the dimension table with a single subselect statement. These IN subqueries are ideal for the use of bitmap indexes because the bitmap can quickly scan the low-cardinality columns in the bitmap and produce a ROWID list of rows with matching values.

This approach is far faster than the traditional method of joining the smallest reference table against the fact table and then joining each of the other reference tables against the intermediate table. The speed is a result of reducing the physical I/O. The indexes are read to gather the virtual table in memory. The fact table will not be accessed until the virtual index has everything it requires to go directly to the requested rows via the composite index on the fact table.

Starting with Oracle8*i*, the requirement for a concatenated index has changed, and the STAR hint requires bitmap indexes. The bitmap indexes can be joined more efficiently than a concatenated index and they provide a faster result.

As I have noted, the star query can be tricky to implement and careful consideration must be given to the proper placement of indexes. Each dimension table must have an index on the join key. In Oracle7 and Oracle8, the large fact table must have a composite index consisting of all of the join keys from all of the dimension tables, while in Oracle8*i* you need bitmap indexes on the fact table. In addition, the sequencing of the keys in the fact table composite index must be in the correct order or Oracle will not be able to use the index to service the query.

Next let's examine alternative index structures and see how they can fit into our physical design.

INDEXING ALTERNATIVES TO B-TREE INDEXES

As you may know, Oracle offers several alternative indexing methods to enhance the standard B-tree indexes. These include bitmap indexes, FBIs, and reverse-key indexes.

Bitmap Indexes

It was a common misconception that bitmap indexes were only appropriate for columns with a small number of distinct values — say, fewer than 50. Current research in Oracle8*i* has shown that bitmap indexes can substantially improve the speed of queries using columns with up to 1000 distinct values, because retrieval from a bitmap index is done in RAM and is almost always faster than using a traditional B-tree index. Most experienced DBAs will look for tables that contain columns with fewer than 1000 distinct values, build a bitmap index on these columns, and then see if the query is faster.

Function-Based Indexes

To use the alternative indexing structures, you must first identify SQL statements that are using the built-in function (BIF). In the next example, we can search the v$sqlarea view to find all SQL statements that are using the to_char BIF.

```
select
    sql_text
from
    v$sqlarea   -- or stats$sql_summary
```

```
where
    sql_text like '%to_char%';
```

Once identified, FBIs can be created to remove the FTSs and replace them with index-range scans.

Reverse-Key Indexes and SQL Performance

There is, however, a major scalability danger with automatically generated synthetic keys. Every insertion to a table requires a corresponding insertion to its primary key index. If the primary key values are being generated in ascending order, then all inserts will need to change the high-order leaf block in the B-tree. There is an obvious danger here of contention for that block of the index, if several users attempt concurrent inserts (whereas the inserts to the table itself can easily be distributed to a variety of blocks by using multiple process free lists).

Prior to Oracle8, the standard strategy to avoid this problem was to ensure that the synthetic key values were not generated in order. This was done by permuting the values generated by the sequence number generator before using them. Various permutation schemes such as adding a leading check digit or reversing the order of the digits have been used. These schemes have the effect of distributing inserts evenly over the range of values in the index, thus preventing leaf block contention. In Oracle8, the same effect may be obtained by using a reverse-key index.

The major disadvantage of distributing inserts in this way is that the data density of index leaf blocks will be typically only 75 percent of capacity rather than almost 100 percent, making fast full-index scans on the primary key index less efficient. However, this access path is not typical and is seldom performance-critical when used. So, reverse-key indexes should be used in general for synthetic primary key indexes.

Index Usage for Queries with IN Conditions

When a query has an IN condition to evaluate multiple expressions, the SQL optimizer will often perform a FTS, but with many variant execution plans. Queries that evaluate multiple conditions can execute with TABLE ACCESS FULL, CONCATENATION, INLIST ITERATOR, and UNION, which all perform the exact same function of returning rows with multiple values. To illustrate, consider the following simple query:

```
select
    ename
from
    emp
```

```
where
    job IN ('MANAGER','PRESIDENT')
;
```

Here you see the execution plan. Note the use of the CONCATENATION operator:

OPERATION		
OPTIONS	OBJECT_NAME	POSITION
SELECT STATEMENT		
CONCATENATION		1
TABLE ACCESS		
BY INDEX ROWID	EMP	1
INDEX		
RANGE SCAN	JOB_IDX	1
TABLE ACCESS		
BY INDEX ROWID	EMP	2
INDEX		
RANGE SCAN	JOB_IDX	1

Now we change the execution plan by adding a first_rows hint and we see an entirely different execution plan:

OPERATION		
OPTIONS	OBJECT_NAME	POSITION
SELECT STATEMENT		1
INLIST ITERATOR		1
TABLE ACCESS		
BY INDEX ROWID	EMP	1
INDEX		
RANGE SCAN	JOB_IDX	1

Of course, this query can also be rewritten to utilize the union SQL operator. Here is an equivalent query:

```
select /*+ first_rows */
    ename
```

```
from
    emp
where
    job = 'MANAGER'
union
select ename from emp
where
    job = 'PRESIDENT'
;
```

Here you see the execution plan using the UNION-ALL table access method:

```
OPERATION
-------------------------------------------------------------------
OPTIONS                       OBJECT_NAME                POSITION
----------------------------  ------------------------   ----------
SELECT STATEMENT
                                                               6
  SORT
UNIQUE                                                         1
    UNION-ALL
                                                               1
      TABLE ACCESS
BY INDEX ROWID                EMP                              1
        INDEX
RANGE SCAN                    JOB_IDX                          1
        TABLE ACCESS
BY INDEX ROWID                EMP                              2
        INDEX
RANGE SCAN                    JOB_IDX                          1
```

Note that we've seen three alternative execution plans for the exact same result set. The point is that there are many opportunities to change the execution plan for queries that evaluate for multiple conditions. In most cases, you must actually time the queries to see which execution plan is fastest for your specific query.

DESIGN FOR ORACLE FULL-INDEX SCANS

In keeping with Oracle's commitment to add intelligence to SQL query optimization, the full-index SQL execution plan has been enhanced in

Oracle9i to provide support for FBIs. With Oracle8, intelligence was added to the SQL optimizer to determine if a query might be resolved exclusively within an existing index. Oracle's IOT structure is an excellent example of how Oracle is able to bypass table access whenever an index exists. In an IOT structure, all table data is carried inside the B-tree structure of the index, making the table redundant.

Whenever the Oracle SQL optimizer detects that the query is serviceable without touching table rows, Oracle invokes a full-index scan and quickly reads every block of the index without touching the table itself. It is important to note that a full-index scan does not read the index nodes. Rather, a block-by-block scan is performed and all of the index nodes are quickly cached. Best of all, Oracle invokes multiblock read capability, invoking multiple processes to read the table.

Oracle and Multiblock Reads

To speed table and index block access, Oracle uses the db_file_multiblock_read_count parameter (which defaults to 8) to aid in getting FTS and full-index scan data blocks into the data buffer cache as fast as possible. However, this parameter is used only when a SQL query performs a FTS and, in most cases, a query uses an index to access the table.

For full-index scans, Oracle imposes some important restrictions:

■ All of the columns required by SQL must reside in the index tree; that is, all columns in the SELECT and WHERE clauses must exist in the index.
■ The query accesses a substantial number of rows. Depending on which expert you ask, this percentage varies from 10 to 25 percent, but this figure depends heavily on the settings for db_file_multiblock_read_count and the degree of parallelism for the query.
■ Because the index nodes are not retrieved in index order, the rows will not be sequenced. Hence, an ORDER BY clause will require an additional sorting operation.

Oracle provides a SQL hint to force a full-index scan. You can also force a fast full-index scan by specifying the index_ffs hint, which is commonly combined with the parallel_index hint to improve performance. For example, the following query forces the use of a fast full-index scan with parallelism:

```
select distinct /*+ index_ffs(c,pk_auto) parallel_
index(automobile, pk_auto)
```

```
     color,
     count(*)
from
     automobiles
group by color;
```

It isn't always intuitive as to whether a fast full-index scan is the quickest way to service a query, because of all the variables involved. So most expert SQL tuners will manually time any query that meets the fast full-index scan criteria and see if the response time improves with the full-index scan.

BASICS OF FBIs

Prior to Oracle9*i*, full-index scans were possible only when the index was created without any null values. In other words, the index had to be created with a NOT NULL clause for Oracle to be able to use the index. This has been greatly enhanced in Oracle9*i* with support for index-only scans using FBIs.

As a quick review, FBIs were an important enhancement in Oracle8, because they provided a mechanism for the virtual elimination of the unnecessary, long-table full scan. Because a FBI can exactly replicate any column in the WHERE clause of a query, Oracle will always be able to match the WHERE clause of a SQL query with an index.

Here, I will use a simple example of a student table to illustrate how a full-index scan would work with a FBI:

```
create table student
(student_name varchar2(40), date_of_birth date);
```

Using this table, create a concatenated FBI of all columns of the table. In this example, the functions are initcap (i.e., capitalize the first letter of each word) and to_char (i.e., change a date to a character):

```
create index whole_student
on student
(initcap(student_name), to_char(date_of_birth,'MM-DD-YY'));
```

With the FBI defined, Oracle will recognize that any SQL statement that references these columns will be able to use the full-index scan. Here is an example of some SQL queries that match the FBI:

```
select * from student
```

```
where initcap(student_name) = 'Jones';
select * from student
where to_char(date_of_birth,'MM-DD=YY') = '04-07-85';
```

INDEXING ON A COLUMN WITH NULL VALUES

One problem with all relational databases is the inability of the software to index on a NULL column. For example, this index definition would ingore those employees with a NULL employee name:

```
create index
    emp_ename_idx
on
    emp
    (ename)
;
```

Whenever a query asking where ename is NULL is issued, there would be no index and Oracle would perform an unnecessary large-table FTS.

```
Execution Plan
------------------------------------------------------------
0 SELECT STATEMENT Optimizer=CHOOSE (Cost=1 Card=1 Bytes=6)
1 0 TABLE ACCESS (FULL) OF 'EMP' (Cost=1 Card=1 Bytes=6)
```

To get around this problem, we can create a FBI using the null value built-in SQL function to index only on the NULL columns:

```
-- create an FBI on ename column with NULL values
create index
    emp_null_ename_idx
on
    emp
    (nvl(ename,'null'))
;

analyze index emp_null_ename_idx compute statistics;
```

Now we can use the index and greatly improve the speed of any queries that require access to the NULL columns. Note that we must make one of two changes:

1. Add a hint to force the index
2. Change the WHERE predicate to match the function

Here is an example of using an index on NULL column values:

```
-- insert a NULL row
insert into emp (empno) values (999);
set autotrace traceonly explain;

-- test the index access (hint forces index usage)
select /*+ index(emp_null_ename_idx) */
    ename
from
    emp e
where
    ename is NULL'
;
-- test the index access (change predicate to use FBI)
select /*+ index(emp_null_ename_idx) */
    ename
from
    emp e
where
    nvl(ename,'null') = 'null'
```

INVOKING THE FULL-INDEX SCAN WITH A FBI

Oracle will always use the FBI whenever possible and will invoke a full-index scan on the FBI. It will do so when the cost-based SQL optimizer statistics indicate that the full-index scan will be faster than a B-tree access via the index.

Here are the criteria for invoking an index-only scan with a FBI. All SQL predicates in the WHERE clause match those columns in the index; the query must return enough rows from the table for the cost-based optimizer to recognize that the full-index scan is faster than a traditional index access. The decision to invoke a full-index scan depends on several parameter settings:

■ Proper statistics for the cost-based optimizer — the schema should have been recently analyzed and the optimizer_mode parameter must not be set to RULE.

- The degree of parallelism on the index — note that the parallel degree of the index is set independently; the index does not inherit the degree of parallelism of the table.
- The setting for `optimizer_index_cost_adj` — this controls the propensity of the cost-based optimizer to favor full-index scans.
- The setting for `db_file_multiblock_read_count` — this parameter factors in the cost of the full-index scan. The higher the value, the cheaper the full-index scan will appear.
- The presence of histograms on the index — for skewed indexes, this helps the cost-based optimizer evaluate the number of rows returned by the query.

An Important Oracle Enhancement

The fast full-index scan on FBIs is another enhancement of Oracle9i. Many databases automatically begin to use this new execution plan when the database migrates to Oracle9i. However, there are several factors considered by the cost-based SQL optimizer when choosing to invoke a full-index scan. It is important that the Oracle professional have the appropriate parameter settings to ensure that the cost-based optimizer does not use a fast full-index scan in an inappropriate fashion.

HOW TO USE ORACLE9i BITMAP JOIN INDEXES

Oracle9i has added the bitmap join index to its mind-boggling array of table join methods. This new table access method requires that you create an index that performs the join at index creation time and that creates a bitmap index of the keys used in the join. But unlike most relational database indexes, the indexed columns don't reside in the table. Oracle has revolutionized index creation by allowing a WHERE clause to be included in the index creation syntax. This feature revolutionizes the way relational tables are accessed via SQL.

The bitmap join index is extremely useful for table joins that involve low-cardinality columns (e.g., columns with less than 300 distinct values). However, bitmap join indexes aren't useful in all cases. You shouldn't use them for OLTP databases because of the high overhead associated with updating bitmap indexes. Let's take a closer look at how this type of index works.

HOW BITMAP JOIN INDEXES WORK

To illustrate bitmap join indexes, I'll use a simple example, a many-to-many relationship where an inventory table serves as the junction between parts

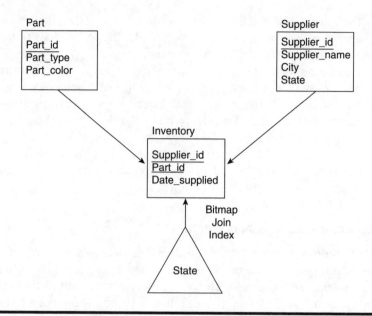

Figure 7.7 A Many-to-Many Oracle Table Relationship with Indexes

and suppliers. Each part has many suppliers and each supplier provides many parts (Figure 7.7).

For this example, let's assume the database has 300 types of parts and the suppliers provide parts in all 50 states. So there are 50 distinct values in the STATE column and only 300 distinct values in the PART_TYPE column.

Note in the listing below that we create an index on the inventory using columns contained in the SUPPLIER and PART tables. The idea behind a bitmap join index is to prejoin the low cardinality columns, making the overall join faster.

It is well known that bitmap indexes can improve the performance of Oracle9i queries where the predicates involve the low cardinality columns, but this technique has never been employed in cases where the low cardinality columns reside in a foreign table.

To create a bitmap join index, issue the following Oracle DDL. Note the inclusion of the FROM and WHERE clauses inside the CREATE INDEX syntax.

```
create bitmap index
    part_suppliers_state
on
    inventory( parts.part_type, supplier.state)
```

```
from
    inventory i,
    parts p,
    supplier s
where
    i.part_id=p.part_id
and
    i.supplier_id=p.supplier_id;
```

Bitmap Join Indexes in Action

To see how bitmap join indexes work, look at this example of a SQL query. Let's suppose you want a list of all suppliers of pistons in North Carolina. To get that list, you would use this query:

```
select
    supplier_name
from
    parts
natural join
    inventory
natural join
    suppliers
where
    part_type = 'piston' and state='nc';
```

Prior to Oracle9*i*, this SQL query would be serviced by a nested loop join or hash join of all three tables. With a bitmap join index, the index has prejoined the tables, and the query can quickly retrieve a ROWID list of matching table rows in all three tables.

Note that this bitmap join index specified the join criteria for the three tables and created a bitmap index on the junction table (INVENTORY) with the PART_TYPE and STATE keys.

Oracle benchmarks claim that bitmap join indexes can run a query more than eight times faster than traditional indexing methods. However, this speed improvement is dependent upon many factors and the bitmap join is not a panacea. Some restrictions on using the bitmap join index include:

■ The indexed columns must be of low cardinality — usually with less than 300 distinct values.

- The query must not have any references in the WHERE clause to data columns that are not contained in the index.
- The overhead when updating bitmap join indexes is substantial. For practical use, bitmap join indexes are dropped and rebuilt each evening during the daily batch load jobs. This means that bitmap join indexes are useful only for Oracle data warehouses that remain read-only during the processing day.

Remember, bitmap join indexes can tremendously speed up specific data warehouse queries but at the expense of prejoining the tables at bitmap index creation time. You must also be concerned about high-volume updates. Bitmap indexes are notoriously slow to change when the table data changes and this can severely slow down INSERT and UPDATE DML against the target tables.

Exclusions for Bitmap Join Indexes

There are also restrictions on when the SQL optimizer is allowed to invoke a bitmap join index. For queries that have additional criteria in the WHERE clause that doesn't appear in the bitmap join index, Oracle9*i* will be unable to use this index to service the query. For example, the following query will not use the bitmap join index:

```
select
    supplier_name
from
    parts
natural join
    inventory
natural join
    suppliers
where
    part_type = 'piston'
and
    state = 'nc' and part_color = 'yellow';
```

Oracle9*i* has introduced extremely sophisticated execution plan features that can dramatically improve query performance, but these features cannot be used automatically. The Oracle9*i* professional's challenge is to understand these new indexing features, analyze the trade-offs of additional indexing, and judge when the new features can be used to speed queries.

DESIGN FOR AUTOMATIC HISTOGRAM CREATION

Please note that the Oracle SQL optimizer has been dramatically changed in Oracle9*i*, release 2 and the most important task for the DBA is collecting good cost-based optimizer statistics. To aid in this, there is a new method_opt in dbms_stats called skewonly. I highly recommend that all Oracle DBAs use the method_opt=skewonly option to automatically identify skewed column values and generate histograms.

Oracle column histograms are important for several reasons:

- The cost-based optimizer needs information about the result set size from multitable joins to determine the optimal join order for tables.
- Oracle needs to know about heavily skewed column values when deciding about whether to use an index versus a FTS.

Here are details about the new automatic histogram generation features in Oracle9*i*, release 2:

The method_opt='SKEWONLY' dbms_stats Option

The first is the skewonly option, which is time-intensive, because it examines the distribution of values for every column within every index. If dbms_stats discovers an index whose columns are unevenly distributed, it will create histograms for that index to aid the cost-based SQL optimizer in making a decision about index versus FTS access. For example, if an index has one column that is in 50 percent of the rows, a FTS is faster than an index scan to retrieve these rows.

Histograms are also used with SQL that has bind variables and SQL with cursor_sharing enabled. In these cases, the cost-based optimizer determines if the column value could affect the execution plan and if so, replaces the bind variable with a literal and performs a hard parse.

```
--***********************************************************
-- SKEWONLY option - Detailed analysis
--
-- Use this method for a first-time analysis
-- for skewed indexes
-- This runs a long time because all indexes are examined
--***********************************************************

begin
   dbms_stats.gather_schema_stats(
```

```
      ownname              => 'SCOTT',
      estimate_percent => dbms_stats.auto_sample_size,
      method_opt           => 'for all columns size skewonly',
      degree               => 7
   );
end;
/
```

CONCLUSION

This chapter has covered one of the most important areas of Oracle physical design, the creation and implementation of high-speed data access structures. The main point of this chapter is that the proper design of indexes can minimize the amount of work performed by Oracle at runtime and reduce overall response time for individual transactions.

INDEX